UNLOCKING
THE PAST

A GUIDE TO EXPLORING FAMILY
AND LOCAL HISTORY IN THE
ISLE OF MAN

UNLOCKING THE PAST

A GUIDE TO EXPLORING FAMILY AND LOCAL HISTORY IN THE ISLE OF MAN

Matthew Richardson

First published in the Isle of Man in 2011
by
Manx National Heritage
Kingswood Grove
Douglas
Isle of Man
British Isles IM1 3LY

Copyright © Manx National Heritage

ISBN 9780901106643

A CIP catalogue record for this book is available from the British Library

The right of Matthew Richardson to be identified as the author of this work has been asserted in accordance with the Copyright Act 1991.

Produced in the Isle of Man by Lily Publications

CONTENTS

A map of the Isle of Man, showing parish boundaries.

FOREWORD BY NIGEL G. CROWE

THE pursuit of family history – what some Manx people used to call 'scraping gravestones' – has evolved rapidly since I became involved in the mid-1970s. New sources have become available, and the technology we use has changed out of all recognition. Other aspects remain constant, particularly the importance and enjoyment to be found in establishing a network of friendly contacts in the course of research. Since 1979, this process has been greatly assisted by the IOMFHS. Looking back, its formation coincided with a widespread upsurge of interest in the subject, but we were brought together partly to respond to the tremendous interest in Manx ancestry generated worldwide by 'Operation Roots', a project that led many people of Manx descent to explore their ancestral connections with the Island.

This volume provides an excellent introduction to the wealth of documentary and electronic resources that are now becoming readily available. It should prove a worthy successor to Mrs Janet Narasimham's invaluable handbook, *The Manx Family Tree*; here will be found details of the records essential to the disciplined process of establishing the necessary proof for each link in your ancestral line, and also in fleshing out the detail of your ancestors' lives and learning about their historical context. The 'vital records' begin with the Ballaugh registers in 1598, whilst the tenure of land can be traced continuously from about the same period and through the association of family names in some cases to around 1490.

Much remains to be learned about the Island's past, and I hope that this book will provide you with the stimulus to begin the study of your own family's place within it. Perhaps, like me, you will be encouraged to explore other aspects of the cultural heritage: language, landscape or folklore. Whatever the outcome, I would encourage you to make a permanent record of your findings, and pass them to the Manx National Heritage Library and the Isle of Man Family History Society. In this way you will be adding to the rich variety of resources on which the next generation can draw.

May I wish you every luck as you get to the truth of those family legends, and share your queries and findings with others. If you are reading these words far from the Island, you can be assured that a warm welcome awaits you when you return to explore, in the words of T.E. Brown, our national poet, to:

Unlock the treasures of the island heart
With loving feet to trace each hill and glen
And find the ore which is not for the mart of commerce

Nigel G. Crowe
Isle of Man Family History Society
Douglas 2011

ACKNOWLEDGEMENTS

THE preparation and publication of this book would not have been possible without the generous help of many people, both within Manx National Heritage and without. I would like to draw particular attention to the staff of the Manx National Heritage Library and Archive Service who have been especially generous with their knowledge of specialist areas: Paul Weatherall, Alan Franklin and Wendy Thirkettle. My colleague Yvonne Cresswell, Curator of Social History, offered much practical advice and also contributed one of the case studies herein. John Caley, Manx National Heritage photographer, prepared many of the numerous wonderful illustrations within the book. Kirsty Neate and Gaynor Haxby helped to steer the project and keep it on track. Miles Cowsill at Lily Publications designed the layout of the book and I thank him warmly for his efforts. From the Isle of Man Family History Society, Nigel Crowe, Priscilla Lewthwaite and Ernie Cleator offered much advice and encouragement. Nigel also kindly contributed the research material for the Joughen case study (see p. 193) Roger Sims provided valuable information in specific areas, Andrew Scarffe was most generous with his specialist knowledge in relation to mining records and Tony Pass was equally helpful in his particular field of architecture. Charles Guard of the Manx Heritage Foundation was most helpful, as were Jan McCartney at the Henry Bloom Noble Library in Douglas, Barbara Gilbert and Roy Swales at the Fleet Air Arm Museum and Joanne Smith at Southampton Arts and Heritage Service.

I would like to thank Stephen Cregeen and David Gallimore at the Isle of Man General Registry for their assistance, and I am indebted to Brian Roberts and Miriam Critchlow at the Isle of Man Public Record Office for their invaluable help with the records of that institution. To the many friends and colleagues who read the text at the draft stage and offered their advice – thank you, you know who you are!

Special mention is due to Janet Narasimham. It was Janet's book *The Manx Family Tree* which really laid the foundations of genealogy as a hobby in the Isle of Man. Now in its third reprint, for many years Janet's book has been the standard work on the subject.

Finally, I am most grateful again to Nigel Crowe for so kindly contributing the foreword to this book. As well as practising as a Chartered Surveyor, Nigel has worked as a professional genealogist and is widely respected in the field of family history in the Isle of Man. It means a great deal to have his seal of approval for this book.

Matthew Richardson
Douglas 2011

INTRODUCTION

THE Isle of Man has a long and proud tradition as an independent nation. Its legal and political framework was established by the Vikings and its legislative assembly, Tynwald, is the oldest continuous parliament in the world, reputedly established over a thousand years ago. The Island has its own language, known as Manx Gaelic. The impact of the Norse settlers was significant, shaping not just political structures but also giving rise to Norse place and personal names. They did not however displace the native language which continued as a *lingua franca* until well into the eighteenth and early nineteenth century, before being displaced by English. This fusion of Celtic and Scandinavian influences has been one of the defining features of Manx culture.

Geographically the Isle of Man is part of the British Isles. As a Crown Dependency, it owes its allegiance to the British Crown (Her Majesty Queen Elizabeth II currently holds the title Lord of Mann). The Island has never been part of the United Kingdom; its relationship with the European Union, of which it is not a member, is under a protocol made when the United Kingdom was admitted. The Island has full internal self government, with Britain merely dealing, at this time, with Defence and Foreign Affairs. It has a Tricameral parliament, Tynwald (comprising an upper house called the Legislative Council, and a directly elected lower house called the House of Keys). The Manx Government has the power to raise its own revenue and sets its own taxation levels. The Isle of Man has its own currency linked to Sterling, its own stamps, its own flag and its own national anthem. Whilst the Crown is represented by a directly appointed Lieutenant Governor, the post is largely ceremonial. The Manx Government has a Council of Ministers and it is led by the Chief Minister. The Island is proud of its growing independence, culture, language and heritage.

Whilst there are obvious similarities between aspects of life on the Isle of Man and life in the neighbouring jurisdictions, there are also significant cultural differences and it is important to understand these. The economy of a small island is also likely to be distinctively different from that of its larger neighbours. That of the Isle of Man has been disproportionately influenced by its geographical location within the Irish Sea. At the same time the Island has been isolated from some of the great trends in British economic history, such as large scale industrialisation, and remains predominantly rural. It has remained largely unspoiled and is a place of almost unparalleled natural beauty. These factors have helped shape a way of life and a people which are in many ways unique. A consequence of these factors has been that at several points in its history there has been emigration from the Isle of Man, to North America, South Africa and Australasia. Today the Manx diaspora makes up a significant proportion of those seeking to trace their family tree through the records held on the Island.

This book is intended both as an introduction to the Isle of Man for those who though having Manx ancestry, may be unfamiliar with the place itself, and as a handbook for those seeking to find their way around the records which make up the Island's collective memory. It offers advice as to which sources are most appropriate and the best way to make use of them. It also provides insights into the Manx way of life, what is special about the Isle of Man and what makes Manx people so proud of where they come from.

Manx family and local records are many and varied, and cover civil registration documents, births, baptisms, marriages and deaths, census returns, manorial records, church records, wills and probate documents, maritime records, and internment, to name but a few. Most, but not all of these sources are held within repositories based on the Island. Manx National Heritage, as the heritage agency of the Isle of Man, is the foremost holder of such records, but other significant collections are also discussed.

Matthew Richardson is to be congratulated on bringing together such a concise survey of what is in truth an enormous subject. However, no project such as this, covering so many areas of expertise, could have been achieved singled-handedly. Recognition is also due to the members of MNH library and archive staff, curatorial staff, custodians of records outside of MNH and indeed experts from the Isle of Man Family History Society and elsewhere who have contributed their knowledge.

Perhaps your family have lived on the Isle of Man for generations, or perhaps you have come to live on the Island recently. Perhaps you live many thousands of miles from the Isle of Man, but can trace your heritage back to the Island. Whatever your circumstances, there is much enjoyment to be gained from the study of the history of the Isle of Man and its people. New technology is making it easier and more rewarding than ever to unlock the past. If you are just beginning your journey, I hope that this book will guide you. If you are an experienced researcher, I hope it will offer you new scope and new avenues for exploration.

G.R.Martin Moore MBE LLB
Chairman of Trustees
Manx National Heritage

A HISTORICAL OVERVIEW OF THE ISLE OF MAN

MUCH of the cultural heritage of the Isle of Man is derived from the fusion of the language and way of life of the native Celtic population, with those of Scandinavian settlers in the tenth century. Evidence of the significant nature of the Norse settlement survives through to the twenty-first century in terms of place names, surnames, political institutions such as Tynwald (the Manx Parliament), settlement patterns and sites, as well as archaeological remains, such as burial mounds. Scandinavian settlements were established both on the Island and throughout the Irish Sea region during the tenth century and over the succeeding centuries, the Island's strategic position in the centre of this region made it both a target and a stronghold for its Norse occupants. Excavations at Peel Castle have confirmed its importance as a Viking settlement in this era. The zenith of Scandinavian influence was the Norse kingdom of Mann and the Isles.

Following the death of Magnus, the last Norse King of Mann, in 1265, Norway ceded the Island to Scotland. The Island became a 'pawn' in the power struggles between the English and the Scottish crowns over the succeeding century. Mann became the property of a succession of English and Scots lords, who were granted the Island as a token of patronage by their respective monarchs. It was finally given by the English crown to Sir John Stanley in 1405, as reward for his loyal duty and support. The Stanleys were appointed the hereditary Kings of Mann, although later during the reign of Henry VIII the title became Lord of Mann. Doubtless aware of Henry's jealous nature, Thomas Stanley wisely decided he would rather be a Great Lord than a Petty King.

The relative stability of the Stanley rule was interrupted in 1642 with the outbreak of the English Civil War.

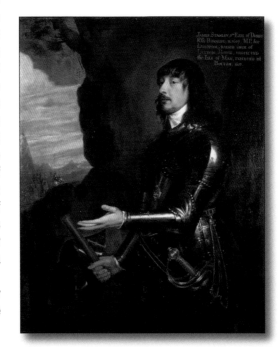

James Stanley, Seventh Earl of Derby, *Yn Stanlagh Mooar.* (1954-7272)

James Stanley, Seventh Earl of Derby, was known to the Manx as *Yn Stanlagh Mooar*, the Great Stanley. An ardent Royalist, upon the outbreak of the English Civil War he placed himself and his properties at the disposal of King Charles I. Following the defeat of the Royalists, the Isle of Man remained an irritating thorn in the side of the Parliamentarian victors in England for five years, until a renewed outbreak of civil war brought matters to a conclusion. James Stanley travelled to England once again to fight alongside the heir to the throne, the uncrowned Charles II, but the Royalists were quickly defeated. Stanley was captured following the Battle of Worcester, and charged with treason for his support of Charles. Found guilty, he was beheaded at Bolton in 1651.

Now Parliament resolved to settle matters in the Isle of Man. A Parliamentary fleet anchored in Ramsey Bay, and as news of its arrival reached the Countess of Derby at Castle Rushen, William Christian (Illiam Dhone), the commander of the militia, and other influential men began secret negotiations for the surrender of the Island. Perhaps they feared that the Countess would do the same thing but acting solely in the interests of her own family. In exchange for certain guarantees, protecting the rights of Manx tenants, Christian handed over Castle Rushen and the rest of the Island's defences without a shot being fired in anger.

Upon the restoration of the Monarchy, the Stanleys regained control of the Island. After a brief trial in 1663, Christian was executed at Hango Hill outside Castletown. He became a martyr to the Manx – a hero who had defied the Stanleys – and his name was commemorated in a heroic Manx ballad. The Malew parish burial register states, 'He died most penitently and couradgeously [*sic*], made a good end, prayed earnestly, made an excellent speech, and the next day was buried in the chancell of Kirk Malew.'

The modern age in the Isle of Man might be considered to begin in the aftermath of the Civil War. The period of Stanley rule that followed is chiefly remembered for the growth in importance to the Island of a prosperous and growing merchant class. In the early 1700s the Isle of Man had its own system of import duties which were considerably lower than those in neighbouring England. Thus it was perfectly legitimate for importers of French brandies, tobacco, tea and other luxury goods to land them in the Isle of Man, and pay Manx duty upon them.

Less legitimate was what happened next; the tea or brandy was frequently decanted into smaller containers, and then rowed across to England, where it was illicitly imported under cover of night. Although this traffic, known as the 'running trade', caused great consternation to the English authorities, the Dukes of Atholl (who inherited the lordship of Man from the Stanleys) maintained it was no concern of theirs. The Westminster Parliament was determined to close this loophole. The Act of Revestment of 1765 was the instrument by which the English Crown bought back the regalities of the Island from the Atholl family, for the sum of £70,000. The Island's trading economy collapsed almost immediately upon removal of the tariff advantage, and a large number of the merchants sold up and left.

Manx sea captains had made a name for themselves on the trading routes of the eighteenth century; The most celebrated Manx seafarer of the Revolutionary and Napoleonic era was undoubtedly Captain John Quilliam. A man of humble origins, Quilliam was born at Ballakelly, Marown. He began his naval career as an ordinary seaman. His rapid rise through the ranks of the eighteenth-century Royal Navy, however, was a testament to its meritocratic nature. By 1805 he was serving as a lieutenant aboard HMS *Victory*, and had come to the attention of Admiral Lord Nelson. On the fateful morning of 21 October 1805 as *Victory* sailed towards the Franco-Spanish line, Quilliam secured his place in history. When a lucky Spanish shot took away the ships wheel, he scrambled below decks and rigged up a temporary system of ropes to steer the ship using the tiller. The prize money from the Battle of Trafalgar established Quilliam as a man of means when he returned to the Isle of Man, and he was invited by the self-elected House of Keys to become one of their number.

With the coming of peace in 1815 the majority of those men serving in the ranks of the Army or below decks in the Navy were discharged onto the labour market. The effect on the Isle of Man was similar to that in most other parts of Britain. There was a general depression, caused by the cancellation of Government contracts, and the surplus of labour meant that the 1820s were difficult times for the Manx.

Against this background of unemployment and unrest began one of the first phases of Manx emigration, with many former agricultural workers seeking a new life in North America. The Manx settled predominantly in Ohio along with other Midwestern states and Canada. Today, there are reputedly more people of Manx descent living in Ohio than in the Isle of Man. The Manx took their ways of life and their crafts with them. The most obvious expression of this was through their patchwork quilts, a tradition brought from the Isle of Man which flourished in the United States.

By the 1840s the ever resourceful Manx people began to turn to a new source of income. The geological make-up of the Island means it is rich in mineral resources, chiefly metal ores. In prehistoric times and in the medieval era attempts were made to extract these ores, at the points at which they were most easily accessible, where the veins broke the surface. By the early nineteenth century, however, mining technology enabled deeper and more lucrative veins to be reached. The mines at Foxdale and Laxey entered a boom era which would last for the next seventy years.

This resurgence in interest in Manx mining lead to the creation of the Isle of Man's greatest industrial monument – the 'Lady Isabella', the Great Laxey Wheel. Built originally to pump water out of the mines, the wheel is believed to be the largest working waterwheel in the world.

Politically the Island entered a new phase in the 1860s when the twenty-four members of the House of Keys voted to allow democratic elections for the first time. The House of Keys Election Act of 1866 handed the vote to all male rate payers holding

This painting, entitled *The Road to Laxey Mines*, dates from the 1840s. It depicts two early waterwheels in the Laxey valley, precursors of the Lady Isabella. (1966-0361)

property valued at £8 per annum. The Keys chose to abolish their previously self-elected status in return for the right to raise their own revenue through taxes. During this period they were particularly concerned by suggestions from England that the Isle of Man should be absorbed into an English county. Embracing democracy, it was felt, would strengthen Manx independence against English interference by increasing the legitimacy of the Island's ruling body.

By the 1860s and 1870s the Island was also booming as a tourist destination. Patronised firstly by the upper classes and latterly by the middle classes, the Island soon became a favourite holiday resort, promising clean fresh air away from the grimy and polluted industrial towns of northern England. The income from the booming 'visiting trade' fed into the construction of much of upper Douglas and the surviving townscape we see today is a direct result of that industry.

The Island's fishing industry, which had been its mainstay in the early years of the nineteenth century, entered its last flourish in the final years of the century. The harbours of Peel and Castletown were so thick with masts that it was said you could walk from one side to the other simply by stepping from one fishing boat deck to another. The main fishing grounds at this time were off Kinsale in Ireland and the Manx vessels made the arduous journey there each summer following the herring shoals. Life on a fishing vessel was extraordinarily hard and full of risk.

The early years of the twentieth century saw an important flourishing of the Arts and Crafts Movement on the Isle of Man. The most significant figure in this was Archibald Knox, the Douglas teacher who drew inspiration from the Norse and Celtic artistic legacy that he saw on the Island all around him. He was particularly inspired by the interwoven designs of the Norse crosses, which he incorporated into his own work. Knox's designs for Liberty and Company of London were turned into exquisite silver and pewter tea services, bowls, clocks and jewellery.

The revival of interest in all things Celtic extended to the Manx language, which had been under pressure for much of the nineteenth century. Yn Cheshaght Ghailckagh (The Manx Language Society) was founded in 1899. The first treasurer was William Cubbon, later second director of the Manx Museum, who went on to become the Society's president. Cubbon's efforts eventually led also to the preservation of Harry

W. Hardie Hay's painting *On the Beach at Douglas* captures the essence of a Victorian seaside holiday. (1984-0302)

Kelly's cottage at Cregneash, which became the first open-air folk museum in Britain. Harry Kelly, one of the last 'native' Manx speakers, also typified a way of life that was in rapid decline by the early twentieth century. It was that of the crofter-fisherman, an almost subsistence lifestyle, by which generations of Manx people had lived. Kelly's two-roomed thatched cottage was seen as the archetypal Manx homestead.

The Isle of Man continued to grow in importance as a holiday destination right up to the First World War. The summer of 1914 was on course to be a record season until the outbreak of hostilities in August of that year. Thereafter, the Isle of Man assumed a new role: that of prison camp for thousands of foreign citizens who were living in the British Isles, and who were interned as enemy aliens for the duration of the conflict. Males of military age from Germany, the Austro-Hungarian Empire and Turkey, some of whom had been resident in Britain for many years, were arrested and interned.

In 1919 after the end of the First World War the camps were closed, and many of the internees were deported to their country of birth, despite the fact that many of them had spent many years in England and some were married to British women.

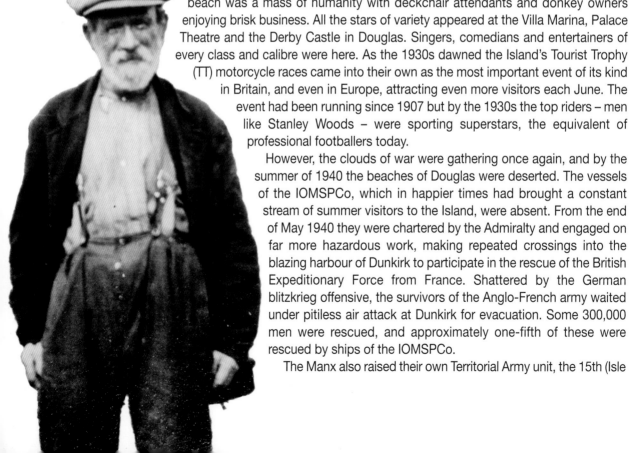

Harry Kelly was amongst the last of the crofter-fishermen, a way of life that was disappearing by the early twentieth century. (Pg659/2)

In the 1920s the Island resumed its role as a holiday capital. Douglas promenade bustled with hotels, restaurants, theatres and cinemas. In high summer Douglas beach was a mass of humanity with deckchair attendants and donkey owners enjoying brisk business. All the stars of variety appeared at the Villa Marina, Palace Theatre and the Derby Castle in Douglas. Singers, comedians and entertainers of every class and calibre were here. As the 1930s dawned the Island's Tourist Trophy (TT) motorcycle races came into their own as the most important event of its kind in Britain, and even in Europe, attracting even more visitors each June. The event had been running since 1907 but by the 1930s the top riders – men like Stanley Woods – were sporting superstars, the equivalent of professional footballers today.

However, the clouds of war were gathering once again, and by the summer of 1940 the beaches of Douglas were deserted. The vessels of the IOMSPCo, which in happier times had brought a constant stream of summer visitors to the Island, were absent. From the end of May 1940 they were chartered by the Admiralty and engaged on far more hazardous work, making repeated crossings into the blazing harbour of Dunkirk to participate in the rescue of the British Expeditionary Force from France. Shattered by the German blitzkrieg offensive, the survivors of the Anglo-French army waited under pitiless air attack at Dunkirk for evacuation. Some 300,000 men were rescued, and approximately one-fifth of these were rescued by ships of the IOMSPCo.

The Manx also raised their own Territorial Army unit, the 15th (Isle

Prisoners rush for dinner at Knockaloe Camp, in this scene painted by an internee named George Kenner. (2006-0063)

of Man) Light Anti Aircraft Regiment, part of the Royal Artillery. It fought in North Africa and Europe, gaining much credit, and the Island itself became an armed camp. As well as the airfields at Ronaldsway, Jurby and Andreas, much highly classified radio interception work and training took place. A number of secret radar bases were also established.

The Isle of Man was once again used to hold interned enemy aliens, but this time there were no purpose-built camps. The internees were held in requisitioned hotels and guest houses, which were surrounded by fences of barbed wire. A large number of the inmates of the camps in the Second World War were Italians. Others were German, Austrian, or Japanese. Significant numbers of Germans and Austrians living in Britain at the outbreak of war in 1939 were in fact refugees from Nazi oppression. Many of them were Jewish. Others were artists deemed to be decadent and un-German, such as Kurt Schwitters. Most of these people were interned on the Isle of Man for only a short time but in the early years of the war a community of exiled German intellectuals and artists grew up in the camps. Some highly important artwork was produced here, including work by Hugo

The crew of the *Mona's Queen* in 1939. Bosun Edgerton Watterson (back row second left) was awarded the Distinguished Service Medal for his bravery during the Dunkirk evacuation. (Pg6698/1)

Dachinger, an Austrian artist, who as both a Jew and a Socialist had been forced to flee Vienna in 1938.

The immediate post-war years were difficult ones. The Island's tourist infrastructure was in a poor state, and few people had money for holidays anyway. Even when the income from the tourist industry began to revive, it was very seasonal. In former times,

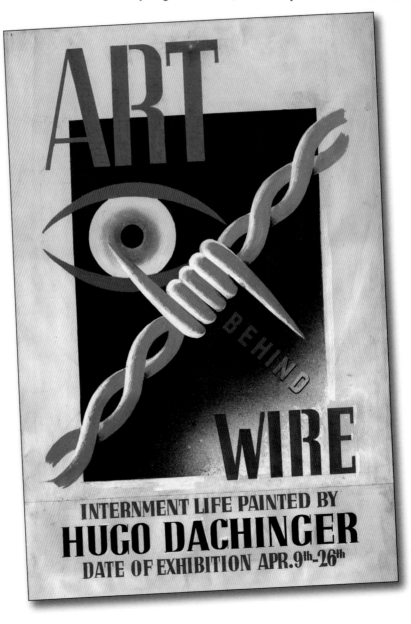

A poster for Hugo Dachinger's exhibition 'Art Behind Wire'. Dachinger was one of the most significant members of the artistic community interned on the Isle of Man. (2002-0103)

alternative winter work had been available to those who worked in the summer in hotels and guest houses. By the 1950s agriculture was also in depression and there was little else on the Island in the way of employment. It was taken as given that anyone who wanted a professional career would probably have to leave the Island to pursue it. In those years the Isle of Man saw one of the greatest periods of mass emigration in its history, and census summaries show a sharp drop in population between 1931 and 1961. Some of those who left went to England, but a great many took advantage of the 'ten pound pom' scheme and took assisted passages to a new life in Australia. In the late 1950s and early 1960s the Manx economy came under further pressure from the growth of air travel and cheap package holidays to Spain, which threatened its traditional markets in the working class north of England.

However, in the early 1960s a number of changes occurred that were to modernise Manx democracy and the constitutional framework. One forward-thinking Lieutenant Governor was Sir Ronald Garvey. Garvey announced in his 1960 budget speech that his priority would be the attraction to the Island of new permanent residents. One of the ways in which he proposed to do this was through changes in the Island's tax structure which would attract wealthy new residents who would either start new businesses or support existing ones. In 1961 the Lieutenant Governor relinquished the position as Head of Government, to be replaced by a Chairman of the Executive Council in Tynwald. This post was the forerunner of that of Chief Minister. The first person to hold this office was Charles Kerruish, the son of a farmer from Maughold who became the Island's most formidable political force.

One legacy of the sixties however that has persisted and which has shaped the character of the Isle of Man over the fifty years since has been the low taxation regime initially introduced by Garvey. This has attracted banks and insurance companies to the Isle of Man, and these in turn have contributed hundreds of millions to the Manx Exchequer over the past few decades. In spite of protests in the 1980s by some local people over the negative aspects of the Island's finance sector, there can be no doubt that it has been the major contributor to the economy over the last thirty or more years. The Isle of Man has always tried to stay one step ahead of the pack, being one of the first to introduce electronic signatures. The Internet and development of electronic technologies have undoubtedly strengthened the hand of the Isle of Man as an offshore financial centre. At the same time the Island has invested a great deal of time and effort in co-operating with regulatory bodies around the world to demonstrate that it is one of the best administered and transparent financial jurisdictions. Unquestionably, like so many aspects of the Island's history before, the finance industry has also changed the population balance of the Island. It has drawn in large numbers of workers, both directly into the banks and also into supporting services, making the population of the Isle of Man of the twenty-first century more diverse than it has ever been.

A GUIDE TO THE MAIN ISLE OF MAN REPOSITORIES

Manx National Heritage Library and Archive Service
The MNH Library and Archive Service is located within the Manx Museum, on Kingswood Grove in Douglas. Full contact details are:

National Library and Archive Service
Manx National Heritage
Manx Museum
Douglas
Isle of Man
IM1 3LY

Telephone: 01624 648000
Fax: 01624 648069
Email: library@mnh.gov.im
Website: www.gov.im/mnh

In 1886 an Act of Tynwald created the Manx Museum as a legal entity, to act as the national repository for the cultural history of the Isle of Man, but the remit of the first trustees initially covered only antiquities and artefacts. It was not until 1906 that the first mention of documentary accessions appeared in the trustees' minutes. In fact, the trustees on that occasion were thanking a certain Mr McLaughlin, the custodian of Castle Rushen, for finding room to store books and manuscripts at his house!

The year 1906 was also significant in that it marked the first chairmanship of A.W. Moore, the great Manx scholar and Speaker of the House of Keys. Under his stewardship the Manx Museum began for the first time collecting books and manuscripts in an organised and systematic way. One of the most significant Manx language documents, the Book of Common Prayer, thought to have been translated by Bishop Phillips in 1610, was purchased in 1909 for £30. By 1914 a library section was an established part of the trustees' report.

The problem of storage however remained. Castle Rushen was increasingly seen as an unsuitable location and the Museum and its library moved to the present site (the former Nobles Hospital) in 1922. At the same time, William Cubbon took up the post of Secretary and Librarian, and began in earnest the task of organising the library collections. Cubbon, a Manx scholar in his own right, was the driving force in establishing the Manx Museum library as the National Library of the Isle of Man. With the purchase of the G.W. Wood collection of printed books in 1923, the aim of holding almost all publications relating to the Isle of Man up to that time was achieved.

By 1960, the growth in the volume of library and archival collections, and the need to store them in conditions that best preserved them for future generations, resulted in the opening of a new purpose-built library and archive building attached to the Manx Museum. For the first time documents were stored in a climate-controlled and protected environment. In 1991 the Manx Museum and National Trust adopted the more manageable trading name of Manx National Heritage (MNH for short).

The iMuseum (Home of Manx Memories – Cummal Cooinaghtyn Manninagh)

MNH opened a new centre called the iMuseum in 2011. Situated on Kingswood Grove and part of the Manx Museum complex, it offers a centralised facility for accessing digital records. The centre is tailored for the family and local history researcher, and acts as a one-stop shop for the key research tools for this. Staff are on hand to assist the public and to provide advice, and the centre provides easy access to family history resources and other records which will gradually increase to include:

Photographs, 1850s–2000s, including several thousand individual portrait photos
Baptism, marriage and burial records from the early 1600s to modern times
Wills and testamentary papers, 1600–1910
Census returns, 1841–1911
Church court records, 1640–1874
Manx newspaper titles, 1790s–1960, providing free text searching of almost 400,000 pages of newsprint
Property deeds, 1695–1910
Land holding records, 1507–1910
Film and sound archive material relating to the Island, 1919–present
First and Second World War internment records
Shipping and crew-list records
War memorial records
TT records covering individual and team entrants, and motorcycle manufacturers.

It is planned that access to these facilities will be available via the Internet by the end of 2011.

iMuseum
Manx National Heritage
Kingswood Grove
Douglas
Isle of Man
IM1 3LY

Telephone: 01624 648000
Fax: 01624 648001
Email: enquiries@mnh.gov.im
Website: www.imuseum.im

The Isle of Man Family History Society Library

The IOMFHS Library is located at:

Derby Lodge
Derby Road
Peel
Isle of Man
IM5 1HH

Telephone: 01624 843105
Email: iomfhs@manx.net
Website: www.iomfhs.im/

Hours of opening are Tuesday, Wednesday and Saturday afternoons from 2pm to 5pm. Access outside of these hours can be arranged by giving appropriate notice to the Librarian:

Mrs Doreen Quayle
17 West View
Peel
Isle of Man
IM5 1BN

Telephone: 01624 843105

The Librarian or a society member will be in attendance to assist with research. The resources of the Library include:

- International Genealogical Index for the Isle of Man, England and Scotland
- Burial registers for the Island and Douglas Crematorium records
- Monumental inscriptions from cemeteries and churchyards on the Isle of Man
- Census records, 1841–1901 on microfilm, microfiche and in publications, with index
- Family trees submitted by members
- Indexes of baptisms, marriages and deaths recorded on the Isle of Man, on microfilm
- Roman Catholic baptisms, marriages and death indexes for the Isle of Man
- Goodwin papers for news of local people
- Manx books
- *Wood's Atlas*
- Journals from other similar societies
- A Strays Index for Manx people born, married or died off the Island
- Books advising on family history research.

Researchers wishing to email the Librarian can do so at: iomfhs@manx.net. Please quote your postal address, and membership number if applicable. It should be noted that although the society has many members worldwide, the team on the Isle of Man comprises a small but dedicated group of volunteers, with no full-time paid staff. For this reason, please allow time for a reply to an email enquiry. Whilst these volunteers are happy to look up an entry from the resources above, it is regretted that they cannot research an entire family tree. A member may also be willing to visit the Manx Museum Library or Registry of Deeds to find an entry, upon request. For those who are not members of the Society, only general enquiries can be answered. The website of the Society is a useful tool in its own right and carries a number of indexes, for example, an index to Braddan burials.

The Isle of Man General Registry

The Registries Section consists of the Deeds and Probate Registry, the Land Registry and the Civil Registry. Each of these is a separate entity with its own key business function within the General Registry. The Registries Section has a commitment to improve customer service, and to extend the use of information technology in a way that will effectively and efficiently contribute to the Section's service and performance. Consequently, the computerised Deeds Index is being upgraded. All records have been computerised from 1989. Records prior to this date will also be computerised, when time allows. In addition, for the first time a Probate Index is available on computer.

All deeds registered from 1911 to the present day are housed in the Deeds and Probate Registry, along with all Grants of Probate from 1950 to the present date. Grants of Probate recorded from 1911 to 1949 inclusive are housed offsite and can be ordered by Deed and Probate staff; this normally takes two to three working days.

All the documents held in the Deeds and Probate Registry are available for the public to view, and have copies of, on payment of the prescribed fee. Exemplified and/or Certified copies are also available on payment of the prescribed fee. Access to all the information is via name-based indexes and therefore it is not possible to trace deeds relating to a property from the address alone. Please note that the deeds and Grants of Probate relate only to property situated on the Isle of Man.

If you do not know who owns a property now, but you do know a previous owner's name, it is possible to trace the deeds to the property by searching under the previous owner's name. If you have neither a current owner nor previous owner's name(s), you can contact the Government Rates Department (telephone: 01624 685661) and providing the property has a rateable value they should be able to confirm the name of the owner(s) or occupier(s).

Where land has no rateable value, such as on some derelict properties or on farmland, enquiries can be made to the Planning Section of the Department of Infrastructure. The Department will be able to establish whether any planning applications have been submitted on the land in question, from which one may obtain a name. Other avenues of enquiry may include local knowledge, for example, from nearby land owners, or by establishing a historical owner from *Wood's Atlas*, which is available to view free of charge in the Deeds Registry. *Wood's Atlas* was published in 1867 and identifies the extent of individual landowners in each parish in the Isle of Man at that time. The name of the landowner can then be used as a starting point to search forward through the deeds housed in the Manx Museum up until 1910, and thereafter in the Deeds Registry up to the present date. This method of searching however can be both time consuming and costly, as there is a fee for production of deeds.

The Land Registry was created to improve on the present system of Deeds Registration and thereby encourage simpler conveyancing procedures; to permit Land Registration information to be made readily available; and ultimately to permit the establishment of a complete Land Information Service (LIS), namely a 'one-stop-shop' for all land-based information, such as planning data, roads and electricity in addition to Land Registration data. It was gradually introduced from 2000 by parish, and roll out for all-Island coverage was completed in 2009. However, properties that have not been sold in recent years will still need to have deed searches carried out in the traditional way.

The Civil Registry contains birth, marriage and death certificates for these events that occurred upon the Isle of Man only. For more information on coverage, see the section on Civil Registration in this book.

The Civil Registry, the Land Registry and the Deeds and Probate Registry are all located at:

Registries Building
Deemsters Walk
Douglas
Isle of Man
IM1 3AR

Telephone: 01624 687039
Website: www.gov.im/registries/

The Isle of Man General Registry is also responsible for the Isle of Man Public Record Office (IOMPRO).

The Isle of Man Public Record Office

The IOMPRO holds mainly twentieth-century records with some from the nineteenth century. The role and functions of the IOMPRO are embodied in the Isle of Man's Public Records Act (PRA) 1999. This came into force on 1 April 2000 and is based on the Public Records Act 1958 in England and Wales. Public records comprise the administrative and departmental records of Tynwald, central government, other public bodies, local government and the courts (as defined in public records legislation). The Act ensures that records of public bodies are selected and retained to become available at thirty years to form a national memory for the benefit of government itself, the public individually and the nation as a whole.

IOMPRO is based at:

Unit 40A
Spring Valley Industrial Estate
Braddan
Isle of Man
IM2 2QS

Telephone: 01624 693569
Fax: 01624 613384
Email: public.records@gov.im
Website: www.gov.im/registries/publicrecords/welcome.xml

The Public Record Office is 2½ miles outside Douglas. There is free parking and it is close to several bus routes.

The IOMPRO website does not contain any lists of holdings. However, it does contain details such as access, location and opening hours. Most records held at IOMPRO are being assessed and listed and may not yet be available under the Public Records Act. Access is usually still possible, although records containing personal information may be closed. It is therefore important to contact IOMPRO in advance of a visit, to ensure that all necessary arrangements are in place.

Public Libraries

Public libraries on the Isle of Man can also be an invaluable resource for research. Port Erin, Castletown, Onchan, Peel and Ramsey all have local history sections including a reference section. The Henry Bloom Noble Library in Douglas has probably the most extensive local studies collection. This includes a collection of Manx books, a range of newspaper cuttings relating to Douglas and plans and pamphlets, some of which are not available elsewhere. There are some electoral records, and an archive of letters and photographs relating to soldiers of the First World War. The library can be contacted at:

Henry Bloom Noble Library
10 Victoria Street
Douglas
Isle of Man
IM1 2LH

Telephone: 01624 696461
Fax no. 01624-696400
Email: library@douglas.gov.im
Website: www.douglas.gov.im/library.asp.

Areas of Research

ADOPTION RECORDS

The Isle of Man Civil Registry maintains the registers of officially adopted children, and this should be the starting point for any enquiry involving adoption. It should be noted however that these records start in 1929, the date upon which adoption was officially recognised. Prior to this there were many cases of informal adoption (often within extended families) but these would not have been legally recognised. MNH holds no records referring directly to adoption of children, but other sources can contain relevant information. For illegitimate children, the diocesan records can be helpful. The orders of court affiliations (MNH archive reference MS 10194) do not contain names of children, but do contain information as to the father of an illegitimate child, if he was ordered to pay towards its upkeep. These records are indexed, and cover the dates 1786 to 1918. The Judicature Amendment Act of 1921 transferred affiliation cases to the responsibility of the High Bailiffs. MS 10050 contains the minute books and order books of cases heard by the High Bailiffs (including orders for affiliation of illegitimate children, maintenance payments as well as information given during the examination of witnesses) for the period August 1921 to February 1942. After this, responsibility for these cases passed to magistrates. Their records extend to 1971, and would normally be closed for seventy-five years. Enquiries from persons seeking their own records would be dealt with at the discretion of the Attorney General's office.

See also:
✿ Church Court Records
✿ Civil Registration

Nancy May Hamilton was adopted in the early twentieth century. As a child she was cherished by her adoptive parents, and in her memoirs (MS 11989) she recalls:

I was born at 12 Mona Terrace, Douglas on 23rd September 1920. My parents, George Elston and May Gladys Elston (nee Bustin), were unable to look after me, and by agreement (there was no court order in those days), I was adopted by Elizabeth and Robert James Harrison who were unable to have children of their own. They lived at 13 Hope Street, Douglas until I was 6 years old . . . When we were not at school and during the school holidays, I spent a lot of time on Southampton Farm at Port Soderick . . . I loved being there when the Mill was there and the corn was being cut. Sometimes I spent a week with my cousin, Kitty Corlett at Castletown . . . We had great fun and she and her brother Tom came to stay with me at Port Soderick . . . Being an only child myself, I enjoyed being with Kitty and Tom.

ART AS SOCIAL HISTORY

For the ages before photography became widespread, the artistic heritage of the Isle of Man provides an invaluable visual record. This record begins in the seventeenth century, and it is generally fair to say that in this early modern period, art was not created for its own sake. Artists usually worked under the patronage of wealthy men, who wanted a visual record of themselves, their families or what they owned, be that landscape, livestock or property.

All pictures in the permanent collections of MNH have been accepted on the basis that they are either works of artistic merit by Manx artists, or they are works depicting Manx scenes. However, a number of these works exhibit an additional quality in that they provide a sometimes unique glimpse of the Island's social, political, topographical or architectural history. Some of the landscapes depicted in these works have changed out of all recognition, or have vanished completely. Many topographical paintings when studied closely reveal fascinating details of contemporary dress, modes of transport or methods of agriculture. This information adds a richness and depth to the surviving written record of the period in question. Likewise, the MNH collection of portraits provides a vivid visual record of some of the major personalities of Manx history.

The earliest known views of the Island are a series of monochrome wash drawings executed by Daniel King of Chester. They represent a series of snapshots from an age of turmoil and intrigue in Manx history, which is still of interest today. Between 1643 and 1651, at the height of the English Civil War, King produced sixteen drawings of important buildings and natural features, adding a short commentary at the bottom of each. These drawings were

This view of Laxey in 1795, by John Warwick Smith, shows linen being bleached by the river. (1954-7226)

subsequently used to illustrate *A Short Treatise of the Isle of Man* by James Chaloner (a Commissioner in Man on behalf of Lord Fairfax, and Governor of the Island from 1657–60), which in turn appeared as an appendix to King's *Vale-Royall of England or the County Palatine of Chester Illustrated*, published in 1656.

The original drawings are housed in the British Library, but MNH has a full series of facsimiles produced in the nineteenth century (Manx Museum accession numbers 1954-5825 to 1954-5828, and 1957-0089 to 1957-0104). King's work clearly reflects the nature of his commission, depicting as it does the important centres of political and religious authority – Castle Rushen, Peel Castle and Bishopscourt. There are, however, works of purely social interest within the collection, for example, a depiction of *the Landskipp of Douglas Towne* (*sic*), which offer important insights into the growth of the town and into ordinary life in this era. The collection as a whole provides a backdrop to some of the most significant portraits in the national collection – those of James Stanley, Seventh Earl of Derby (Yn Stanlagh Mooar), painted by a follower of Van Dyke (1954-7272), the charcoal study of his wife Charlotte de la Tremouille (1954-7822) and the painting of epic proportions depicting William Christian (Illiam Dhone) (1954-6561), their nemesis.

The next major artistic study of the Isle of Man was that undertaken by Moses Griffith in 1774. Griffith visited the Island with a party of artists and antiquaries and recorded views and locations such as Balasala Abbey (*sic*), Tynwald Hill, Ballaugh church and Peel Castle. The collection remained unpublished and largely unknown until the library of Griffiths' patron, the noted Welsh antiquary Thomas Pennant, was sold in 1938. The works were acquired by the Manx Museum at this point, as were other works that subsequently came to light. They are now held as 1954-5140 to 1954-5697.

The third collection of important topographical works is the set of twenty-six watercolours executed by John 'Warwick' Smith around 1795 (1954-7201 to 1954-7226). The works by Smith in the Manx national collection were probably commissioned by the Fourth Duke of Atholl, who was Governor of the Island from 1791. The paintings had been lost from public view until in 1950 the then Director of the Manx Museum discovered them adorning the walls of Blair Castle in Perthshire. The transfer of the paintings to the Isle of Man was subsequently arranged. It would be hard to overstate the importance of this collection in terms of Manx social history. Smith's depiction of Laxey in 1795 shows linen laid out on the river bank to dry after bleaching, and his watercolour of the promulgation of laws on Tynwald Hill the same year is believed to be the earliest depiction of the Manx national assembly.

From this same era the portrait collection includes important figures from the

Island's political and ruling classes, for example, Lieutenant Governor Cornelius Smelt (1954-1689) and Bishop Thomas Wilson (1954-7823), two men who did much to endear themselves to the Manx people during this period. There are also representatives of the merchant classes, for example, the magnificent portrait of Thomas Durie (1956-0403), the Douglas merchant, and those of Captain John Taubman (1973-0070) and his family painted by George Romney, probably the greatest English portrait artist of his age.

The burgeoning coverage of the Island's maritime heritage in this era is well represented by Richard Wright's painting *The Squadrons of Thurot and Elliot in Ramsey Bay, 1760* (1954-7451). During the Seven Years War a sharp naval engagement between a raiding French squadron and a British force sent to subdue them took place off the Ballaugh coast. The captured French vessels were brought into Ramsey for repairs where they were painted by Wright, a self-taught artist born in Liverpool around 1720. As well as the obvious importance of this work in terms of maritime and naval history, the artist has captured a wealth of detail, perhaps best exemplified by the small boat full of sightseers shown in the foreground.

By the nineteenth century the flourishing of art in the Isle of Man (particularly

Richard Wright's *The Squadrons of Thurot and Elliot in Ramsey Bay, 1760* shows captured French warships being inspected by onlookers. (1954-7451)

that of home-grown artists) means that there is a rich and vibrant gallery of work illustrating almost every aspect of Island life. Fishing and fishing vessels were popular subjects for artists such as John Holland. Agriculture and rural scenes have been copiously portrayed; the watercolour painter Robert Evans Creer captured many rural scenes and rural activities, including the cutting of turf from a turbary. His 116 works are held by MNH as 2006-0074, and the collection has been published as *Gold Dust and Calm* (2007) by Val Cottle. Even the mines at Laxey and Bradda Head have been covered by painters. The growing tourist industry received extensive coverage, from the magnificent paddle steamers bringing visitors to Douglas, and painted by Samuel Walters, to the newly constructed townscapes of terraced streets which sprang up to cater for the thousands of summer visitors. One of the most iconic paintings in the collections of MNH is *On the Beach at Douglas* (1984-0302), painted in 1894 by W. Hardie Hay. It shows a group of children watching a Punch and Judy show, a more typical image from a Victorian seaside holiday would be hard to imagine. Two of the greatest Manx artists, John Miller Nicholson and Archibald Knox, worked in this era and have left a magnificent body of work, including both bustling harbours and open countryside.

In the twentieth century, John H. Nicholson took up his grandfather's mantle, and painted many scenes not otherwise documented by photography. He was particularly interested in industrial landscapes, and in the 1940s captured scenes such as abandoned mine workings at Foxdale, quarries and derelict farm buildings resulting from agricultural emigration. However, it might be argued that from the perspective of reflecting the social history of the Island, the greatest artistic contribution of the twentieth century came from a cartoonist, Harold 'Dusty' Miller. His cartoons for the *Isle of Man Weekly Times* cover the 1930s to the 1950s, and although some (particularly in wartime) were comments upon international developments, the vast majority of his body of work details the quirks of life on the Isle of Man. The topics range from the squabbles between the House of Keys and Douglas Corporation, the lack of preparedness of the Island's air raid precautions (and who was to blame), who bore the burdens of taxation and aspects of the visiting industry. A number of original cartoons are held by MNH as 2005-0069 and 2005-0220.

MNH is in the process of digitising the national art collections with the long-term view of making these images available through the iMuseum. There are currently plans to make some 200 works available in this way by late 2011, including local views from the early twentieth century by William Hoggatt and Archibald Knox.

A typical thatched
Manx cottage near
Greeba Bridge,
around 1900.
(Pg11779)

BUILDINGS AS HISTORICAL EVIDENCE

Although people have lived on the Isle of Man for thousands of years, the earliest examples of ordinary dwellings that still exist were built within the last three or four centuries. The vast majority of houses are from the period since 1830, but there may yet be hidden clues to more ancient fabric in and around existing dwellings, particularly in the countryside where demolition was rare and very little was wasted.

One important link between family history and Manx buildings is in the names they were given. Many farmsteads and rural cottages bear the name of the family that lived in or owned them over a long period, for example, Ballacallin, the farm of a family named Callin. Sometimes there may be two adjacent farms of the same name, such as Ballacallin Mooar and Ballacallin Beg. In most cases, this would indicate that a smaller farm has been created from a larger one, perhaps for a son or a tenant. The simplest

dwelling type to survive in use today is the single-storey, two-room unit typified by Harry Kelly's Cottage at Cregneash. There are many local variations of this type, depending upon the district and the available materials, but typical examples are 9–10m long and 4.5m wide with central doorways, small windows and simple roofs (building timber being scarce). Very few still have their original thatched covering as they were re-roofed when imported slate became available, but many retain the *bwid suggane* – slate pegs embedded below the eaves by which the thatched roof could be roped down. Others still have the original slate flashings – *lhiack* – set into the chimneys which were intended to stop driving rain penetrating the thatch.

Whilst there appear to be only a few unaltered examples of the two-room cottage, it should be remembered that the Manx were resourceful house improvers. Extensions and 'makeovers' were common, so that many buildings now have lean-tos and upper storeys which make the original structure hard to recognise from the outside. Sometimes a house was built around an existing dwelling, for example, the Grove at Ramsey, where an impressive early Victorian mansion was built around a stone mariner's cottage. One telltale sign of this practice is the thickness of walls in the original fabric, which may well differ from later construction. Quite a few dwellings were downgraded when families became larger or richer, so that many a country farmyard will have outbuildings, perhaps now housing animals, which were lived in by people before a newer, larger home was built. Sometimes the only evidence of former habitation is a long disused *chiollagh* or traditional fireplace.

Until about 1830, most of the Manx population were rural, but examples can be found of early town houses, which are often rather more sophisticated than those of a similar period in the country. By the 1700s, the gentry were importing such 'polite' features as vertical sash windows, classical door cases and symmetrical facades which we now associate with Georgian architecture. Most of the towns, the old capital Castletown in particular, have examples of this style which is just as distinctive on the inside with features such as classical cornices, panelling and elegant staircases. The ground floors of some houses were shops or offices, and still retain their impressive shop fronts and grand front doors. Within a generation or two this style percolated down to the less well-to-do and it was to survive well into the Victorian era.

The same style was easily adapted for terraced housing. Although there are earlier examples of this type around the harbours, the era of the terraces began in the second quarter of the nineteenth century when developers sought to cater for middle-class town dwellers, some of them genteel 'comeovers', many more from the rising professional and trading classes. In the terraces of Upper Douglas

William Blundell, of Crosby in Lancashire, described the homes of the ordinary Manx country people (whom he described as 'tall of stature and of a strenuous bulk, but boorish . . . having their wits as gross as their ayre') in 1657 in his *History of the Isle of Man*. These consisted in this era not even of stone-built dwellings but instead of sod cottages, made from earth. All of these have now vanished from the landscape, save for occasional marks still discernable in the fields. He writes:

These men's habitations are mere hovels, compacted of stones and clay for the walls, thatch'd with broom, most commonly containing one room only. Very few have 2 rooms, have no upper rooms, such as in their towns they call lofts, nor any ceiling but the thatch itself, with the rafters, yet in this smoking hut, like ye wild Irish, of whom many opine them to be antiently descended, doth the man, his wife, and children, cohabit, and in many places with ye geese and ducks under ye bed, the cocks and hens over his head, the cow and calf at the bed's feet . . . (p. 57)

As for the towns of Douglas and Castletown, he stated:

The houses in all these towns are of one fashion, low built, being not contiguous, much less continuous, in placing of them, observing no order either of uniformity or proportion, only Castle Town hath some little formality more than the rest. The materials of these structures are of small stones and lime, as those in the country which I described before, and thatch'd as those also, with this only difference, that these are 2 stories high, that is, they have an upper room above ye lower, which the country houses for the most part have not, the lower rooms they call cellars, for they have none underground; their upper rooms they call lofts, and they are long and narrow, which they thus order; in the middle is ye door, over against that on the other side there are commonly placed 2 beds at each end of the room, one on the other side, at ye upper end of all is the chimney, . . (pp. 68–9)

Mrs Mary Gilrea of Jurby, outside her sod cottage in 1897. The 1901 census shows her as a 77-year-old widow, living on parish relief. She spoke English and Manx. (Pg12695)

are well-preserved examples with handsome frontages protected by railings. There are various grades of accommodation from the lavish classical ranges of the squares to the humble but well-proportioned terraces with their front gardens, and within each house would be well-defined areas to accommodate the family, their servants and the workspaces associated with Victorian living.

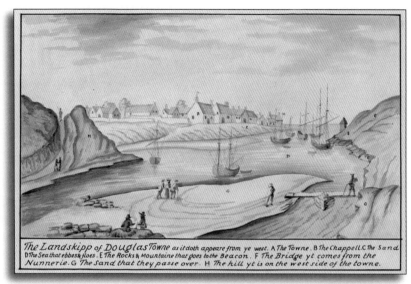

The Landskipp of Douglas Towne as it doth appeare from ye west. A The Towne . B The Chappell. C The Sand. D The Sea that ebbes & floes . E The Rocks & Mountaine that goes to the Beacon . F The Bridge yt comes from the Nunnerie. G The Sand that they passe over . H The hill yt is on the west side of the towne.

Daniel King's *Landskipp of Douglas Towne* shows the type of houses in the area around the harbour, c. 1651. (1957-0101)

The Island pioneered mass tourism in the same period, and the terraced layout, enlarged, proved to be well-suited for the visiting industry. By the 1860s and 70s better communications, improved harbourworks and the new railways increased the flow of visitors to a summer flood. As demand grew, the old landed estates around Douglas and elsewhere were sold for development, and large commodious properties were built, with minor variations, to an overall plan. Large parts of upper Douglas were built solely to cater for this summer trade, and entire terraced streets were built as guesthouses, each one run as the family business by the landlady. The era of the terraces lasted throughout Queen Victoria's reign. The Isle of Man can claim to have a place in the next development, that of suburban living. The work of Mackay Hugh Baillie Scott and Armitage Rigby is well known in the history of the Arts and Crafts Movement. It was to inspire a new style of living typified by the 'garden suburbs' of Douglas. Although the Arts and Crafts style was short-lived, it went on to influence house building throughout the twentieth century.

Information about the former occupiers of a house may be found in a variety of sources. Directories are useful for the nineteenth and early twentieth centuries, particularly if the property in question is a former boarding house, for which specialist directories exist. Newspapers often carried information about property available to rent. Census returns will record at ten-yearly intervals the occupants of a property. However, the information was gathered in an era before postcodes and house numbers, so it can sometimes be difficult to relate this to an existing building, particularly in rural areas. If no copies of the deeds to the property are available, then provided that the name of the present owner is known, a 'backwards' search can be made in the 'grantees' index held at the General Registry, Douglas. These indexes go back to 1911. The MNH Library and Archive Service holds property deeds from the late seventeenth century to 1910. These are indexed by parish and then by name of the 'grantor' or seller. Some of the deeds held by MNH have been digitised and are being indexed for future release through the iMuseum. Deeds held by the General Registry from 1989 to date are available both through public-access terminals at the registry and in the future also at the iMuseum.

Wills are another good source of information not only about real estate proper, but also about possessions, because these are often shown in an inventory of goods which sometimes accompanies a will. The MNH Library holds indexed wills for the period c. 1600 to 1916. These have been digitised and will be available at the iMuseum in due course. Later wills may be consulted at the General Registry. Wills sometimes describe a property in useful terms, for example, 'all my large house, formerly occupied by William Cubbon as a farm'. A considerable number of properties were formerly part of a larger estate so estate papers, such as leases, rentals, surveys and notices of sale, may also help to research a property.

The MNH Library and Archive service holds a photographic survey of farmhouses and cottages, carried out in the 1930s. The collection is listed as PG 5647 in the photographic archive. These photographs, numbering over 700, can be particularly useful if researching even a modest rural property. Some of the cottages that were thatched at the time of the survey will have been re-roofed since, so there are useful clues about the original appearance of a building. Also numbers of the buildings photographed were already derelict at the time, and will have since been demolished altogether. These photographs will be available digitally through the iMuseum from 2012.

William Blundell's *History of the Isle of Man* (1657, reprinted 1876) offers one of the earliest descriptions of the homes of the Manx. Copies of both volumes are held by the MNH Library and Archive Service as MS 00049 and MS 00050, and the work was reprinted by the Manx Society as Volume XXV. John Kitto's book *Historic Homes of the Isle of Man* (1990) offers a good survey of the major dwellings inhabited by the great and the good up to the beginning of the twentieth century; the book is well illustrated, with many interior shots. These are particularly interesting, as it should be noted that most of the houses illustrated are not open to the public.

See also:
✿ Land and Property Records
✿ Wills and Probate

CASTLE RUSHEN (PRISON) PAPERS

Extensive records relating to the use of Castle Rushen as a prison are held by MNH. The bulk of the collection is held under MS 09783 and a hand list and guide to the records exists in the Library and Archive Service Reading Room of the Manx Museum. The records are many and varied, and cover such things as the prisoners' diet and rations, and punishments for offences within the prison. The account books (MS 09783/9-14) record the work upon which prisoners were set within the prison, including breaking of stones and production of oakum. This classic Victorian prison punishment involved the unpicking of worn-out rope on a fixed metal spike to produce loose fibres. These were then sold by the prison to provide caulking for ships, the fibres being rammed between the planks to make them watertight.

The Visiting Magistrates' minute book (MS 09783/8) and the Gaoler's journal for July–August 1872 (MS 09783/7/4) document the final days and execution of the last person to suffer capital punishment on the Isle of Man, John Kewish, who was hanged in the castle for the murder of his father.

Castle Rushen during the era in which it served as the Island's gaol, up to 1891.(Pg9395)

Of particular interest to family historians will be MS 09783/1/1-2, 'An account of the prisoners confined in Castle Rushen', with offenders and debtors listed concurrently. Columns are arranged by the prisoner's name, date of confinement, the cause of detention such as a writ of contempt or order by the Deemster and its date; also the amount of any demand and costs, the date of release and reason for discharge. This covers the dates 1836 to 1850.

Also of interest will be MS 00762C, an admission and discharge register covering the years 1825 to 1832. A register of imprisoned debtors containing the name of the individual, age, date of imprisonment, cause of detention, the date of the order, at whose suit, the amount of the demand and costs and the date of discharge. There are also notes of those prisoners who were transported to the Australian penal colonies. This register is currently being indexed, with a view to the information being made available through the iMuseum in the future. Prisoners from Castle Rushen who were transported to Australia in this era may also be mentioned in the

See also:
✿ Court
   Records
✿ Prison
   Records

Manx Sun newspaper, which is also available through the iMuseum.

MS 09783/2 is an 'offender's book', running from April 1849 to July 1855, and November 1876 to December 1878. This again records the date of imprisonment, the prisoner's name, age and offence, the term of imprisonment and the date and reason for discharge.

Records of prisoners from the period 1807 to 1825 are held by the MNH Library and Archive Service in the Atholl Papers 146, sub folders 1 to 6 (MS 09707). These consist of weekly returns of prisoners together in some cases with the name of the person who was maintaining the prisoner, and the reason for imprisonment. This gives a fascinating insight into prison life before the work of the Victorian prison reformers regularised conditions in British prisons, and attempted to introduce an element of reform. In those early days the standard of life for a prisoner depended very much upon his station in life, and wealthy friends or family were not just permitted but were actually expected to provide for a prisoner's diet and other needs. An incident in March 1823 offers a fascinating insight into the 'ad hoc' nature of prison life in this period. A letter from the Visiting Magistrate Robert Kelly informs the Lieutenant Governor: '. . . that I have sent to your Secretary a petition and complaint against William Corrin [of Castletown] one of His Majesty's Constables for having when on guard at the Gaol taken one of the prisoners there out to a Public House to drink ale' (Atholl Papers 120-55).

The Visiting Magistrates' book (MS 09783/8) for 1 August 1872 records in the words of the High Bailiff the execution of John Kewish, the last prisoner to be executed on the Isle of Man:

I was present this morning at the execution of John Kewish for the murder of his father. He was expected immediately after the clock struck 8 in the morning, on a gallows erected in the debtors yard attached to the castle. The execution was performed by William Calcroft. The death of the unfortunate convict was instantaneous the body hung for an hour and was then lowered and placed in a coffin which had not been seen by the convict. A black flag was hoisted at 8 o'clock to the top of the flagstaff and lowered half mast when he was being removed for execution. When the body was taken down the flag was again raised to the top and after the burial, which took place in the criminals yard, it was lowered and taken down. An inquest was held on the body. All the melancholy arrangements were ably carried out by the gaoler and officers of the gaol and by the persons employed for the constructions and erection of the gallows.

John Kewish, convicted of the murder of his father, was executed at Castle Rushen in 1872. (Pg1219)

CEMETERY RECORDS

A survey of the Island's tombstones and their inscriptions was first carried out by John Feltham and Edward Wright in the summer of 1797. It was published as *Memorials of God's Acre being Monumental Inscriptions in the Isle of Man* by the Manx Society in 1868. Aside from highlighting the fact that very few people at this time appear to have been able to afford a headstone, this document is of great value as in the intervening years many of the headstones will have been lost or become illegible through weathering. This document is held at F75q by the MNH Library and Archive Service and a working copy is available in the Reading Room. MNH also holds transcriptions of monumental inscriptions, compiled by the IOMFHS, from all of the churchyards and cemeteries of the Isle of Man. These are held in the Reading Room, and are indexed. Monumental inscriptions are of tremendous value in establishing what relationship persons within the same household and perhaps sharing the same name had to one another. They can also offer information as to cause of death, which can be particularly useful before the introduction of civil registration.

Headstones in Lezayre churchyard, painted by Robert Evans Creer in 1888. (2006-0074)

See also:
❀ Parish Records

Also of value to family historians are burial plot registers. Information on who bought a grave plot is often recorded and this can shed further light on family relationships. MNH holds some registers of burial plots but others are still held by the parish concerned. Those held by MNH are generally held amongst the papers of that particular parish, for example, for the parish of German, the register recording the sale of burial lots is held as MS 10974/17. Malew burial ground plot conveyances are held at MS 09761/12, whilst the plot register for the Glebe Yard covers the years 1865 to 1896. The most detailed is for the large Braddan (new) cemetery, which from around 1850 served most of Douglas (particularly interesting are MS 09306/3, a book containing records of the sale of private burial plots from 1888 to 1934, and MS 09306/5, a similar book covering the sale of plots in area 2, from 1885 to 1930).

MNH also holds Defunct Returns from 1884 to 1921. These are lists of people who died in each parish in a given period. They are extracts from burial registers sent by vicars to the High Courts of Justice, and are a continuation of an earlier practice prior to civil registration where vicars reported to the courts the names of those who had died, for the purposes of probate. There are anomalies in these records in as much as they sometimes include those who have died in a particular parish but are not buried there, but the typical information includes the name, age and date of burial of the deceased. These series (MS 10216 and MS 10623) are in the process of being digitised and volunteers are currently working on the documents, extracting names to form an index which will be available through the iMuseum.

Burial registers are in many cases to be found with parish records, and are discussed elsewhere in this book.

The headstone of Robert Hutchinson, a Laxey miner, reveals that he was originally from Northumberland, and had held the position of Past Provincial Grand Master (PPGM) within the Oddfellows organisation. (Courtesy of Andrew Scarffe)

CENSUS RECORDS

Early Manx census records tend to be of individual towns, rather than of the whole Island. The earliest known record of this type is William Harrison's Douglas census of 1730 ('List of householders in the town of Douglas, with their names', found in the parish register of St Matthew's, Douglas, which is held by MNH (MS 09888). Other early census records exist for Castletown in 1751 (MS 01770C) and Andreas in 1757 (MS 01164C), however these latter two whilst naming the heads of families and their wives, list only the numbers of children and servants. The record for Andreas was collated by Church authorities as part of the 1757 visitation of all parishes, but appears to be the only one which survives. A census of Peel (1814) and for the parish of German (1814) also

The 1841 census for the Grove, Ramsey reveals the names not just of the Gibb family, but also of their servants. The ages of both Duncan Gibb and his wife Janet are shown incorrectly. Such errors were not uncommon in an age when precise dates of birth carried less importance than they do today.

survive, these were conducted by the Reverend James Gelling at the behest of the Bishop of Sodor and Mann. Both are held in manuscript form only by MNH (within the records of the parish of German at MS 10974/16) but a transcript is available on the Manx Note Book website at: www.isle-of-man.com/manxnotebook.

Microfilm copies of the Isle of Man census returns for 1841 to 1881, and microfiche of the 1891 and 1901 census enumerations are available in the Reading Room of the MNH Library and Archive Service. These returns record each person in a 'household', the relationship of every person to the 'head of household', their ages, occupations and places of birth. For the 1841 census MNH is unusual in that in addition to the official transcripts, for some parishes it also holds the original volumes in which the information was recorded (MS 10052). These have been microfilmed, and the originals would not now normally be produced due to their fragile nature. The 1841 census contains additional valuable information, as it also required informants to identify the parish of their birth. The 1901 census returns for the Isle of Man differ from those of England in that they also contain information about language; a column indicates whether the person spoke English, Manx or both.

The 1911 census was released early, in 2009, as part of a project between the The National Archives (TNA) at Kew and Find My Past (Bright Solid), albeit with certain personal information withheld until 2011. Initially, it is only available on a pay per view basis through the Internet, although it is available free at TNA and in six selected public libraries in England. Discussions at the time of writing are still in progress as to how MNH can provide access to visitors, by means of a library package or subscription, but it is hoped that some form of access will be made available from 2011 when the full data is released. Further details about this are available from MNH.

The 1911 census also contains extra details not recorded previously. Informants were asked to state how long they had been married, how many children had been born of their current marriage and how many of those children were still alive. Also researchers using this census can see for the first time digital images of the original return sheets, as filled out by their ancestor in their own handwriting. This contrasts with the census of previous years, where researchers can only look at pages from the book filled out by the enumerator, after he had visited the households. This in itself provides an interesting degree of insight into the standard of literacy of one's forebears.

Another difference in the approach taken with the 1911 census concerns individual households. In previous decades, it is possible to see the name of everyone living in a particular building, regardless of their relationship to one another. With the 1911 census, records are made available on a household by household basis. Therefore, a lodger renting rooms in a house is not shown on the return of the main family owning or occupying that dwelling, but rather is shown on a separate sheet as a householder in his own right. In the previous census years it is also worth paying attention to how many rooms a family are occupying. In the towns, poorer people may be occupying two or three rooms in a large house, indicating that they are sharing with other families. Check if the enumerator has used single or double lines in the margin. A single line divides households or families within the same property. A double line indicates a new household in a separate property. In rural areas, if a family are shown as occupying two or three rooms, this can often be taken to indicate they live in a traditional Manx cottage, with a living room doubling as a kitchen and one main bedroom with a cockloft above. Harry Kelly's cottage at Cregneash is typical of this type of dwelling.

Information about the various census records available can be obtained via a number of websites:

- www.1911census.co.uk – records for Britain, Isle of Man, overseas military and overseas naval personnel
- www.1901.censusonline.com – records for England and Wales only
- www.nationalarchives.gov.uk/census/ – background information only
- www.ancestry.co.uk – records for Britian and Isle of Man (1841–1901)

The IOMFHS has published transcripts of all of the 1851 and 1881 census. Indexes to the 1841, 1851, 1861, 1871, 1891 and 1901 census, compiled by the late Brian Lawson, are available in paper form in the MNH Library and Archive Service Reading Room and also via the IOMFHS website at:

www.iomfhs.im/default.aspx?CategoryID=22.

The Genealogical Society of Utah has name-indexed the 1881 census and a microfiche copy is held by MNH. In addition, some parishes and the town of Ramsey have been indexed for other decades by private researchers and these hard-copy indexes are available at the library enquiry desk. The indexes to the 1841, 1851, 1861, 1871 and 1891 census can be searched electronically through the iMuseum, where the 1911 census will also be available.

Census records relating to Ontario in Canada and Ohio in the United States are also worth consideration when researching Manx ancestors. Both areas saw large influxes of Manx settlers in the nineteenth century, indeed the statement bears repeating that there are reputedly more people of Manx descent living in Ohio than there are in the Isle of Man. It is not unknown for an ancestor missing from one of the Isle of Man census returns to be picked up on the Ohio census, having emigrated permanently or perhaps just visiting family.

The 1850 census of Ohio is available on microfilm in the Reading Room of the MNH Library and Archive Service. The 1880 census of Ohio (and those of other American states to 1930) and the 1881 census of Canada are available via a number of websites including: www.familysearch.org and www.ancestry.co.uk. This latter website holds other extensive records relating to the state of Ohio, which may well include Manx forebears.

CHILDREN'S HOMES

The earliest children's homes on the Isle of Man were founded as charitable institutions, on private initiative. This was in response to the high numbers of children who having lost their parents had no means of supporting themselves, and were in danger of falling into vice or criminal activity. The Douglas Home Mission was started in December 1868, and was first instituted with a view to aiding the large number of destitute children who were without parents, relatives or friends and needed help with regard to their food, clothing, lodging and education. The home was first situated in James Street, Douglas but in May 1869 it moved to larger premises in Woodhouse Terrace on the South Quay. At this time it provided a home for twenty-two children between the ages of 6 and 14 years. By May 1870, the Mission needed to move again and took Mountain View on Glencrutchery Road for an annual rent of £40. When the children were brought to the home, a form had to be signed by the surviving parent or guardian agreeing to give up all claim to them, and not to interfere with their upbringing in any way.

The Douglas Industrial Home for Orphan and Destitute Children was founded in 1868, and in 1871 it merged with the Douglas Home Mission. In 1881 it changed its name to the Isle of Man Industrial Home for Orphan and Destitute Children. Once in the home the children had to work in order to bring in income, in addition to their schooling. They manufactured paper bags, hearth rugs and firelighters for sale, and a tailor was employed once a week to teach the boys to mend their clothes. Some 16 acres of land were cultivated as a kitchen garden. Some of the boys worked as errand boys and as market porters on a Saturday night. The children commenced their day at 6.00am when they were given a small piece of bread. They would then attend lessons and prayers until 8.30 when they would stop for breakfast, which would consist of porridge and milk. They were then allowed a little time to brush their clothes, clean their shoes and have a short play.

It was then work again until they were given a midday meal which might consist of boiled rice or Irish stew (made with potatoes and meat). Then they returned to work, followed by more lessons until time for tea at 5.15. If they were lucky, tea might consist of herring and bread, or just bread and butter, with tea, milk and sugar. After the meal the children would be allowed to play in the grounds, read or amuse themselves with toys until their evening prayers and Bible lesson before going to bed. Every day each child learnt to read and repeat from memory a text from the Bible. When they were old enough the boys would be apprenticed and they would then live in their Master's house. He would feed, clothe and train them for their future occupation.

In 1881 there was a major change in the financial status of the home, as it obtained money from the charity established by the will of Pierre Henri Joseph Baume, an eccentric French immigrant. This money meant the home was no longer operating on a hand-to-mouth basis and enabled it in 1882 to buy Strathallan Hall in Onchan, which allowed for accommodation for ninety children. The youngsters were given a good education and although it was known as an industrial home, the work in which the children were engaged was of a self-supporting nature. They had a market garden and glass houses and in inclement weather they assembled paper bags which were sold to local shopkeepers. From the late 1880s it became associated with the Quarrier Homes of Scotland and sent many children to Canada, via the scheme administered by these homes. In 1910 the home and its occupants moved to Glencrutchery in Douglas, and later became part of the National Children's Home organisation.

Ramsey Children's Home had its origins in a temporary Ragged School established in the winter of 1862 for the well-being of the destitute children. The instigator was Miss Susanna Gibson, daughter of T.C. Gibson who owned the Ramsey shipyard. The success of this temporary expedient led to the establishment of a permanent home in 1863. This became the Ramsey Industrial School. Thwaites' *History and Directory* of 1863 stated:

An Industrial School has just been erected at North Ramsey, but at present no master is appointed. The object of the founders of this institution is the instruction of those children who have been entirely neglected by their parents, or prevented by other circumstances from partaking of all other means of instruction and improvement. In cases of extreme destitution, it is intended to provide food as well as education. The

A letter from A. Cowley, living in Adolphustown, Ontario, Canada was published in the 1891 report of the Home for Orphaned and Destitute Children. Part of it reads:

Dear Mr Campbell, I write to let you know that I am glad to hear you are coming out next spring, I will be very glad to see you. We are having some very cold weather here. We have had it thirty below zero, and we have had lots of snow. We are drawing up our wood now, and it is a fine job too. . . . I was going to school, but the school is nearly three miles from where I live, so I can't go, but I will go soon . . . I hope all the rest of the boys and girls are well; give my love to them, and tell them I wish they were out in this country . . . Give my love to the Governor and Mrs Walpole, tell them I hope they are well; and the High Bailiff Mr Barber, and the rest of the Committee. I hope you will have a big crowd this year, and get enough money to send all the boys and girls out to this beautiful country, for I know they will not want to go back.

object chiefly in view at present is the rescue of poor girls for whom, if left without a home, (as is the case in many instances,) there is absolutely no rescue and no hope. These girls will be trained to habits of order and industry, and every way fitted for domestic service. The school will be supported by voluntary contributions. The number of children received will, therefore, depend upon the amount of the subscriptions. With the exception of two very little children, whose extremely destitute condition first suggested the idea of the school, no provision at present is made for boys. It is, however, to be hoped that the institution will meet with that patronage it so justly deserves, so that in a short time not only the poor girls, but the most destitute of the male children may be received, clothed, and educated within its walls.

In 1878 this home became part of the Methodist Children's Home and Orphanage (founded in 1869). By 1880 a new home, Ballacloan ('Children's Estate' in Manx), had been built near the Mooragh Park. In its later years this home was run by the National Children's Home. By 1881 there were twenty-seven children resident, of whom only eight were Manx. In total some 400 children were admitted before 1914, and many of these came from the London area. Most were aged 4 or over and stayed some five years at Ramsey. Girls were trained for domestic service, whilst many of the boys were sent to Canada. The home could accommodate about forty-five children. From 1904–17 only girls were admitted, but in 1917 an additional home, Dalmeny, was acquired and this became the girls' home. Boys were henceforth readmitted to Ballacloan. In 1956 Ballacloan was sold, and all the resident children were transferred to Dalmeny. By 1989, with major changes in the way children in care were accommodated, all residential care was transferred to Douglas. Dalmeny was kept open only for special needs' children. Further background information on Dalmeny can be found in Constance Radcliffe's *Shining By the Sea* (1989).

MNH holds no records of individuals from children's homes. Records relating to the National Children's Home on Glencrutchery Road in Douglas are available, if appropriate for release, from:

Isle of Man Children's Centre
Woodbourne House
38 Woodbourne Lane
Douglas
Isle of Man
IM2 3LG

These take the form of an admission register, dating from 1888. The information contained within it covers the child's name, age, parents and the reason why the child was placed in the home. Many of the children were apprenticed to businesses in Douglas or on the Island and some of course were sent abroad, and this is sometimes

Ballacloan, the children's home near Mooragh Park in Ramsey.

noted. The records of the National Children's Home in Ramsey (Dalmeny) were transferred to the NCH North West Office in Warrington some years ago. The National Children's Home is now known as Action For Children, and the organisation's website www.actionforchildren.org.uk has a page dedicated to records which it holds and what level of access to these is available.

The Isle of Man Home for Orphaned and Destitute Children did receive an endowment from the Henry Bloom Noble Trust, and some administrative (rather than personal) records relating to this may be found in Noble's papers, held by MNH (MS 09196). The MNH Library also holds the annual reports of the Home for Orphaned and Destitute Children (Reference D50/4). Although these reports make reference to the fund set up in order to send orphaned children to the colonies (and list the subscribers to this fund), there are few names of those who were actually sent abroad contained within them. The reports do contain some printed letters received by the organisation from children formerly in the home, reporting on their new circumstances. Most are only initialled but some do show the full name.

The British Home Child Emigration scheme ran from 1870 to 1957. During that time some 100,000 British Home Children (alleged orphans) were sent to Canada by over 50 British child-care organisations. These 4–15-year-old children worked as indentured farm labourers and domestic servants until they were 18 years old. The British child-care organisations professed a dominant motive of providing these children with a better life than they would have had in Britain, but many have come under critical scrutiny since from some of the children and their descendants, who allege that they also had monetary incentives. They state that when the British authorities 'sold' these children to Canadian farmers, they not only rid themselves of an unwanted section of their society but also profited financially.

What is undeniable is that children in care in Britain were often permanently separated from their extended families by being sent abroad. Siblings were then separated from each other when they reached Canada. Most never saw their brothers and sisters again. Many spent their lives trying to identify their parents and find their siblings and most were unsuccessful. An unknown number of children ran away from their indentured labour in Canada to the United States. It is estimated that there are now 4–5 million Canadian and American descendants of the British Home Children.

Perry Snow in Canada has undertaken much research on the British 'Home Children'. His database holds details of 375 children from the Isle of Man who were sent to Canada. His contact details are:

Perry Snow BA (Hons) MA Clinical Psychologist
4103 Centre Street
NW Calgary
Alberta
Canada T2E 2Y6

Telephone/fax: 00 1 403 288 4477
Email:persnow@shaw.ca
Website: www.freepages.genealogy.rootsweb.ancestry.com/~britishhomechildren/surnames.htm

An article entitled 'Emigration of Manx Children to Canada 1884–1928' appeared in the Isle of Man Natural History and Antiquarian Society (IOMNHAS) *Proceedings*, Volume 10, 1–10. In addition, the National Archives of Canada holds information about the so-called 'Home Children' and this has been indexed by the British Isles Family History Society of Greater Ottawa (BIFHSGO). The information can be accessed online via the Society website (www.bifhsgo.ca/). The postal address is:

BIFHSGO
P.O. Box 38026
Ottawa
Ontario
Canada K2C 3Y7

See also:
✿ Adoption
Records

CHURCH COURT RECORDS

Diocesan courts had a wide range of functions including trying parishioners for offences against Church law. Whilst today it is difficult for us to appreciate the amount of control the Church held over many aspects of people's lives, these records can be a mine of information for family historians. One record series, the Presentments, contain matters to be dealt with by the court, brought by churchwardens and vicars for misdemeanours. Another series, the Libri Causarum (literally the 'books of causes'), lists these cases and the content is wide and varied. These records include disputed wills, cases of non-attendance at church (which was punishable by a fine), fornication and illegitimate children. Approximately 10 per cent of births in the eighteenth and nineteenth centuries were illegitimate. If a record of a baptism records only a mother's name this may be an indication of illegitimacy, and it may then be worth consulting presentments in the ecclesiastical court records. In these cases the plaintiff (usually the mother of an illegitimate child, or sometimes its maternal grandfather) claimed that a particular person was the father. If the Church believed this to be the case, it made an affiliation to the father and might order that 'lying in' costs be paid to the mother. The child is not normally named in these records, but the father's name may appear as the defendant. The Presentments span 1659 to 1874. Those prior to 1790 are available on microfilm in the Reading Room, and are being indexed.

Another series, the Church Court Orders, spans 1786 to 1918, and contains a brief outcome of each case. They are a useful resource from which to obtain the names of fathers affiliated to a child and who were possibly charged with lying in expenses. An index by name for orders from 1815 to 1918 can be checked by consulting library staff, as it is not yet publicly available. Because of the significance of this resource for family history research (enabling fathers of children to be identified) the original documents have been earmarked for future digitisation. In the interim it is hoped that the existing indexes will be suitable for delivery through the iMuseum.

The Presentments, Libri Causarum and orders of court are all part of diocesan deposit MS 10194 at the MNH Library and Archive Service. A particularly interesting case from the Diocesan Presentments of St George's chapel, Douglas for 1808, held in this series, concerns Captain John Quilliam of the Battle of Trafalgar fame. In the documents he was named as the father of an illegitimate child: 'At a Chapter Court Holden at Douglas June 21st 1808. Elizabeth Gelling has deposed on the Holy Evangelists that Captain John Quilliam now of the Isle of Man is father of her illegitimate child.' Quilliam chose to ignore the charge, and at another hearing held at Marown in 1809 he was found to be in contempt of the court. The child however was baptised at St Matthew's, Douglas and the entry here reads: 'John Quilliam son of Jn' Quilliam and

See also:
✿ Folklore
✿ Court
   Records

Elezth Gellin [*sic*] I'llegit. Baptised May 8, 1808. Sadly, the little boy died the following year, and it is further recorded that: 'John Illegit child of Elizabeth Gelling and John Quilliam buried at Kirk Braddan 14th January 1809.'

The case against Quilliam appears to have been dropped by the Church following the child's passing, but an interesting sidelight is cast upon Elizabeth Gelling, for she appears twice more in subsequent church court records with illegitimate children, in each case naming a person of wealth as the father, and it is tempting to speculate that she chose to name John Quilliam as the result of his substantial fortune following the award of Trafalgar prize money.

Another part of the church court records is held at MS 03640. This is an account of the members of the Castle Rushen garrison (male and female) tried by diocesan courts between 1601 and 1720. It includes references to punishment by imprisonment, the stocks, penance and payments towards repairs to Castletown chapel and bridge. There is also a reference to a woman placed in the stocks, and a man sentenced to wear a bridle for cursing.

Another fascinating story from the

The cover of a guidebook produced by the witchcraft centre, Castletown, around 1960.

One of the charges brought before the church courts was 'charming', which seems to have been the survival of a form of folk magic. The idea of a 'wise woman' able to cure minor ailments, a figure that had probably been a part of most rural communities since time immemorial, did not sit easily with the paranoia of the seventeenth-century Church. The Kirk Malew parish register contains a document that was published in the *Journal of the Manx Museum* (Volume III, 39), one of many such in the collections of MNH:

*Whereas Mrs. Jane Cesar hath bene accused upon suspicon of whitchcraft charminge or sorscerie wherupon certaine examacons have beene taken And the said case beinge putt to the triall of a Jurie, they the s*d *Jurors (after examinacon of the business) have this day cleared and acquitted ye said Jane Cesar of the accusacon aforesaid as by theire Answere may appeare.*

*Nevertheless that the said Jane Cesar may declare her inocencie of such practizes and that shee doth renounce the same as diabolicall & wicked; she is hereby ordered to acknowledge the same before the Congregacon of Kk Malew parish the next Lords day to the end that others may be admonished to relinquish detest and abhor such delusions wch are of great inducemt to greater temptacons and are too frequently practized in this Island as is dayly observed of w*ch *if any one shall be hereafter accused and the same lawfully proved such persons are to be severely fined, and punished, or otherwise proceeded against accordinge as the law doth p*rvide *in such cases.*

As late as the nineteenth century J.J. Frowde noted that some professional charmers still made a speciality of curing ringworms, others of stopping the flow of blood from severe cuts, whilst yet others devoted their powers to the removal of warts. He transcribed an account given to him personally:

I can well remember when about ten years of age being taken to Laxey . . . from thence up into the country to a cottage on the mountains, where dwelt an old woman by repute a highly successful charmer. The journey was undertaken for the purpose of having her supposed powers brought to bear on a longstanding ringworm on my head. On entering the hut I was placed in a low chair before the fire and the old crone began by moistening her thumb which she rubbed in the ashes on the hearth and then transferred to my head, rubbing the adhering dust well into my scalp at the same time muttering a charm or incantation of some sort. When this operation was over the ceremony was complete, and having paid the fee we departed.

In the 1950s there was a temporary revival of interest in witchcraft in the Isle of Man. The Witches' Mill at Castletown was established by Gerald Brousseau Gardiner as an occult and folk-magic museum. The history of the mill and its supposed connections with witchcraft however were entirely invented by Gardiner in order to attract tourists.

diocesan courts concerns the eighteenth-century case of Bahee Kaighin, who was accused of witchcraft. The presentment record gives a full account of her trial and subsequent acquittal through lack of evidence. In fact, there seem to have been numerous cases of persons brought before the church courts upon charges of witchcraft in the mid-seventeenth century. Witchcraft in the Isle of Man was considered as prevalent, if not more prevalent than elsewhere in Britain at this time. The foremost scholar on this topic, Professor Ronald Hutton, has stated that 'In the Middle Ages the Isle of Man had the reputation of being the part of the British Isles most steeped in sorcery'. The reason for this is generally believed to be the far greater survival of what might be termed 'folk magic' in the Isle of Man. The cases make for fascinating reading. Diocesan court records from 1666 record the fact that Elizabeth Kewin, alias Cubon, was tried by Kirk Arbory chapter court, the charge being that she was: 'Goeing abroad the country and bringing home with her burdens of corne, meale, fish, etc and suspected to have gotten the same for sorcery and wicked practices, and by deluding poor ignorant people; also (by report) many resorting to her house to get of her sorcery, and bad signes seen by credible persons . . .'. The records of her trial are very detailed with many witnesses named and indeed quoted verbatim. Although she was convicted of sorcery, she was merely given a penance to perform.

By the later seventeenth century it seems that the authorities were aware of the fact that malicious charges of witchcraft were easy to make and difficult to refute. They did not want a repetition of the incident, which the Libri Scaccarii record in 1617, when a woman and her adult son were burned at the stake in Castletown for witchcraft, their screams apparently audible in Ballasalla. Contrary to the situation in other parts of the British Isles, this incident seems to have dampened rather than fuelled the fervour for witch burning. The trial in 1617 was unusual in its seriousness, in that witchcraft was alleged to have caused a death, thus making it a capital offence. Subsequently, in the Isle of Man, witchcraft trials were always held in the church courts, rather than the criminal courts, and it seems that the Manx authorities were very careful to ensure this, as the church courts could not hand down a death sentence.

Even as late as the 1700s we find another John Quilliam (church warden and grandfather of the famous seafarer) earning notoriety when his neighbours were brought before an ecclesiastical court for 'turning the sieve' at the Quilliam family home, Ballakelly in Marown. This was a form of sorcery used to find the truth of a statement – apparently they were attempting to catch a thief!

A final part of the church court records concerns Orders on Claims (MS 10194). This series concerns claims from creditors against the estates of those who had died, and which were assessed by an archdeacon or the bishop's representative. This material is being photographed with a view to digital access via the iMuseum.

See also:
✿ Parish Records
✿ Church Court Records

CHURCH RECORDS

The MNH Library and Archive Services Officer holds the position *ex officio* of Methodist archivist and keeper of records for the Isle of Man District. Methodist records are extensive, and include such things as roll books from Rosemount and Pulrose Methodist churches in the 1950s (MS 08558), marriage registers from Methodist New Connexion Derby Road chapel, Douglas and United Methodists church, Parliament Square, Ramsey, 1896–1909 (MS 08644), and numerous account books, minute books and log books. Many of the records relate to Sunday schools and in some cases these include registers (discussed in the School Records section). A partial hand list of Methodist records held by MNH is available for consultation in the Reading Room.

Equally extensive are the records of the Anglican diocese of Sodor and Mann. The archives of the Manx Church (as the Church of England is known on the Island) are also held by MNH. Some interesting material survives amongst early church records, including, for example, the list of seat holders in Douglas chapel (Old St Matthew's) in 1735 (MS 00959), a diagram of the interior of Ballaugh church, with names of pew-holders, around 1826 (MS 01618/2) and a document from Santan church regarding the rebuilding of the chancel and the right to pews therein in 1774 (MS 04817). Pews were usually purchased by prominent families, and could equally well be sold, so numerous deeds exist regarding the sale and purchase of seats in churches in this era.

In the 1920s the Vicar General deposited a large quantity of early correspondence, official papers and administrative papers relating to the fabric of buildings, reporting procedures and the twice-yearly reports from the parishes. Church records cover the diocesan level, which are mainly administrative, and also the parochial level, and it is this latter material that is much more likely to hold information of interest to family historians. As an example of the type of material that is held at this level, MS 11101 covers the parochial records of St Mary's, Castletown. This includes minutes, accounts, correspondence, deeds and minutes of the Parochial Church Council. It is well worth remembering that in the nineteenth century the parish as a unit had many administrative roles now performed by local government, and the nature of the records will reflect this. This particular deposit also contains copies of electoral rolls – those who attend church are usually given a form to complete, which registers them to vote for the Parochial Church Council. It was once also a requirement that a parishioner had to have been baptised in the parish. These rolls are of rather limited use for family historians because they are often short, though this depends upon the size of the church. In this deposit there is also information about bequests to the church, and indeed it is not uncommon in the nineteenth century and earlier to discover that people left property to the church in their will.

Church records include applications for marriage licences signed by Bishop's Surrogates. These are not parochial records, as they cover several parishes together, and are not licences themselves but the actual application. They cover the end of the nineteenth century and the beginning of the twentieth century and are held under MS 11099.

The records of the Anglican diocese of Sodor and Mann include at MS 12019 the records of the Diocesan Board of Finance (DBF). Most of this material is rather mundane administrative records such as bank statements, but the deposit does contain amongst other things detailed and extensive lists of those young people who were confirmed in the Church of England and thus able to partake of Holy Communion. Generally speaking, these lists contain just names. There are no places of birth or addresses. However, those for Douglas in the early 1940s are particularly interesting as they cover HMS *St George*, the Royal Naval training establishment for boys which was established on the Isle of Man during the Second World War. Literally hundreds of boys passed through the establishment during the years it was in operation and many were confirmed whilst in training on the Island. The records are broken down into Howstrake, Majestic and Cunningham Camps, the main accommodation centres making up HMS *St George*. These records offer one method of establishing if a forebear with Second World War naval service had trained on the Isle of Man. The records extend to the 1980s but later years will be closed.

MNH does not hold records of the Catholic Church on the Isle of Man in any official capacity, but does have permission to hold the records of the Catholic Church of St Mary of the Isle in Douglas (part of the archdiocese of Liverpool). These records include registers of baptisms, 1860–1942; registers of defuncts, 1862–85, 1913–98; and registers of defuncts, 1876–83, 1961–73 (all under MS 11988), and under MS 10857 the following:

- Baptism and marriage registers (mixed), 1817–56
- Baptism registers, 1856–1920
- Indexes to baptisms, 1856–1928
- Notice books, including some banns of marriage, 1862–1995 (with gaps)
- Cash books, 1852–79, 1923–29
- Bench rent account books, 1855–1937
- Donation book, 1852–73
- Mission accounts and parish accounts books, 1903–64.

CIVIL REGISTRATION

See also:
✿ Parish Records

Voluntary civil registration of births and marriages was introduced in the Isle of Man in 1849, and provided a means for persons who objected to or who declined the offices of the Established Church to make a registration of a birth or a marriage. This removed the anomaly whereby a baptism performed in a dissenters' church was not accepted in a court of law as proof of parentage. However, it was not until 1878 that registration of births became compulsory, some forty-one years after the equivalent legislation was passed in Britain. Compulsory civil registration of deaths was also introduced to the Isle of Man in 1878, and compulsory civil registration of marriages on the Island followed in 1884. Although the registration of marriages had taken place from an early date, the 1884 Act of Tynwald transferred this responsibility from the Ecclesiastical to the Civil Registry. Copy certificates of births and deaths are available from the General Registry. Prior to these dates, researchers are dependent upon parish records (discussed in the Parish Registers section).

A microfiche copy of the index to civil registration records of births, marriages and deaths is kept in the MNH Library Reading Room. This index is divided into four districts prior to 1979, and then is further subdivided into two series of Established Church and Nonconformist records, so in some cases it may be necessary to check eight sets of records in order to

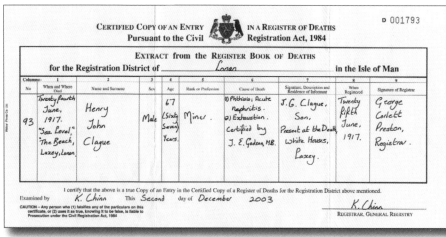

find the desired entry. The records cover the whole island from 1980 to 1993. This index is useful for confirming when and indeed whether such an event took place on the Isle of Man. Full certificates can then be obtained from the General Registry. Unfortunately, some marriage entries for the eastern district are only indexed by the male name, which can make checking difficult. Because the Isle of Man has its own General Registry it is not therefore included in the indexes to the British registries for civil registration or probate. By the same token, it is not currently possible to search Isle of Man births, deaths and marriages online via www.ancestry.co.uk, though some other websites do appear to have Isle of Man records, for example, www.ukbmd.org.uk/.

A certified copy of an entry in the Register of Deaths, produced by the Isle of Man Registries. It shows that Henry John Clague, a miner, died of the lung disease Phthisis in June 1917.

COURT RECORDS

Court records dating from before 1800 are held by the MNH Library and Archive Service, which also has microfilms of many later records. The post-1800 records are held by IOMPRO or the General Registry and access to them will depend on whether there is a microfilm copy available for public use, the date of the record and the confidentiality of the contents so, as with other records at IOMPRO, application should be made in advance. For nineteenth- and early twentieth-century records first check whether a microfilm is available at MNH.

Two good background sources are A.W. Moore's *History of the Isle of Man* (1900) and J.R. Dickinson's *The Lordship of Man under the Stanleys* (1997), both of which cover the administration of the Island through the courts. The current organisation of the courts can be seen on the Courts of Justice website: www.courts.im.

Court judgments from recent years are available to search via the Internet, on the website www.judgments.im. This contains a free online database providing access to the judgments delivered by the Isle of Man Courts of Justice. Currently, the site lists all judgments handed down from 2002 onwards, of which some of the earlier ones are in PDF format, and the majority of judgments delivered in 2000 and 2001 in PDF format. At present, a search cannot look at the contents of a PDF document, only the titles and party names.

Paper copies of pre-2000 judgments can be obtained from the General Registry Library (telephone: 01624 687593) and the Tynwald Library (telephone: 01624 685520). Copies of judgments are subject to the current charge for photocopying. Links to Manx judgments delivered by the Supreme Court for the Isle of Man, the Judicial Committee of the Privy Council and relevant judgments made by the European Court of Human Rights can be accessed via the 'Other Judgments' section on the site. Judgments will normally be published within ten working days of the judgment being handed down, with the exception of judgments that need to be 'de-personalised' prior to publication, which may take longer.

The Criminal Court in the Isle of Man is known as the Court of General Gaol Delivery. Originally, this court was presided over by the Governor, members of the clergy and House of Keys. This continued until 1823, when responsibility passed to the Deemsters and in 1921 to the Second Deemster. The first records begin around 1500, and those up to 1799 are held by MNH, which also has on microfilm the Criminal Books from 1848 to 1902 and the Criminal Court Entry Books (lists of cases by date) from 1848 to 1970.

The Civil Courts were the Chancery Court, the Exchequer Court, the Common Law Courts, the Admiralty Court and the Northern and Southern Deemsters' Courts.

Deemster Roy Eason presiding over Court session at Castle Rushen, in the 1960s. (Pg7828)

In 1883 the High Court of Justice was established with three Divisions – Chancery, Common Law (including the previous Exchequer and Admiralty jurisdictions) and Staff of Government (appeals from other divisions). Changes in the twentieth century included the addition of a Family Division in 1991.

The Chancery Court was established in 1578. Its main records were called the Libri Cancellari (also known as Lib Canc). Those from 1578 to 1799 containing actions, decrees, etc. of the Chancery Court and petitions and enrolled deeds of

Deemster John Taubman, appointed to the post in 1739. (1973-0073)

Quiggin's *Illustrated Guide to the Isle of Man* (1841) notes that:

THE COURT OF GENERAL GAOL DELIVERY is held twice in the year for the trial of felonies. In this court the Governor presides, attended by the Deemsters and Council. It was formerly held in the open air, within the outer gate of Castle Rushen, and the Governor, Council, and Deemsters sat there with the twenty-four Keys; and if any criminal were indicted for felony, four men out of each parish, amounting to sixty-eight, were summoned for the purpose of trying the felony, and if the person indicted, when put upon his trial, pleaded not guilty, four men out of one parish were brought before him in order that he might select such of them as he thought proper; and in case he did not choose the said four or any of them, then four others out of the next parish were in like manner brought before him, and so on until he had chosen twelve out of the number returned to the court, who were sworn to try the felony; and the Attorney-General proceeded to examine the witnesses on behalf of the crown, and the person accused made his defence. After the proceedings had been gone through, and the jury were ready to deliver their verdict, one of the Deemsters demanded of the foreman of the jury, in the Manx language, 'Vod fir charree soie?' in English, 'May he who ministers at the altar continue to sit?' or, 'Whether such of the council as are Ecclesiastic could remain in court or not?' and if the foreman of the jury gave for answer, they could not, then the clergy withdrew; whereupon one of the Deemsters asked the jury if the prisoner was guilty or not guilty, and upon the jury declaring him guilty, one of the Deemsters pronounced sentence of death. The law and constitution of this court are now the same, except that the right of challenge has been put under considerable limitation by an act passed in 1813, for amending the criminal laws, and that it has been adjudged by the King in Council that the Keys do not form an integral part of the court.

bargain and sale are held by MNH as MS 10071. The remainder, which continue until 1896, are at IOMPRO. The other Chancery Court records available on film at MNH are Chancery Petitions, 1806–1851 (GL803-822) and Chancery Petitions indexes, 1800–1935.

The main records of the Exchequer Court were called Libri Scaccarii (Lib Scacc). These are available on microfilm in MNH from 1580 to their end in 1847, along with Exchequer and Staff of Government to 1895 and Staff of Government to 1896 to 1916. There is a filmed index covering Lib Scacc and its successors from 1799 to 1925.

The Common Law Courts are now divided into Superior and Summary jurisdictions, but originally covered any kind of action between subject and subject, including real or personal estate. The early records are called Libri Placitorium (Lib Plitor) or Books of Common Pleas. These are on microfilm at MNH from 1496 to

William Blundell, in his *History of the Isle of Man*, says:
These deemsters in the Isle of Man are but two in number, and but seldom sit both together upon any cause whatsoever, for their power is distinct, dividing the Island between them into two parts, as it were by a line crossing the Island from east to west to Peeltown, in the west side of the Island, from Douglas Town in the east; ye one deemster having jurisdiction in the north part, the other in the south part of the Island, the Island being long, and in the midst very narrow. The deemsters are chosen out of the natives of the Island, but not by the natives themselves ... they have ever been elected by the kings and lords of the Island ... The lord maketh chief of ye deemsters of the most sufficient, judicious, and of men of ye greatest understandings, yet best know ye laws and customs of ye Island, for he ought to be perfect and speak the Manks language, whereby he may be able to give that charge to the juries in the courts of ye sheedings to pronounce sentence of life and death at their head courts, to give the oath to the crowner and moors, and to understand ye plaintif and defendants pleading before him, etc., and for this cause there were never any deemsters chosen but such as were of ye Manks breed only, and those of the best and ye most antient families, as I noted before in the Christians and Cannals.

A list of known Deemsters from 1408 to 1960 appears in the *Journal of Manx Museum*, Volume VI, 160. The list is compiled from the *Liber Juramentorum*, the *Isle of Man Statutes*.

See also:
✿ Castle
   Rushen
   (Prison)
   Papers
✿ Church
   Court
   Records
✿ Wills and
   Probate

their end in 1901, followed by Common Law Division records from 1902 to 1916 (GL687 to GL690). A filmed index is also available covering 1948 to 1952 (GL773). Of particular interest in Lib Plitor are the earlier records of those criminals who were sentenced to transportation to the Australian penal colonies during the nineteenth century. A full list of those sentenced to transportation also appears in Hampton Creer's *Never to Return* (2000). A parallel series of records of those who suffered transportation exists at TNA in the Home Office Convict Transportation Registers (HO 11); this material has been indexed and is available via both www.ancestry.co.uk and the website of the State Library of Queensland (www.slq.qld.gov.au/info/fh/convicts/about). In both cases it is possible to extract the names of Manx convicts.

Within the MNH Library and Archive Service, MS 10050 contains some of the records of the office of the Clerk to Isle of Man Justices (Magistrates and High Bailiffs). Most of the documentation consists of judgments handed down by the courts of petty session, for minor offences, and the punishments consist mainly of fines. These records begin in 1849 and go up to 1971, so later volumes will be closed under the seventy-five-year rule. They are organised by town, and also include material relating to licensing. Other such records are held by IOMPRO and General Registry.

IOMPRO also holds licensing court records from 1818, bankruptcy proceedings records from 1872 and Guardians of Court accounts from 1848.

Enquests were courts of enquiry with a far wider scope than English inquests, although they do include enquiries into deaths. Records of Enquests from 1688 to 1916 are on film in the MNH Library and Archive Service, along with indexes to 1829 and entry books from 1830 to 1941. Later, possibly in the nineteenth century, the term was anglicised to inquest. Some inquest information is confidential and, as with most records in IOMPRO, requests for access to post-1916 records must be made in advance so that the relevant authority is obtained. Recent inquests are not usually available for public inspection, although extracts from files may be made available upon special permission from the coroner. It is also worth remembering that inquests are often covered in local newspaper reports which sometimes go into considerable detail. Many inquests were held during the Second World War, covering such things as fatal aircraft crashes on the Island or into the sea nearby. Steve Poole's book *Rough Landing or Fatal Flight: a History of Aircraft Accidents On, Over and Around the Isle of Man* (1999) adds background information on many of these incidents. Frequently, there were inquests into deaths of enemy aliens held in internment camps on the Island.

CREW LISTS

Crew lists are the records of the crew serving on ships of a certain size for a certain period – usually a voyage or half-year. Smaller vessels under a minimum tonnage were not required to keep crew lists, so the records do not cover fishing boats, for example. The documents are more properly called Crew Lists and Agreements. Most of those relating to the Isle of Man are held by MNH under MS 09800, however there are some gaps, as years ending in 0 and 5 were extracted as a sample prior to deposit, and are now held in the Newfoundland Maritime History Archive (www.mun.ca/mha).

The masters of British-registered ships were (and still are) required by law to keep records of their crew and return them to the authorities (in the late nineteenth century this was the Board of Trade, a department of the British Government). Failure to make returns promptly could result in delays to the ship and fines for the master, and compliance with the regulations seems to have been good. As a result, the Board of Trade accumulated a large volume of documents (possibly numbering into millions), most of which have survived to the present. Unfortunately, the quantity of documents for the period after 1861 became so unwieldy that these volumes were eventually dispersed to nearly fifty different repositories. This can make it cumbersome to access records for individual ships.

However, the documents can provide detailed information on the comings and goings of all ranks of seafarers. A typical document contains information about the ship, for example, its name, official number, port and date of registry, owner's name and address, master's name and address, and the tonnage of the vessel. Each crew member's full name, age or year of birth, place of birth, date of signing on and off, capacity in which employed and the name of the ship in which previously served should also be recorded. There should also be a list of voyages with dates and sometimes details of the ship's cargo.

The most interesting item of information in the entry for a seafarer is likely to be 'Ship in which previously served'. In theory, this allows the researcher to trace back the career of a seafarer step by step, through a series of crew lists, until he or she comes to the entry that says 'first ship'. In practice, however, the chain is likely to break down sooner rather than later. Nevertheless, it should be possible to trace back at least a few ships.

Ships sailing in British coastal waters filled in crew lists every six months, recording all the crew who had sailed on the ship during that time. Some of these lists were made up from temporary records which were held on the ship. Ships that made any voyage outside British coastal waters completed an agreement for that voyage only. Seafarers signed on at the start of the voyage and also on or off (or deserted) at ports where the ship called. Entries in these documents were usually signed by the seafarers themselves.

Where a vessel sailed mostly in British waters but made occasional foreign-going trips, there may be both lists and agreements for the same period. Agreements for

See also:
- Shipping Company Records
- Shipping Records

foreign-going ships included sections to record disciplinary matters, for example, where seafarers deserted or were dismissed. There are also official logs which record similar details and also events such as accidents and wrecks. These official logs do not include day-to-day journals of the working of the ship and they do not survive (if they ever existed) for many voyages, presumably the uneventful ones. However, since the events that are recorded are sometimes dramatic and are described at the time in the master's own words, where they exist they make fascinating reading. On signing off from a ship, a seafarer would be given discharge papers recording the voyage and comments on their work and conduct. A small number of these documents survive, as family heirlooms, in record offices and occasionally amongst bundles of crew lists.

In order to find records of a merchant seafarer on crew lists of British-registered vessels for the period 1861 to 1913, it is possible to use the original documents. In order to do this, however, it is first necessary to find the whereabouts of these, as the original documents are dispersed. In order to find an ancestor on an original crew list, it is necessary to know:

- The name of the ship that they sailed on
- Her official number
- The year(s) that the seafarer served on that vessel
- Where the crew lists for that ship and dates are archived.

It may also be helpful to know the ship's port of registry. If the ship's name is not known, it then becomes necessary to try the indexes that list seamen's names. Information on how to do this is held on the Crew List Index Project (CLIP) website: www.crewlist.org.uk/findingonindexes.html. Recently, this material has been digitised, and is now available through www.findmypast.co.uk, on a pay as you go basis or by subscription. This has been a great step forward, as it is now possible to search for a seafaring forebear simply by using the name of an individual, and without needing the name of a ship. Details of Manx vessels are available on a database available in the Manx Museum Reading Room.

On the crew list index is listed Ned Maddrell, the well-known Manx speaker who lived at Cregneash, and whose voice was recorded by the Irish Folklore Commission in 1947. Maddrell went to sea as a Merchant Mariner before and during the First World War. On the index he is shown as Edward Maddrell, born in Port St Mary in 1877. He is recorded as aboard the *Capellar* in 1904 before moving to the paddle steamer *Prince of Wales*, an IOMSPCo vessel operating between Douglas and Liverpool. He was aboard the *Lady Bell* for a brief stint, before returning to the *Prince of Wales* in 1912.

Ned Maddrell of Cregneash served as a Merchant Mariner before and during the First World War, and appears on a number of crew lists. (Pg6909-1)

CUSTOMS RECORDS

As Britain grew wealthy in the years following the restoration of Charles II, demand for tobacco, rum, brandy and wine grew. In later years, it was tea that became perhaps the most sought after commodity of all. A system grew up by which goods were landed on the Isle of Man, duty to the Lord of Mann was paid, and the goods were then re-exported to England or Scotland, thus avoiding higher rates in those countries. The Manx merchants – quite legitimately – made a considerable profit by taking advantage of the lower import duties on the Isle of Man. Supplying this demand was a highly lucrative trade and quite legitimate in the eyes of the Manx authorities, who could not care less where a cargo was destined for once Manx duty was paid and after it left the Island. The Manx referred to it as the 'running trade', but this activity was the source of increasing tension between 'the British Government and the Earls of Derby (and later the Dukes of Atholl). A Royal proclamation dated 9 August 1661 condemned 'a sort of people called smuckellers – who made it there [sic] trade to steal and defraud His Majesty and Customs!' The Royal Navy frequently stopped Manx vessels in the Irish Sea which they suspected of smuggling, only to find that goods were being lawfully carried and that the correct documentation existed.

MNH holds extensive records of Ingates and Outgates, that is Customs Books giving details of vessels entering and leaving the ports of the Island, and of the cargoes which they were carrying, in the series MS 10058. The records cover the period 1579 to 1755. From 1523 revenue was payable to the Lord of Mann on goods landed at the Island's ports. On arrival at a Manx port in the seventeenth century a merchant had to produce a list of goods and was obliged to report personally to the Comptroller at Castletown. The merchant was then directed to go to the Water Bailiff who was responsible for keeping the Customs Book, to make an entry, a copy of which was returned to the Comptroller for signature. Only then could goods be unloaded. The records are divided into sections covering the four main ports, Douglas, Peel, Ramsey and Castletown, and the sections for each port are then subdivided into 'in gates and out gates'. For the period 1578 to 1654 Books of Licences and Entries survive. The information contained is similar to that within the Water Bailiff's accounts and they list export licences and tickets of entry issued to merchants.

Further customs records are held by MNH as part of the Castle Rushen papers, and these cover goods entering the ports of Douglas, Peel, Ramsey and Derbyhaven, between the dates of 1703 to 1765. They are held as MS 10637 and should be used in conjunction with records of Ingates and Outgates. These records effectively document how the 'running trade' worked in practice.

The foremost of the Manx merchants in the eighteenth century was Paul Bridson (1694–1771). He was also the deputy customs officer for Douglas. (1978-0155)

The accounts usually record a date, the name of the merchant or ship's master, the cargo and the amount of duty collected. Unfortunately, pre-1690 records provide no details about either ports of origin or destination. In most cases the names of captains and owners of vessels are recorded. A typical entry would read as follows:

17 October 1719 Ramsey
Paul Bridson enters of board [*sic*] the Ann of Dublin, William Corkill Master
Four hides leather
16 calf skins
4 doz wood poles

Paul Bridson was a noted Manx merchant, Captain of the parish of Braddan and part of a growing and prosperous merchant class in the Isle of Man in the early part of the eighteenth century. The Commission of Inquiry for the Isle of Man which was established in 1791 to examine the laws and governance of the Island refers several times to Bridson and his commercial activities, including the evidence of a William Crebbin, a fellow Douglas merchant between 1758 and 1765, who noted that Paul Bridson, 'carried on trade to a great extent'. This was borne out by John Quayle, Clerk of the Rolls and formerly under the Atholl rule, collector of customs, who upon taking

Joseph Train in *Historical and Statistical Account of the Isle of Man* writes:

Although the contraband trade from the Isle of Man was nearly suppressed before I was stationed as an excise officer in Galloway, my duty occasionally brought me into contact with some of the remaining landloupers of the free trade, a term by which the Manx smugglers were known in the south of Scotland . . . Myles Crowe was for many years a schoolmaster in the Isle of Man, but he was at length induced to embark his little capital in the free trade, at that time carried on to a great extent by the Islanders . . . At the time to which I allude it was the fashion for gentlemen to wear very wide small clothes, buckled immediately below the knee and Myles Crowe being then a gay fellow, that part of his dress was smuggled nankeen. He had an idea that the most convenient mode of smuggling a few pounds of tea out of the Island was by filling the vacuum of his small clothes on his person with that article. He accordingly filled them up to the waistband, but unfortunately, just as he was about to embark, having made a long stride from the quay to the vessel, his nankeen dress was thereby rent from side to side, and instantly his whole cargo of fine congou showered into the water, to the no small amusement of a large assemblage of fashionable spectators, with whom the quay of Douglas happened to be at that time crowded. (Author's copy with corrections and inserts, MS 06903)

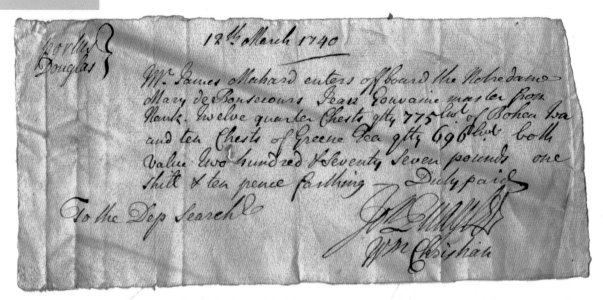

This document, dated 12 March 1740, records the import of ten chests of green tea by James Merchard. They were landed by the *Notredame Mary de Bonsecours* at Douglas.

up the post in 1755, 'found Mr Bridson in trade, and a factor for others'. In fact, Bridson was in the curious position of being both deputy customs officer for Douglas and a merchant in his own right. He was in effect both poacher and gamekeeper! Close study of the customs archives would allow a researcher to build up a detailed picture of the commercial activities of men like him during this period.

The situation led ultimately to the Act of Revestment of 1765, by which the British Crown took over responsibility for the administration of customs duties relating to the Isle of Man. By the removal of the Island's tariff advantage, the British Government hoped to close the Manx loophole and recoup lost customs revenue, and indeed many of the Island's merchants sold up and left as a result. However, there can be little doubt that smuggling persisted in the Irish Sea for many decades after Revestment. Microfilm copies of customs records pertaining to the Isle of Man which are held by TNA are also to be found in the MNH Reading Room. These include letter books containing correspondence with customs officers at Castletown in the early nineteenth century (MIC 2). Joseph Train, author of the *Historical and Statistical Account of the Isle of Man* (1845) spent his working life as a Customs Officer in Galloway, and offers a fascinating glimpse into life in this era, and the characters he encountered, not least of which was a smuggler named Myles Crowe. A useful article exploring Crowe's background and ancestry through Manx records is Ann Harrison's 'Myles Crowe the Smuggler', *Journal of Manx Museum*, Volume VII, 234. The most extensive research in recent years into the Isle of Man's role in smuggling, and into the lives of the main characters involved, has been carried out by Frances Wilkins. Her research has resulted in a number of publications, notably *The Isle of Man in Smuggling History* (1992).

DIRECTORIES

The Isle of Man did not have an equivalent of the Kelly's series of directories found in parts of Britain. However, the Island has featured occasionally in some early British directories. A few directories of the Island were published in the nineteenth century, though not on a regular basis. Some examples of those held in the MNH Library and which can be found under library reference L10 are:

- Holden, 1811
- Pigot, 1824, 1837, 1843
- Slater's, 1846, 1852, 1857
- Thwaites', 1863
- Brown's, 1882, 1894
- Porter's, 1889
- Bent's, 1902, 1907
- Barrett's (Borough of Douglas), 1955
- Barrett's (Isle of Man), 1963.

This type of record will chiefly be of interest to those seeking middle-class ancestors, or those in trade or farming. The information contained within the directories in the early nineteenth century predominantly concerned professional people, tradesmen or farmers and many earlier directories are organised alphabetically by trade or occupation rather than by surname. Some others also contain the names and addresses of persons of quality. The type of information recorded in directories changed over time. By the late nineteenth century the coverage was wider and often includes house by house information. The 1894 *Brown's Directory* is particularly useful as it lists householders street by street, and includes labourers and members of the lower classes as well as professional people, including interesting details such as the occupants of the widow's house on Big Well Street in Douglas. Later directories are particularly useful for researching boarding house and hotel keepers as these are listed in detail. It is also possible to locate people who just rented the odd room to visitors in summer through these records. The directories published by the Isle of Man Tourism Board and Publicity Board in the late nineteenth through to the mid-twentieth centuries are also fairly comprehensive for the visiting industry. These list all registered hotels and guest houses, giving the name of the proprietor, their rates and the facilities that the premises offered. The larger hotels sometimes also took an advertisement in the directory, and this may include a photograph or sketch

Mrs and Mrs Guard, proprietors of the Hydro Hotel in Douglas. (Courtesy of Charles Guard)

Hilary Guard ran the Hydro Hotel in Douglas as a family business in the 1960s. He was interviewed in 1999:

Well, there was reputed to be up to a hundred [bedrooms], but of course with the bathrooms and things putting in, that reduced to about seventy or eighty. The maximum number we ever took, and we reached that figure three times, was 200. We never got to 201 but we got to 200 three times. Now the dining room would seat 180 people and from the time we opened in TT week until we shut in September you could say, virtually, there was 180 people in and we had [extra] tables which we had in the smoke room downstairs, or the television room, and we used to seat them there, the odd ones in the bar room as well. . . We got a good mixture of youngish people in their thirties – twenties and thirties. And we never used to advertise, only in the Guide, we found that the brochure that the Tourist Board issued was the only advert needed. I used to laugh when I saw many of these adverts, some of them a whole page, talking about the golf course and all this sort of business and the electric trams and the steam railways and horse trams, which had got nothing to do with the hotel. If people are coming to my hotel, well I didn't call it a hotel, I called it a good class boarding house. I was getting up to sixty enquiries a day, sixty, and only in the Guide, because in the Guide I just put about the hotel.

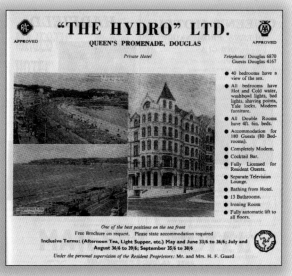

The advertisement for the Hydro Hotel in the 1969 *Isle of Man Official Hotel and Travel Guide*, issued by the Isle of Man Publicity Board.

of the premises. In some cases the advert also featured a photograph of the proprietor, emphasising the fact that these establishments were very much family businesses. The MNH library has an extensive set of these directories at B266.

It is also worth mentioning in this context the yearbooks produced by both the *Isle of Man Examiner* and the Norris Modern Press in the twentieth century. The *Examiner Annual* was published from 1907 to 1979, whilst the *Norris Modern Press Yearbook* covers 1906 to 1972. Volumes in both series contain a directory section listing, for example, public officials, the members of various boards, the local secretaries and officers of friendly societies, postmen and police officers. They also carry numerous advertisements which may be useful in tracing commercial ancestors. Both titles are available in the Manx Museum Reading Room (Library reference L6).

Peel was the subject of a number of directories produced in the early 2000s by Hanneke Young-Tammel. These were published by the Leece Museum in Peel, and used various other sources to reconstruct lists of residents in the city on a street by street basis. Copies of these volumes are again held by MNH (Library reference F74).

Telephone numbers originally appeared in the general directories and the earliest dedicated telephone directory held by MNH dates from 1899. Whilst telephones did not become widespread until probably the 1960s, telephone directories are still useful for confirming the dates at which a certain address was occupied in the mid-twentieth century, particularly for the decades in which census information is not yet available. Some of those held by MNH are in photocopy form, but the run is fairly complete from 1924 to the modern era, with the only significant gap occurring during the Second World War. Telephone directories are held under library reference B102.

DISSOLVED REGISTERED COMPANY FILES

The records of dissolved companies were created by the Isle of Man Companies Registry. All files contain a registration certificate; memorandum and articles of association; certificate of incorporation; particulars of directors or managers; summary of capital and shares; appointment of receiver; receiver's statement of receipts and payments; striking-off notices and dissolved notice. Some files will have additional

Gelling's Foundry on South Quay, Douglas, as it appeared in 1972. (Pg5359/10)

Gelling's Foundry was one of the best known companies on the Isle of Man, in part because of the sheer range of items that it produced. These varied from cast-iron hearths, fireplaces and kitchen ranges, to the smaller iron castings on the Laxey Wheel, to net winches for fishing vessels. Located on South Quay in Douglas, the site is now occupied by garages and tyre bays.

information, and this may include: return of allotments; annual returns; mortgage details; resolutions passed at extraordinary general meetings. It is important to note that the contents and procedures documented within these files have changed over time, so not all will be the same. Likewise, some files are more extensive than others. Typically, the useful information contained within these files centres around who was the chairman of a company, who served as its directors, when it was in operation and where its registered office was located. A selection of Dissolved Registered Company files from 1970 to 1982 are held by the MNH Library and Archive Service. Dissolved Registered Company files from c. 1865 to 1970 and samples from 1982 are held by IOMPRO. Files are retained by the Companies Registry for twelve years after dissolution.

Some examples of the companies for which IOMPRO holds files include Gellings Iron Foundry (1877–1919), Clinchs Brewery Ltd (1897–1948), Rushen Abbey Hotel Company Ltd (1898–1911), Glenfaba Brick Company Ltd (1900–31), Bradda Mines Ltd (1882–1923) and Clucas Laundry Ltd (1920–47). These records offer a great deal of potential in terms of

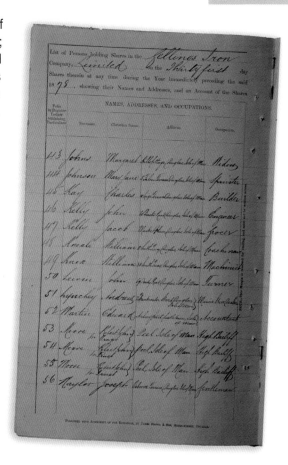

A list of shareholders in Gelling's Foundry Ltd, Douglas. (Courtesy of IOMPRO)

research into the history of a town or locality and the nature of the businesses that would have been the major employers there in the second half of the nineteenth century and the beginning of the twentieth century. What they will not do however is offer much in the way of insight into the social conditions within a company, what it was like to work in a particular industry, nor indeed do they provide the names of employees of the company, unless they happened also to be shareholders in it.

In the case of Gellings Foundry the most useful documents are perhaps the Memorandum of Association, which states that in 1877 George W. Dumbell, William Todhunter and James Adams purchased the business carried on by Richard Gelling of Windsor Terrace at the Iron Foundry, Douglas, the business thenceforth to be known as Gelling's Iron Foundry Company Limited. A further document dated 21 March 1919 confirms the liquidation of the company, and the registration of a new company known as Gelling's Foundry Limited.

See also:
✿ Directories

DIVORCE RECORDS

MNH holds a considerable number of marriage contracts, dating from the seventeenth and eighteenth centuries, and these might be considered as being an early form of pre-nuptial agreement. A marriage contract was a device for recording which property, including land, would be transferred to a couple by their respective parents upon marriage. Until 1867, land could not be disposed of by will (it had to go to the eldest son); a marriage contract was thus a way in which land could be transferred to an heir during the lifetime of the parents. Child marriages were also covered by such contracts, for example, that of 1674 between John and Joney Cannell, who were promised by their respective families to be married when they came to 14 years of age, and if either had died before that age, then another child from that family would have taken their place. Not surprisingly, some betrothals contracted in this fashion were unhappy and were dissolved, for example, in 1657 in Lonan the planned marriage of William Stole and Joney Quirk was cancelled 'on request of both ptys & Tho Quirk the father's petition setting forth that tho his daughter was by him brought to church she utterly refused to consent & accept of Stole for her Husbd and so are freed of each other and to dispose of themselves as pleaseth God to direct them'. This subject is covered by J. Roscow in 'Manx Marriage Contracts 1600–1736', IOMNHAS *Proceedings*, Volume X, 3–16. Frances Coakley has also prepared a provisional index of marriage contracts, and more information on this is available from the Manx Note Book website: www.isle-of-man.com/manxnotebook/famhist/genealgy/mctrcts.htm).

Two early cases of divorce are known, one from the Andreas presentments of 1637 granting a separation to John Quirk from Joney Faragher on grounds of adultery, and one from Jurby from the same year, when William Gawen was granted a separation from Ann Kellie by a church court. However, these appear to be isolated instances. Generally, if a couple had married, a divorce in the formal sense was practically impossible to obtain. Certainly this was the case for ordinary people in the nineteenth and early twentieth centuries. Because of the much shorter life expectancy in former times, many bad marriages were ended by the demise of one or the other parties, but there were still many cases of abandonment. In an age before the welfare state, a husband who abandoned his wife and children was condemning them to a life of poverty and misery. The difficulty in obtaining a divorce explains the many cases of bigamy that occurred in the nineteenth and early twentieth century. The offence was taken very seriously and the resulting court cases were followed with great interest. Bigamy cases were frequently reported in the newspapers, often in great detail.

Divorces in the Isle of Man in the late nineteenth and early twentieth century were by Act of Tynwald, and the procedure for obtaining one was described in the 1930s as 'archaic', 'cruel' and 'unjust'. The petitioner had first to take proceedings in the Chancery Court. He or she had then to present a petition to Tynwald asking to introduce a bill. After a bill had been prepared and passed by both houses (it was invariably passed within a matter of minutes without a division) the act was promulgated by being read aloud on Tynwald Hill, a deeply embarrassing occasion for the parties involved. For those seeking records of divorces in this era, each one will be indexed in the Proceedings of Tynwald for the year in question, and there will be a printed Committee report on each. These records can be accessed through Tynwald Library, though the total numbers are very small.

The cost of obtaining a divorce by this method was so expensive as to be out of reach of ordinary people, prompting the 1937 Judicature (Matrimonial causes) Bill which brought the law in the Isle of Man into line with that in England, and made divorce easier to obtain. There was however considerable opposition to the Bill, both from the Church and from women's groups. The eventual reform of the law in the Isle of Man – and perhaps also the strain of wartime separation – did, as opponents had argued, lead to an increase in the number of people seeking a divorce in the 1940s.

Even as recently as the twenty-first century, newspapers in the Isle of Man regularly reported the details of local divorces. No blushes were spared as the names of all parties, and the grounds for the divorce, were printed in full. Up to 1960 these reports can be accessed through the Manx newspapers available via the iMuseum, or for later years in the MNH Reading Room.

See also:
✿ Newspapers

ELECTORAL ROLLS

The earliest electoral records known to exist are amongst the Castle Rushen papers. One example relates to an election that took place on 25 June 1700 when the voters of Douglas, Conchan, Lonan and Maughold appointed Mr Ewan Christian as their representative to treat with the Earl of Derby over the question of land tenure. The preamble reads: 'Wee whose names are hereto subscribed of ye Garfe Sheading being conveind together to give our votes for one selected man in ye Sheading to make known our requests and treat with our Honorable Commissioners touching our holdings under his Honourable Lord have given our mutuall consents.' Beneath this about 200 men of the Sheading have signed the document, together with 3 women – a remarkable fact when women were considered not to have had voting rights for a further 200 years. (A transcript of this document appears in the *Journal of Manx Museum*, Volume III, 17). Similar documents exist for those entitled to vote upon this issue in the sheadings of Glenfaba, Rushen, Kirk Michael and Ayre. These too are transcribed in the *Journal*, on p. 23 of Volume III. Copies of the *Journal* are available for consultation in the MNH Reading Room.

MNH holds electoral rolls under the reference MS 09842. They include voters' lists and poll books for the following periods: 1867–1915, 1919/20, 1950–84 (incomplete). The current electoral rolls from 2004/5 onwards are also held under MS 11110.

Poll books are slightly different from electoral rolls in that they actually record the name of the person who was voting and who they voted for. Secret ballots were not introduced for some time after the reform of the House of Keys in 1867. This was because there was a widespread belief amongst Victorians (not just on the Isle of Man) that voting was an important civic responsibility, and one should stand up openly and be counted in elections.

Voters' lists from 1989 are held at IOMPRO (except for the current year and the previous year, which are held at General Registry and are available by prior appointment).

On the Isle of Man the franchise was extended in the following sequence:
- 1866: Male property owners and tenants
- 1881: Female property owners (widows and spinsters) and male lodgers
- 1892: Female occupiers (widows and spinsters)
- 1903: Female lodgers (widows and spinsters)
- 1919: Adult suffrage (age 21 and upwards) and ex-servicemen aged 18–21
- 1971: Persons aged 18 and upwards
- 2006: 16–18 year olds (the Isle of Man being the first place in the British Isles to enfranchise this age group).

It should of course be remembered that the Isle of Man is not represented at

Westminster, so researchers will not (for example) find an electoral roll for the December 1918 'khaki election' (these are also sometimes known as Absent Voters Lists, as they contain the details of servicemen entitled to a postal vote). For fuller details of the extensions of the franchise to Manx voters, see the relevant Acts of Tynwald at D200/1 in the MNH Reading Room. In addition to House of Keys elections, the MNH Library and Archive Service holds records of voters in local elections, for example, the Douglas borough voters' list of 1891, held at MS 01635.

It is also worth noting that prior to the 1970s a system of plural voting existed in the Isle of Man, whereby ownership of property sometimes entitled a person to a second vote. Some electoral records are therefore also effectively records of property ownership. The Douglas Burgess Roll of 1924/25 (MNH Library reference F71/16x) shows the voters of Douglas and identifies those entitled to vote on the basis of property ownership (even if they are not the occupier). The Henry Bloom Noble Library has the Douglas Burgess Roll for 1925/26 amongst others.

An irony of history is the fact that if Emmeline Pankhurst, leader of the Women's Social and Political Union, had grown up on the Isle of Man, where her mother was born, she would automatically have been entitled to vote and might not have become involved in the suffragette movement. An alternative view of course is that it was the knowledge of the more advanced rights of women on the Isle of Man that spurred her on. *Manx Quarterly*, Number 9, 826 (October 1910) noted:

On Friday afternoon, April 22nd, at 5 o'clock, Mrs Sophia Jane Goulden, of 9 Strathallan Crescent, Douglas, passed away. She had been in poor health for some months. She had an attack of double pneumonia, from which she partly recovered, although it left her very weak. Unfortunately, on Thursday afternoon she had a relapse, which ended fatally, as stated above. Mrs Goulden, who was 75 years old, was the only daughter of Mr and Mrs Craine, who lived in Lonan, where she was born. They afterwards came to reside in Douglas. Miss Craine, who was an unusually good-looking young lady, was married when only 18 to Mr Robert Goulden, of Manchester, and went to live there. Her mother (Mrs Craine), who lived in Christian Road, finally went to live at Strathallan Crescent. To Mr and Mrs Goulden were born six sons and five daughters . . . [one of whom] Emmeline . . . married Dr Richard Pankhurst, the eminent barrister and jurist. Since Dr Pankhurst's death, about ten years ago, Mrs Pankhurst's career has been well-known as the founder and leader of the Women's Social and Political Union, for the enfranchisement of women . . .

EMIGRATION RECORDS

Despite the fact that Manx émigrés would first have to leave the Isle of Man before obtaining a passage to the New World or Australasia, there are no surviving records of passengers departing from the Island. If such records were kept by the IOMSPCo at the time (which is doubtful) they were not retained. Occasionally in the early nineteenth century, Manx newspapers would carry advertisements for ships departing for the New World, with the date upon which they were due to sail. Even more occasionally, newspaper articles actually carried the names of those departing for foreign parts. It is possible to search these newspapers electronically in the iMuseum, and the most useful titles are probably the *Manx Sun* or *Mona's Herald*.

On the whole it is usually easier to find a record of a relative departing from a British port for a new life abroad. The website www.findmypast.co.uk holds passenger lists for those departing from all major British ports between 1890 and 1960, including Liverpool which one assumes would be the obvious point of departure for Manx émigrés. Passenger lists contain details of the name, age and occupation of passengers as well of course as their destination.

Wisconsin Indians hunting buffalo in the winter. (Courtesy of Wisconsin Historical Society)

See also:
✿ Census
Records

It is also often far easier to find a record of a forebear entering their adopted country, than leaving their old one. For those whose ancestors settled in the United States between 1892 and 1924, the records of Ellis Island immigration centre are an invaluable resource. These records have been digitised by the Genealogical Society of Utah and are now available on line at: www.ellisisland.org/sign/index.asp. As with all such databases created by the transcription of original records, it is not infallible, and if an ancestor who should be present cannot be found right away, it is often wise to employ a certain amount of lateral thinking. Different spellings of surnames are worth trying, as are different abbreviations of Christian names. The Ellis Island records can also be searched on a ship by ship basis if necessary, though this is laborious.

The census records of the adopted country are also a useful resource for tracing those beginning a new life abroad, and these are discussed elsewhere in this book.

A fascinating series of letters survive giving a flavour of émigré life for the Manx in the New World. These were written by Thomas Corlett, who emigrated with his mother, father and five brothers and sisters from Orrisdale, Kirk Michael to Ohio in 1827, and are held by MNH (MS 05281 et al.). Similar records are the series of letters from the Crebbin family in Victoria, Australia to their family at Ballakillowey, Rushen in the 1870s (MS 06333) and the diary of Manx emigrant J. Qualtrough's journey to New Zealand in 1859.

In the twentieth century, emigrants and their activities in their new homelands were frequently the subjects of reports in the Manx newspapers. If they returned to the Isle of Man for a visit this was considered even more newsworthy, and a card index exists in the MNH Reading Room specifically covering newspaper references to émigrés between 1957 and 1994. Newspapers up to 1960 are available in the iMuseum, and a simple search, for example, using the word 'Ohio' brings up numerous hits in this context, including a report of the golden wedding anniversary of a Manx couple, an obituary of a Manx woman, and a Manx professor at an Ohio university.

R.H. Kinvig's article 'Manx Settlement in the USA' (*Proceedings* of the IOMNHAS, Volume 5, 436–55) is a useful source for research. Equally important is John Quirk's book *The Manx Connection* (2007), which explores contemporary Manx societies in North America and Australasia, and contains useful insights into the size and strength of Manx communities in these parts of the world. If a forebear is known to have emigrated it may well be worthwhile contacting local history societies (or even Manx societies) in their adopted home to ascertain what records are available there. Frances Coakley's Manx Note Book website contains a good overview of the sources available for researching Manx émigré ancestors, as well as analysis of the patterns that emigration took (www.isle-of-man.com/manxnotebook/famhist/genealgy/emig.htm).

Thomas Corlett
of Orrisdale.

Thomas Corlett of Orrisdale wrote a series of letters to his family in the Isle of Man, describing his experiences in the United States. In one letter dated 26 January 1857 he writes to his uncle to tell him that he has now moved on to Baraboo, Wisconsin:

"... there are many Indians still around us. They often come into our little village and traffic with us. They are dressed in skins and blankets. They are of a copper color, long features, high cheek bones, long straight black hair – they look savage. They often camp out in the commons and amuse us with their wild whoops and yells and war dances. We have no fear of them, though we often travel 50-60 and hundreds of miles alone, pass through their hut villages and eat of their venison.

The prairies here are very fine. There are thousands of acres as fine land as the sun ever looked upon, still in their wild state. The winters are very cold and long. There has been two feet of snow on the ground since the second of Dec and they tell us it will keep on the ground till the last of March..."

Using American records on the www.familysearch.org website it is possible to identify Thomas Corlett's marriage to Mary Hart Parmelee at Franklin, Portage, Ohio on 10 May 1862. The 1880 United States census also shows his brother William Corlett, no occupation shown, residing at Cleveland, Cuyahoga, Ohio along with his brother John, also born in the Isle of Man and shown as a carpenter.

ENTERTAINMENT

For more than fifty years, during the golden age of variety, the Isle of Man could lay claim to competing with London as one of the entertainment capitals of the British Isles. It had a rich music-hall tradition, and during the summer seasons when thousands of visitors flocked to the Island, it attracted some of the biggest names in stage and theatre. In the pre-Second World War era Douglas boasted venues such as the Pavilion (now the Gaiety) Theatre, Grand Theatre, Villa Marina, the Palace Ballroom and the Derby Castle, all of which hosted live entertainment. In its heyday the Palace Ballroom boasted the largest undercover dance floor in Europe, and the complex was opened by the singer Vesta Tilley in 1913. Other places of entertainment included Douglas Head where there was an open-air auditorium, which staged Pierrot and minstrel shows, and White City on Onchan Head which hosted similar performances. In the years either side of the First World War the singer Florrie Forde had a summer residency, and owned a holiday home at Niarbyl on the west coast of the Island. In the 1920s and 30s Wilson, Kepple and Betty performed regularly, and the top touring shows started their run in Douglas, before moving on to other seaside resorts across Britain. Comedians such as Billy Danvers, Ethel Revnell and Gracie West (a popular female double act), Sandy Powell (catchphrase: 'Can you hear me mother?') and Liverpool comedian Jack Edge honed their acts in front of summer season crowds in Douglas. Wilfrid Pickles, the comedian and radio star, was a sell-out at the Villa Marina. The only major comic talent produced by the Isle of Man itself in this era was Harry Korris, born Henry Corris in Douglas in 1891.

Joe Loss and his orchestra performed regularly at the Villa Marina, whilst Ronnie Aldrich and his Squadronnaires played in theatres. In the 1950s Ivy Benson and her all-female orchestra were also popular. A number of cinemas, such as the Picture House on Strand Street, the Regal cinema on Victoria Street, Royalty cinema on Walpole Avenue and the Pier Pavilion Kinema showed the latest films.

The Bee Gees and Pete Townsend of The Who were all products of the Isle of Man's music and entertainment industry, as they were brought to the Isle of Man at a young age, when their fathers played in orchestras and bands in Douglas hotels. Even into the 1960s the

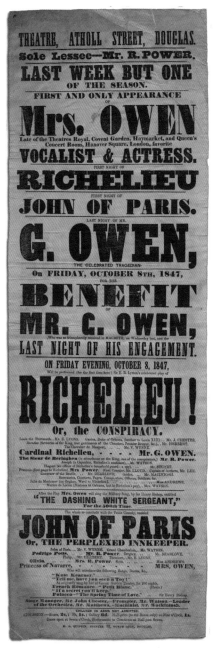

A bill from a
Douglas theatre.

Wilson, Kepple and Betty appeared at the Derby Castle, with their famous Sand Dance, in 1939.

Isle of Man was still able to attract big name acts, with the Rolling Stones performing at the Palace Ballroom, and Freddie and the Dreamers playing a summer season on the Island in 1964. The Isle of Man's music and theatre tradition continues into the twenty-first century in the person of Samantha Barks, who has appeared on television and on stage both in London and the Isle of Man. In his later years the Isle of Man was home to Sir Norman Wisdom, hapless star of the Ealing comedies.

MNH holds an extensive collection of theatre programmes and play bills, going back as far as the 1820s. Theatre posters record the acts performing (and their hierarchy), whilst photographic archives record the changing face (and eventual demolition) of most of the theatres and cinemas. MNH also holds the records of the Strand Cinema Theatre Company Limited (MS 11965), and the archives of the Palace and Derby Castle Company (MS 09398). The digital newspaper archive at the iMuseum is a rich resource for entertainment history, featuring not just articles but also advertisements from theatres and cinemas. The *Douglas Weekly Diary* (1928–77) provided a comprehensive listing for all Island entertainments, and copies are held by MNH (Library reference L6/DOU).

Worthy of mention in its own right is the collection of photographs deposited with MNH by Eva Kane in 2007. Eva's mother (known as Kanie) ran the Falcon Cliff Hotel. As a former stage performer herself, she was well known in the world of variety, and many of the stars of the 1920s and 30s' theatre lodged with her whilst performing in Douglas between the wars. Her collection of over 120 signed photographs of performers is held by the MNH Library and Archive Service.

See also:
✿ Newspapers

FOLK LIFE SURVEY

See also:
✿ Folklore
✿ Manx Gaelic
   Records

In the 1950s the Manx Museum began an ambitious project which grew from the efforts of field workers to capture the Manx language before it died out. This new venture was the Folk Life Survey, and field workers visited older people across the Island on behalf of the museum. They either asked the respondent to write down, or in some cases transcribed their earliest memories. As these people were mostly in their eighties their memories stretched back well into the nineteenth century. In some cases they recalled stories told to them by their grandparents, which went back almost to the eighteenth century. The information covered particular aspects of Manx life such as traditional methods of agriculture, folklore, crafts such as shipbuilding and blacksmithing, and notable events such as coronations, wars and epidemics. There were stories about press gangs roaming the island, and traditional folk stories such as the appearance of the death carriage. Information was also collected about field names, which may have applications both in the study of language and also land use and ownership. Due to the age of the respondents at the time that the material was collected, the bulk of the content refers to a period of time roughly from the 1870s to the early 1900s.

A large quantity of personal information relating to identifiable individuals was also collected, including nicknames of people which might in a few cases have been considered offensive or disrespectful. This resulted in the survey being closed to the public for fifty years, in order to protect the informants and also to avoid causing offence. However, plans are now underway to digitise and fully index the information contained within it. The survey can be consulted at the MNH Library and Archive Service Reading Room.

Additionally, and linked to the Folklife Survey are the Sound Archives of MNH. The earliest recordings are of Manx speakers, created on wax cylinders, and are in most cases simple recitations (for example, of the Lord's Prayer in Manx). However, the oral history archive in its fullest extent covers military subjects, for example, the Women's Land Army and the Manx Regiment, the TT races and the Tourist industry. The collection is in the process of digitisation, and over 600 individual recordings will be made available through the iMuseum by 2014.

FOLKLORE

There is probably no other part of the British Isles as steeped in folklore as the Isle of Man. The reasons suggested for this are varied, but it might be argued that the history of the Island favoured the survival of pre-Christian, Celtic beliefs into the modern era. The belief in superstition and magic might also be the product of an existence that at times bordered on the subsistence level. Examples include farming marginal land, where the loss of a sole animal such as a previously healthy cow to apparently inexplicable forces might spell disaster for a family already on the edge of starvation, and might lead to a belief in ill-wishing or supernatural forces. Likewise, fishing in treacherous waters, where the sudden appearance of a gale or a squall could take vessels and their crews to the bottom, required the appeasement of potentially sinister forces. Even in good weather, fishing was a chancy business, and a boat returning without a catch could have dire consequences for a fisherman's family. It is no surprise therefore that of all areas of Manx life, fishing is perhaps the one surrounded by the greatest degree of superstition. Fishermen would carry the *crosh*

A miner's funeral procession passing through Laxey in the 1890s. (Pg5222)

Antiquarian J.J. Frowde, writing around 1890, described one of the more common superstitions, that of the 'funeral sign':

Late one night a miner was coming through the village of Laxey on his way home when he suddenly heard the sound of a funeral hymn being sung in front of a house he had to pass, where there lived a man he knew. On nearing the spot from where the sound proceeded he felt himself surrounded by an invisible throng of people and was immediately forced along in the midst of a procession. Just in front of him he could see a blue light moving, and the thought immediately occurred to him that he was involuntarily taking part in some man's 'funeral sign' a thing of which he had often heard but had never before seen. This idea was strengthened when the procession turned up a narrow road leading to the parish church, on arriving at which the throng vanished, the light disappeared and the man was at liberty to proceed on his way home where next morning he was informed that the person before whose house he had heard the hymn being sung was seriously ill and by noon that day was dead. This is just a sample – the form of the story may vary a little, but in nearly every instance the mysterious blue light plays the leading part. (Frowde papers) bollan to ward off the threat of drowning; it was considered unlucky to mention any animal on a fishing boat; it was unlucky for a vessel to be the third to leave harbour, so the second and third would leave tied together; it was unlucky to whistle, for this could summon the wind; the list goes on and on.

Another aspect of Manx folkore is the belief in fairies (known as 'themselves'). Today this manifests itself in the rather quaint practice of saying 'good morning' to the fairies when passing over the Fairy Bridge at Santon, but this disguises a more sinister reality. In Manx belief, fairies are not the pretty, harmless creatures of modern popular culture. Instead, they are potentially malevolent spirits that must be placated (or at the very least not antagonised). It was widely believed that fairies lived in Tramman (elder) trees, and to cut one down was to invite dire retribution from the inhabitants. A pair or iron tongs placed over a cradle would prevent 'themselves' from taking the child and substituting a changeling.

It could be further argued that the strong Manx connections with the smuggling trade in the seventeenth and eighteenth centuries further reinforced many of these beliefs, as they provided useful cover stories for the nocturnal activities of those involved in illicit trade. Lights seen after dark in a churchyard could be explained as fairies. A coach with muffled wheels making no sound as it crossed the countryside at night could be explained as the death carriage – a harbinger of mortality. Such stories would have had the added advantage of scaring off anyone who might have been interested in finding out more about what was going on. It is interesting to observe that many locations around the Island that are associated with smuggling, such as Niarbyl Bay, are also some of those with the strongest associations with folklore and folk tales.

It is perhaps easy for modern researchers to scoff at these beliefs and to think of those in the past as in some way 'backward', but to those who lived in former times these beliefs formed a very real code, a framework by which they lived their lives. For those wanting a greater understanding of what motivated our ancestors, what they believed in and what was important to them, then study of folklore is an important part of unlocking the past. Many places on the Island are intimately associated with folk legend, for example, the Moddey Dhoo of Peel Castle, or the Buggane of St Trinian's, and these stories are very much part of their heritage.

Many folklorists in the nineteenth century collected and recorded the Island's substantial body of folktales and superstitions. Charles Roeder was an early collector, whilst A.W. Moore published *Folklore of the Isle of Man* in 1891. The most celebrated book of this genre, Sophia Morrison's *Manx Fairytales* (1911), features illustrations by Archibald Knox. William Cashen's book *Manx Folk-lore* was published in 1912. Cashen was the custodian of Peel Castle and he was born in a thatched cottage at Niarbyl, and was a fluent Manx speaker. The most comprehensive modern survey of the subject is probably Margaret Killip's *The Folklore of the Isle of Man* (1986). Much unpublished material will be found in the Manx Museum's Folk Life Survey, discussed in the Folk Life Survey section.

See also:
✿ Folk Life Survey

FRIENDLY SOCIETIES

The welfare state, introduced by Clement Atlee's post-1945 Labour Government, offered people for the first time social security from the cradle to the grave. This was paralleled in Tynwald by legislation such as the National Health Service (Isle of Man) Act 1948, but prior to this working people had attempted to provide this cover for times of sickness and bereavement through self-help groups. The chief amongst these in the Isle of Man were the Rechabites, Foresters and Oddfellows. Sometimes derided as mere 'funeral clubs' for the poor who wanted to avoid the stigma of being buried in a pauper's grave, at their height these societies were far more than this. They were a means of mutual support for working class communities who faced summary dismissal from their employment without any recourse to redundancy payment, potentially crippling medical bills if they fell ill and, until the 1920s, no state pension in their old age. In return for a small weekly contribution, the friendly societies provided insurance against many of these pitfalls. As well as social and welfare benefits they provided a temperate social life. They were part of a drive on the part of the working classes for self-improvement, by encouraging working men not to drink or gamble their wages away but to provide for their families instead. Their symbolism reflected this, in particular the use of the beehive. Bees were seen as industrious and hard working, and honey was the reward of their labour.

The first of the main societies to become established on the Island were the Independent Order of Oddfellows, who organised themselves into Lodges. The Oddfellows opened their first Lodge on the Island, the Loyal Mona Lodge in Douglas, at the Saddle Inn in Queen Street in 1830. However, the Isle of Man in the nineteenth century was also one of the greatest strongholds of the Rechabites anywhere in the British Isles, and it is perhaps no coincidence that one of the strongest districts in the Isle of Man was Laxey, where the main source of employment was also one of the most dangerous, namely mining. The annual or bi-annual parades of the Oddfellows and Rechabites through Laxey, the members wearing sashes and regalia and with banners flying, was one of the highlights of the year.

The Rechabites drew their name from the biblical tribe that had foresworn alcohol, and which feature in Chapter 35 of the Book of Jeremiah. Indeed they

A commemorative medal awarded by the Ancient Order of Foresters court number 907, the 'Star of Mona' on the Isle of Man, marking its golden jubilee year in 1890. (2002-0212)

based much of their structure and language on Old Testament terminology. The individual districts were known as 'Tents', after the tents in which the original nomadic Rechabites had lived in the deserts of Palestine. The latter day Rechabites were also closely linked to the Methodist church, and to the temperance movement, and (on paper at least) the society disapproved strongly of alcohol. Its motto was 'We Shall Drink No Wine', but it was a standing joke that after having been sworn in, often the first thing that happened to a new member was that he was taken to a pub for a drink! In 1836 the first Manx Tent, the Mona Union, was opened in Douglas. By 1914, in the *Examiner Annual*, it was listed as having 525 members and a capital sum of £13,354.

The main sources of information for family historians are held by MNH, contained within MS 09417, MS 09746, MS 09866, MS 10043 and MS 10044. These records refer in the main to the Isle of Man Rechabite district and were formerly held at Allan Street Rechabite Hall, in Douglas. They also cover the Star of Mona Tent (Peel), Rising Star Tent (Glenmaye), Mona Daniel Tent (Castletown) and Mona Rushen Tent (Colby). The records typically contain rule books, minutes of meetings, accounts, including records of members' contributions and sick-fund payments, funeral payments, etc. Registers of members (for example, MS 09417/138 covering the Sons of Mona Tent at Laxey between April 1900 and October 1971) are perhaps most likely to be of use to family historians. A useful hand list for Rechabite records exists in the MNH Reading Room.

For those seeking a wider understanding of the Rechabite movement, the archives of Healthy Investment, the mutual society by which the Rechabites are now known, was recently placed in the care of the Senate House Library, part of the University of London. This archive includes board minutes, 1864–1975; minutes of districts and tents; *Rechabite Magazine*, 1864–73, 1878–1925, 1925–77; *Junior Rechabite Magazine*, 1890–1925, 1927–77; conference reports and papers, 1839–1998; directories, 1887–1916; song books; ritual books; tent books and case files. The box list for this archive is available online as part of the University of London Research Libraries archives catalogue at: www.archives.ulrls.lon.ac.uk/ (email: shl.specialcollections@london.ac.uk).

The last of the three main groups were the Foresters, who organised themselves into Courts. The opening of the Free Forester Court 'Queen of the Isle', no. 1356 was reported in the *Manx Sun* of 11 December 1841:

On Wednesday evening last, a new Court of the Ancient Order of Foresters, was opened at the house of Mr Proctor, Yorkshire-house Lord Street, in this town, the Court was named, Court 'Queen of the Isle', no. 1356. After the initiation of a number of respectable individuals, the company sat down to an excellent Supper, provided for the occasion by Host Proctor. After the cloth was withdrawn, our respected townsman, Dr Sale, was called to the chair. Many patriotic and suitable toast[s] were given, and several excellent songs sung, accompanied by an excellent violin. The party separated at a late hour, highly delighted with the meeting.

GENEALOGIES

When embarking on family history research, it is important to remember that it is not always necessary to re-invent the wheel! There is always a possibility that at some point a family tree will converge with one that has already been mapped out. A great deal of time and effort may be saved if a conclusive link can be made to such a family tree (and assuming that the existing genealogy is accurate of course). Sometimes surprising links between family trees can be discovered. In 1997, research revealed that one of the descendants of Paul Bridson, the Douglas merchant, was none other than Tony Blair, the British Prime Minister, with a Mayor of Bolton thrown in along the way!

The MNH Library and Archive Service holds many family trees ranging from almost complete genealogies down to odd scraps of family history information. Many of the early deposits of this type of information were brought together under classmark MD20. Perhaps the most significant is the Kewley of Ballafreer Commonplace Book (MS 00037) written around 1763, which is '. . . an account of the women that have been married in (Ballafreer) for many years past, who they were, of what kindred they descended, And from what parrishes they came as far as we could hear by our antecessours brought down by word of mouth from father to son to this present year of o'er Lord'. This most significant early record of a Manx family was probably compiled by John Kewley, a descendant of Doncan McKewley who is recorded in the Manorial Roll of 1511.

There are also works by a number of individual researchers in this field, which are worth noting. A few in particular stand out, amongst them the Goodwin brothers of Peel. Edmund and George Goodwin went to a great deal of trouble to trace the family trees of notable Manx families, during the 1920s. Their four volumes of scrapbooks have been microfilmed and are available in the MNH Reading Room (reference RC 3 and 4, with original material at MS 00334/1-4C). They contain several hundred names. *Some Manx Pedigrees* by J. Alfred Brew is a more recent work, compiled in the 1990s, and is also worthy of mention in this respect. Brew again traced the lineage of notable Manx families such as the Quayles of Castletown. This is available in the MNH Reading Room (MS 09671) and can be checked by staff upon request if a particular name is supplied, and if an extensive search is not required. Constance Radcliffe traced the lineage of a number of Maughold families, and copies of these manuscripts are also in the collections, for example, the Kerruishes of Maughold 1511 to 1967 held as MS 06444.

There is a large body of published material relating to Manx family trees. Notable amongst this is *The Yesterdays Behind The Door* by Susan Hicks Beach (1956), which charts the history of the Christian family of Milntown. Other works held by the MNH Library and Archive Service include *Seed of Isaac* by R. Kissack, a history of the Kissacks on the Isle of Man. Helen C. Moody's *Meet Your Relatives* (1973) is a history

Amongst the families covered by A.W. Moore in his series '*Old Manx Families*' in his Manx Note Book were the Quayles of Clychur, the ancestors of George Quayle of Castletown. Of them he wrote:

Quaile, Quaill, MacQuaile, Quale, Quaylle, and MacQuayle are the forms in which this name is found in the early manorial records and parochial registers until the middle of the seventeenth century, after which it is usually spelled Quayle. In Ireland, whence the name came to us, it is found in its uncontracted form of MacPhail (Paul's son) at a very early date. Gilbert MacQuaile was a Member of the House of Keys in 1422, and Quayle and MacQuayle are Abbey tenants in Malew, in 1540. The first member of the above family, whom we find settled in Clychur, is Thomas Quale, who was possessor of Clychur in 1581, and Member of the House of Keys in 1593. Nicholas Quaile, his son, is entered as owner of the property in 1601, and it was afterwards held in succession by Thomas Quaile, Nicholas Quaile, entered in 1615, Gilbert Quaile, 1630, and Thomas Quayle, 1646 (buried November 2, 1669, Malew).

Captain George Quayle, a member of the House of Keys for fifty-one years. His yacht Peggy is now preserved in the Nautical Museum, Castletown.

of one branch of the Corlett family in the United States, whilst *The Corlett Family in America* by Elsie Catherine Hamilton covers similar ground. John Stowell Kenyon's *A Manx Family* (1972) examines the Gells and Gills of Kenna and Malew. Branches of both the Costain and Cowell families have been written up in the twentieth century.

In the 1880s A.W. Moore's *The Manx Note Book* (published in several volumes) included a section on old Manx families. Much of this information is also now available via Frances Coakley's Manx Note Book website (www.isle-of-man.com/manxnotebook). The IOMFHS Library also holds numerous copies of existing genealogies.

INTERNMENT RECORDS

Tracing family members who were interned during one or other of the two world wars has been one of the fastest growing areas of amateur genealogy in recent years. Indeed, it is probably fair to say that enquiries concerning a forebear who was interned on the Isle of Man now make up a large proportion of the correspondence received by the MNH Library and Archive Service. Directly after both world wars there was a certain stigma associated with having been identified as an enemy alien, which meant that many people did not talk about their experiences, even with close family. This has in part fuelled the desire by their descendants to find out more about what happened to them on the Isle of Man. The Island was chosen as a centre for the internment of enemy aliens in both world wars firstly because, owing to the lengthy sea journey, it would be relatively difficult for internees to escape from, but also because there was a ready supply of accommodation provided by the Manx tourist industry.

MNH holds an original register for Douglas Camp (the former Cunningham's Young Men's Holiday Camp, requisitioned for internees), listing the names and serial numbers of those held there. This comprises around 6,000 entries, but is slightly less than this in terms of individuals, as some received more than one number. No similar register exists for Knockaloe, but a database is being created to hold the names of known internees at Knockaloe. This has been compiled from the many camp newspapers, sports programmes and other documents held in MNH archives, and the numerous items of

A view of Knockaloe Camp, painted by George Kenner, a German internee who later emigrated to America. (2006-0067)

craftwork held in the collections of MNH. This database is available through the iMuseum. A series of glass-plate negatives of photographs of internees at Knockaloe and Douglas camps, numbering in excess of 3,000 items, also survives. These plates have been scanned and are available to view at the iMuseum. They feature camp activities such as drama and cultural events as well as individuals.

The records of the British Government Foreign Office, in particular the Prisoners of War and Aliens Department correspondence files, are held by TNA under FO 383. These files contain many references to Knockaloe and in addition to general reports upon conditions in the camp and suchlike, there are also numerous letters relating to named individuals held within the camp. The indexes to these files may be searched via TNA website at: www.nationalarchives.gov.uk.

Two memoirs published in the 1930s shed an interesting sidelight on the experience of internment on the Isle of Man in the First World War. In 1932 Paul Cohen-Portheim published *Time Stood Still*, whilst in 1933 Major Paul Stoffa, an officer in the Hungarian army, published *Round the World to Freedom*.

In the Second World War, a number of hotels were requisitioned to house internees.

Major Paul Stoffa had been captured by the Russian army on the Eastern Front. After escaping from a Russian POW camp, he disguised himself as a merchant seaman and it was in this guise that he was again captured by the British, aboard a merchant vessel. Unable to prove his identity at the time, he was treated as a civilian and interned at Alexandra Palace, which served as a transit camp for those on their way to Knockaloe. In *Round the World to Freedom* (1933) Stoffa wrote:

After the usual formalities we were distributed to the various camps: my new home was Camp III. As it was mercifully dark, camps and compounds conveyed little to us: I was taken to one of the many army-huts, each divided into three sections with a double row of bunks ranged alongside the wall. My first thought was that I was back in the fo'c'sle, only on dry land. The sea of mud round the camps provided a substitute for the missing element ... I soon discovered why the camp at Knockaloe inspired such dread amongst the inhabitants of the Alexandra Palace. Here internment was reduced to its simplest elements: barbed wire, huts and mud. There were no 'frills', no panorama of London stretching for miles, which in itself was an element of qualified freedom, no permanent buildings and no visitors, it was the home of make-shift, grim, cold and monotonous. The incessant drizzle outside supplied the key-note of our existence. In a sense, it was almost a replica of the prison-camp at Shkotovo: it gave one the same feeling of utter isolation, a complete severance from the outside world. No wonder that so many men degenerated here by degrees into something near a state of savagery: the decent majority struggled hard to keep afloat in a sea of hopeless despondency – many went under, insanity claiming not a few.

FEMALE. 2778

REGISTRATION CARD.

(1) NAME (Surname first in Roman capitals).

PROBST, *Martha Alwine Auguste.*

ALIAS

(3) NATIONALITY *German* Born on *18 July 10* in *Boomum.*

(4) PREVIOUS NATIONALITY (if any)

(5) PROFESSION or OCCUPATION *General maid.*

(7) Address of last residence outside U.K. *Gartenstrasse 28, Elze, Hanover.*

SINGLE or MARRIED *Single*   Husband's Name and Serial No.

(8) GOVERNMENT SERVICE

(9) PASSPORT or other papers as to nationality and identity.

German Pft. 3802
London. 5.9.8.

(2) IDENTITY BOOK OR REGISTRATION CERTIFICATE.

No. *511242.*
Date *25 Oct. 33*
Issued at *Slough.*

(6) Arrived in U.K. on *23 Oct. 33.*
Pt. 18-7-40

(11) SIGNATURE OR LEFT THUMB PRINT.

Martha Probst

RNJZ-384-3

The registration card of Martha Probst, a German-born maid interned on the Isle of Man in Rushen Camp. (Ms09310)

The camps were located in Douglas, Onchan, Peel, Ramsey, Port Erin and Port St Mary. This time both males and females were arrested. The largest groups were of German, Italian and Austrian nationality. About a hundred Japanese were also held, and a number of Finns. Many of those interned in 1940 were in fact refugees from Nazi persecution who had fled to Britain in the 1930s. After a vetting process, those who were not Nazi sympathisers were largely released and many made a vital contribution to the Allied war effort. In addition to internees, British fascist sympathisers and IRA members were detained under Section 18b legislation, in the Peveril Camp at Peel. They were supervised by members of the Metropolitan Police. Records relating to those detained under Section 18b are held by TNA, though these are closed for 100 years.

MNH holds around 4,000 original index cards for female internees from the Second World War, many of which include a photograph. Females were held in the Rushen Camp, along with children under 16 (some of whom were born in the camp). The index cards for the male internees were largely destroyed after the war, though it has been possible to reconstruct a partial database from other sources (the only male index cards that appear to have survived are those for Vichy French soldiers and civilians, held on the Isle of Man following the fall of Madagascar to the Allies in 1942). In total some 15,000 names of Second World War internees are held by MNH, and these are available through the iMuseum. More information about the holdings of MNH in relation to internment may be found at: www.gov.im/mnh/heritage/library/bibliographies/internment.xml.

The Association of Jewish Refugees has released through its website the complete back archive of its *Journal*, from 1946 to present. The text is key word searchable, and many Jewish refugees who were interned on the Isle of Man will be mentioned by name. It can be found at: www.ajr.org.uk/pdfjournals.

Papers relating to former Second World War internees who did not return to the country of their birth, and who underwent naturalisation as British subjects following the end of the war, are held by TNA under HO 405, although it is believed that this series is only partially complete. More information on this can be found on the TNA website, in particular the research guide: www.nationalarchives.gov.uk/records/research-guides/naturalisation.htm. The names of those who opted for naturalisation may also sometimes be found in the *London Gazette* in the years from 1946 to around 1948. The entries usually state the country of birth of the individual together with the address at which they were living at that time, and their occupation. Back copies of the *Gazette* have been digitised and can be accessed via the website at: www.gazettes-online.co.uk. The *London Gazette* may also be useful in tracing the appointments of officers who served on the staff of internment camps during both world wars. During the First World War, enlisted camp guards were predominantly members of the Royal Defence Corps and were quite often veterans of Victorian colonial wars, or men found not physically fit for front-line service in the trenches. If they had no front-line service in the First World War, they will not appear on the Medal Index Cards (discussed elsewhere in this book). They may however have papers in the WO 97 series at TNA (if they had served in the Army prior to the First World War) or in the WO 377 series.

Some information on camp civilian staff is held by the MNH Library and Archive Service. This comprises two lists: Knockaloe Aliens Camp Roll of Headquarters Staff, as of 28 July 1917 (comprising 13 pages, and covering around 235 staff, including A. Knox as Chief Parcel Censor) and Douglas Aliens Camp staff as of 8 July 1917 (2 pages and covering around 44 staff). Both are bound into a scrapbook under B.114/2xf Military.

The service papers of enlisted guards from the Second World War internment camps will still be held by the Ministry of Defence, and may be applied for if the subject can be shown by means of a death certificate to have been deceased for twenty-five years or more.

See also:
✿ Military and Naval Records

LAND AND PROPERTY RECORDS

A good understanding of the Manx system of land division is essential before beginning to examine land and property records. The Manx people have traditionally considered themselves 'northsiders' or 'southsiders'. The physical barrier presented by the mountain chain running diagonally across the Island has resulted in parallel administration, of the northern side of the Island from Peel, and of the southern side from Castletown. Each had its own castle, its own courts and Deemster. The *Chronicles of Man* attribute this division to the Battle of Sky Hill in 1079, when it is said that Godred Crovan took the southern portion of the Island for himself, and left the surviving Manx chiefs to the north. The Island is subdivided into sheadings. The origin of these are unclear, but there are six sheadings and the term may be a derivation of the Norse 'sixthing' and parallel the term riding (thirding) in Yorkshire. The Island is then further divided into seventeen parishes, with in most cases three parishes to a sheading.

Parishes are split into treens (or it might be argued that a number of treens were grouped into parishes, probably in the twelfth century). It may be that this division into treens reflects an earlier Celtic system of land holding. The number and size of the treens varies from parish to parish, but a treen generally contained four quarterlands (or farms) and was used as a convenient fiscal division with the annual tax (the Lord's rent) payable according to its size. Each treen would have had its own small chapel or *keeill*. Land that was not considered of great farming value was left as common land. Later enclosures of such land formed what is known as the *intacks* (literally 'intakes'). Generally the boundaries of the treens followed natural divisions such as streams and watersheds. With the exception of the Marown/Santan boundary (and these parishes seem to have been formed much later than the others by the division of Marown) parish boundaries followed those of the treens.

Manorial records cover tenancy of land and the transfer of these tenancies. They are of great value to those studying Manx ancestry, because the surviving records of the manorial courts contain the names of all tenants, their respective land holding and the nature of the tenancy transfer, during the period from 1507 to 1913 when the system ended. Because land traditionally tended to be passed from father to eldest son, the records documenting this can be useful in helping to construct a family tree. Broadly speaking the manorial records fall into two distinct periods: those up to 1704 and those afterwards. Prior to 1704, the bulk of the landmass of the Isle of Man was owned by the Lord of Mann, who leased parcels of land to tenants in return for specific services and rent. The mode of tenure was known as 'the Tenure of the Straw'. This was because a tenant wishing to return his lands to the Lord or to pass the tenancy on did so simply by going to the manorial court and delivering a straw. A record was then made of the transfer.

A tradition grew up on the Island whereby in almost every case the eldest son succeeded his father as tenant. So entrenched did this become that the system of granting leases by the Lord virtually ceased, and families came to regard their tenancies as sacrosanct. Realising that this custom was developing, in the 1640s James Stanley, Seventh Earl of Derby, tried to revert to the old system by a mixture of incentives and coercion. A forty-year struggle between the Derby family and the leading Manx families ensued, which was finally resolved with the statute of 1704. This statute provided for fair rent, fixity of tenure and free sale. It ended the threat of the arbitrary imposition of fines by the Lord when land changed hands, and allowed for the sale of tenancies by tenants by private treaty. The widespread use of conveyance deeds also grew up in the Isle of Man after 1704. The Lord retained the right to collect rents and fines until 1826 when these passed to the British Crown. They were finally abolished in 1913 after which all land became freehold.

The rolls listing the names of tenants for the purposes of collecting the Lord's rents are contained in four series of volumes held by the MNH Library and Archive Service. All are available on microfilm in the Reading Room. They consist of:

- Libri Assedationis, or setting books (c. 1507–1911), containing the names of all landholders and the rent they paid to the Lord of Mann
- Libri Vastarum, sometimes called 'Wast' Books (1511–1916), recording the admissions, entries and titles of landholders and the alienation fines and rents paid by them
- Composition Books (from 1593), describing each tenement and recording all fines paid
- Libri Episcopi, two books covering 1511–1760 and 1761–1922, recording the tenants of the Bishop's Baronies
- Libri Monasteriorum, or Abbey Books (1579–1890), containing the rentals of Rushen Abbey and of the various lesser baronies.

There are also tenant books in the MNH collections from the Barony of Bangor and Sabal. Some smaller deposits also refer to tenants, in particular the Nunnery estate rental ledger, which is arranged by tenant and covers the period 1829 to 1861 (MS 09926), or to landowners, for example, that covering the northside parishes from 1850 to 1860 (MS 05442). There is also a substantial collection of deeds from the seventeenth century to 1910 held in the MNH Archive, under MS 09494. These are indexed by parish and then by the name of the grantor (i.e. seller). These records are currently in the process of being digitised, though initially at least this will only cover the period from 1847 to 1910. Those after 1910 are held by the Deeds and Probate Registry. These are also indexed by grantee (purchaser). Further information about how to use these records is available on the MNH website, or at the MNH Reading Room. It is worth mentioning, however, that deeds prior to 1847 are divided into four classes. These are north-side sales, south-side sales, Castletown deeds (which cover the whole Island) and mortgages. Each has a separate index, in which those of each parish are listed chronologically with the names of vendors and purchasers. The north-side and south-side sales are separately indexed. After 1847 this system was abolished in favour of a central registry of deeds in Douglas which was charged with registration of all titles and claims to any land whatsoever lying within the Isle of Man. Deeds were then indexed by individual parish, with deeds organised alphabetically by the surname of the vendor. It is hoped that digitisation of these important records will simplify searching these records and obviate the need to consult many different indexes. As an additional finding aid, a project is currently underway to index the Registration Books relating to deeds held by MNH. This project seeks to draw out the names of both parties involved (grantor and grantee), the date of actual deed (several months might elapse before it was actually registered) and other details about property involved. The current coverage for this project is 1890–1910, but it is proposed to continue further back to 1880 in due course.

Deeds after 1910 are held in the Isle of Man Registry of Deeds, where they can be examined upon payment of a fee. Deeds are being digitised, and those from 1990 to date are currently available through public-access terminals at the Isle of Man Registry of Deeds and the iMuseum. IOMPRO also holds property records, in particular Isle of Man Government Property Trustees minutes and files from 1892 to 1987, and Assessment Board Rate books from 1902 to 1976. Other land and property records are held by TNA. These are known as CREST (Crown Estates) records and cover the period from when the British Crown assumed the land right of the Atholl family in 1826 through to 1949. They consist of the usual records of leases and grants of land to tenants but also include an 1829 survey of the border between Dalby and Glen Maye.

MANX GAELIC RECORDS

Towards the end of the nineteenth century a small number of Manx patriots, scholars and enthusiasts became increasingly aware that traditional ways of life on the Isle of Man were irrevocably changing, and that the people who were the bearers of the old traditions and customs were slowly disappearing. A movement began to collect and record this 'unwritten history'. People like Sophia Morrison, William Cashen of Peel and Charles Roeder collected folk tales. However, alongside this, and inextricably bound up with it, was the need to capture and record the native language of the Isle of Man, for this was the first language of many of the informants.

Professor Carl Marstrander made wax-cylinder recordings of the Manx language in the 1920s, but the need and impetus to collect and record the language was given a boost with the opening of Harry Kelly's cottage at Cregneash, in 1938. After the Second World War, in 1947 the Taoiseach of Ireland, Eamon De Valera, visited Harry Kelly's cottage in the course of an unofficial visit to the Island. On hearing of the declining number of Manx speakers and the Manx Museum's lack of any suitable recording equipment to preserve this fragile aspect of the Island's heritage, De Valera offered to make available the mobile recording equipment used by the Irish Folklore Commission. This offer was eagerly accepted and in due course a van with recording equipment arrived in the Island to begin recording. The resulting body of material formed the core of the MNH sound-recording collection.

The MNH Library and Archives service holds a large quantity of written material both about and in the Manx language. A Manx Gaelic bibliography containing around 900 entries is available to researchers upon request. For those interested in background information, Brian Stowell and Diarmuid O'Breaslain's *A Short History of the Manx Language* (1996) is a useful introduction. In 2003 the recordings made by the Irish Folklore Commission were digitally enhanced and released by MNH as a five-disc CD compilation, with an accompanying book giving biographical information about the informants, as *Skeealyn Vannin – Stories of Mann*.

Several sound recordings in Manx from the National Sound Archive have been digitised and will be available through the iMuseum, along with a selection of Manx language films from the National Film Archive.

See also:
✿ Folk Life Survey

In 1984 Kevin Danaher recounted his own memories of travelling with the Irish Folklore Commission in 1948, to record the surviving Manx speakers:

We spent some weeks going up and down the Island, meeting people and working with them. I have very happy memories of the people who helped us at the time . . . and the old people we went to – I've very happy memories of those, such friendly people. Ned Maddrell probably was the chief one but there was also Yn Gaaue Doo, John Kneen from Ballaugh, and John Tom Kaighin who was a blind man from the north side of the Island, a very nice and gentle person. And Harry Boyde who was a tremendously fluent speaker of Manx . . . in fact the difficulty was to get him to stop talking! And several others. I mean we had a delightful meeting [at the Kinvigs' house] close to South Barrule where half a dozen of the old people got together and had a tremendous evening there talking. And also on another occasion, we brought Yn Gaaue Doo over to meet John Tom Kaighin and the two of them sat down and conversed in Manx because the old people at that time didn't have very much opportunity to speak to their contemporaries with difficulties of travel and so on . . . and to get into the same natural fluency which they had. And, of course, when you got these two old boys going it certainly was worth listening to. We recorded at least part of their conversation . . . They were the first good voice-recordings made in the Isle of Man.

Manx speakers John Kneen (second left) aged 95 and Harry Boyde (second right) aged 78, being recorded in 1948. (Pg12278)

MANX MUSEUM MANUSCRIPT COLLECTION

The MNH Library and Archive Service holds numerous collections of documents that have relevance for family and local historians. Some of the larger collections such as the Castle Rushen papers are referred to elsewhere in this book. Some of the smaller collections are highlighted in the *Journal of Manx Museum*, which is available in the MNH Reading Room. A few of the more interesting examples include:

- The Atholl papers (MS 09707) – this extensive collection covers every aspect of the administration of the Isle of Man in the eighteenth century by the Dukes of Atholl and their agents. A card index to persons named within the documents is held in the MNH Reading Room, together with more detailed printed summary lists and microfilm copies of the papers
- The Claghbane papers – these include a petition to James Stanley, Lord of Mann in 1648 from the parishioners of Kirk Maughold for the appointment of William Christian as clerk of the parish. The petition is signed by about a hundred men from Maughold parish (a transcript of this document was also published in the *Journal of Manx Museum,* Volume III, 54, and subsequently on the Manx Note Book website)
- The Derby papers (MD 401) – some papers of the Stanley family relating to the administration of the Island are held under MD 401 with microfilm copies in the series DP1-21. A hand list is also available
- The Libri Scaccarii (MS 10071) – the books of the Exchequer Courts. These contain the records of the Vigil of Mann – the watch that was set up in each sheading in 1497 to guard the coasts. The document gives the names of the men from each sheading charged with this task. A transcript appears in the *Journal of Manx Museum*, Volume III, 16, together with notes attributing the names to individual treens
- The Ellesmere papers (MS 00242) – these papers were originally part of the estate of Lord Ellesmere, before being sold to an American library. Copies were obtained by the Manx Museum and these include a book of fees and wages paid to members of the Castle Rushen garrison, from 1575. The roll lists by name soldiers, the schoolmaster, the slater, the falconer and a host of others. These papers were the subject of an article in the *Journal of Manx Museum*, Volume III, 53–5.
- The Harrison/Stevenson papers – this disparate collection is held under MD 436. A card index exists in the MNH Reading Room. The material covers the eighteenth to early nineteenth centuries, including some documents relating to the Stevenson family.

MAPPING

John Speed's map
of the Isle of Man,
dating from 1610,
shows many
important details,
including larger
houses, churches
and castles.

Maps and plans are an invaluable source for the study of the history and development of the Island, providing information on place names, settlements, development, coastal erosion, land divisions and estates, mines and railways. From a family history point of view they are also extremely useful, often providing information on which family lived where at a particular point in time.

Prior to the Ordnance Survey a number of cartographers surveyed the Island, at a variety of scales. Some of the best known examples include that by John Speed produced in 1610, and the very precise work of Peter Fannin, the former Sailing Master in the Royal Navy who had drawn up charts for Captain Cook on his South Sea voyages

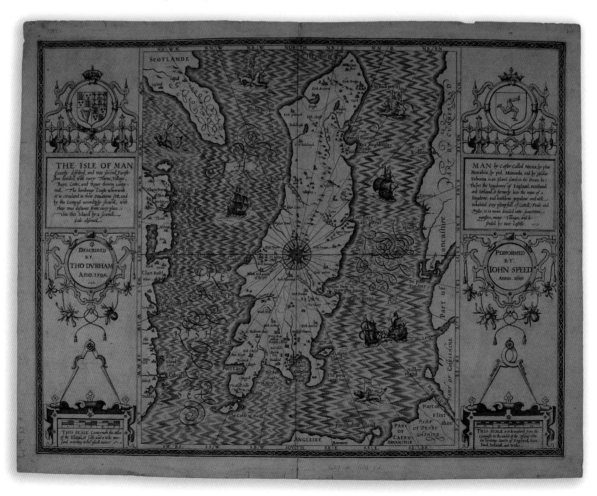

and who spent his retirement mapping the Isle of Man. These maps are recorded in *Early Maps of the Isle of Man* (1994) by A.M. Cubbon. Some of these maps are also illustrated in a volume of facsimile maps published by Shearwater Press entitled *Maps of the Isle of Man 1280–1760* (1975). In addition, a cartobibliography of printed maps covering the Island has been prepared by Frances Coakley. It is available in draft form for consultation in the MNH Reading Room and also via the Internet, on the Manx Note Book website at www.isle-of-man.com/manxnotebook/maps/index.htm.

The Ordnance Survey was commissioned by the British Government to survey the Island and between 1866 and 1871 a series of maps was produced, at the following scales:

- 1:500   Douglas and Ramsey only
- 1:2500   Whole Island by Parish (25in = 1 mile)
- 1:10560   Whole Island (6in = 1 mile)
- 1:63360   Whole Island (1in = 1 mile).

There is a reference book for the 25in plans arranged by parish which states the acreage and use of each plot of land whether arable, wood, house and garden, rough pasture and so on. This is available in the MNH Reading Room (Library reference O.11). This relates only to the 1st edition of the series, and was abandoned for later editions as the acreage was then printed directly on the maps.

Unfortunately, the large-scale mapping was not revised until the 1950s and so there is no equivalent of the County Series for England, with its frequent revisions. This is a particular problem when trying to chart the development of urban areas such as Douglas, where growth was rapid. With such a wide gap between surveys, buildings can easily have sprung up and been swept away again by later development without ever having appeared on a map or plan. Of particular note in the case of Douglas is the fact that the Ordnance Survey maps predate the various promenade extensions and harbour developments.

Other maps and plans worthy of note are the 1842 Copper Riot Plan. Up to 1840 the Manx penny was valued differently from the English penny, there being fourteen of the former to the pound. Plans to assimilate the two (and thus devalue the Manx penny) led to riots in Douglas. In order to compensate those shops and businesses that had sustained damage (and also to encourage citizens to be more active in quelling future riots) a rate was levied on properties in Douglas and Braddan. A surviving plan shows every dwelling in the town, with a rateable value ascribed (it is not known if a similar plan was drawn up for the parish but if it was, it does not appear to have survived). This plan, known as the Copper Riot Plan, is held at the IOMPRO. Each property on the plan is drawn quite accurately in terms of footprint and has a running number. This number relates to a document held amongst court records, 63/1842 Libri Scaccari, noting who the occupant was. There were also riots in Peel and a similar rate was proposed for the citizens of that town as a result. It is not known if it was ever imposed, and if it was no surviving plan is known to exist.

However the Leece Museum in Peel does hold an 1894 rating map of Peel seafront, drawn up by a James Connell. Unfortunately, this does not show the names or the

---

Joseph Train's *Historical and Statistical account of the Isle of Man* (1845) states that:

The greater part of the copper currency of the Island, between the years 1830 and 1838, was of foreign mintage, which, in a great measure, displaced the copper pence and halfpence struck in the tower of London, and designed solely for circulation in the Island, being of less value than the copper coinage of Great Britain. A British shilling was equal to fourteen pence of Manks copper; and one pound three shillings and fourpence Manks was equivalent to one pound sterling. All negociations for money, therefore, if intended to be according to the British standard, were so expressed, otherwise Manks currency was understood.

Such an immense quantity of base copper was in circulation in 1838, that the insular legislature deemed it necessary to prepare a bill to assimilate the copper currency, with that of the United Kingdom, which, having received the royal assent on the 3rd January, 1840, was promulgated at St. John's on the 17th March following … the lieutenant-governor issued a proclamation calling in the old copper, which was to be completed on the 21st September 1840, on and after which, the copper currency of the Island was to pass at the rate of twelve pence to the shilling.

So great was the excitement caused by this alteration, and such was the hostility to the innovation, manifested by the lower orders of the inhabitants, that, upon its introduction, a riot took place at Douglas and other parts of the Island. The windows and doors of the houses of the legislators, and of those shopkeepers who were favourable to the change, were demolished; the riot act was read, the military called out, and the principal portion of the respectable inhabitants sworn in special constables; but it was not until a company of soldiers had arrived from Liverpool that the Island was restored to its wonted tranquillity. The new copper now circulates quite freely, and is looked upon by the inhabitants as a great benefit in facilitating commercial intercourse.

owners or occupiers of the properties but does indicate the respective values of properties. The curator of the museum may be contacted at:

The Leece Museum
Old Courthouse
East Quay
Peel
Isle of Man
IM5 1AR

Telephone: 01624 845366
Website: www.peelonline.net/leece/

Geological Survey

This was conducted by G.W. Lamplugh between 1892 and 1897 and published at 1:10560 scale. It was accompanied by *The Geology of the Isle of Man* published by the same author in 1903. This latter volume is useful for background information on the mining industry and is in part available on the Manx Note Book website. Also available in the MNH Reading Room are copies of the Drift edition at 1:63360 for 1898, 1913 and 1966. A more recent Drift edition (1975) at 1:50000 was published by the British Geological Survey. A new edition was produced in 2001. The MNH Library reference is O43.

Annotated/Antiquarian Maps

A hand-annotated version of the 1:10560 scale Ordnance Survey of the 1860s is available in the MNH Reading Room with notes from research by Cubbon, Kermode, Savage, Craine, Megaw and Lamplugh. This shows archaeological sites and place names around the Island, which have not been recorded by the Ordnance Survey.

Goad Plans

These are detailed street plans of the main shopping area of Douglas and currently cover the period from 1971 to 2006 at roughly three-year intervals. They name the occupier of each shop unit and chart the development of the retail centre which makes them an invaluable source for students. The MNH references are pDG 69-77M and pDG62-64L.

Department of Infrastructure Plans

A series of Local and Strategic Plans with accompanying written statements have been produced in recent years by this department of the Isle of Man Government, and are held under the MNH Library reference B60: Local Plans for Arbory and East Rushen; Braddan Parish District; Castletown; Douglas; Foxdale; Kirk Michael; Laxey;

Onchan; Peel; Port Erin; Port St Mary; Ramsey; St John's; Sulby. Strategic Plans for Eastern Sector; North Eastern Sector; North Western Sector; Southern Sector; Western Sector.

Kay Plans

These were purchased by the MNH Library in 1953 from an architectural practice based in Athol Street, Douglas. They consist of a series of hand-coloured maps with amendments up to the 1940/50s and are based on the first large-scale Ordnance Survey (1:500 or 1:1250). There are about forty sheets covering Castletown, Douglas, Laxey, Onchan, Peel, Port Erin and Ramsey. It should be noted however that there is not a complete set for each area.

Land Utilisation Survey

At 1:63360 for 1932 and 1963, based on the Ordnance Survey map. There is also a report of the survey for 1932 updated by Norman Pye to 1939 which was published in 1941.

Abandonment Plans/Non-Coal Mines

These vitally important plans dating from the mid-nineteenth century to around 1914 record the position of individual mine shafts and plot the geographical location of underground workings in the Isle of Man. All Abandonment Plans are held by MNH on deposit from the Health and Safety Executive, HM Inspectorate of Mines.

Soil Survey

Mapped by B.S. Kear and drawn onto the 1969 1:63360 Ordnance Survey Map with accompanying book. MNH Library reference A224/37 and pXX.21.L. See also *Soils of the Isle of Man* by Fullen et al. MNH Library reference A224/78q.

Wood's Atlas

James Wood was a surveyor for the Asylum Board who compiled a new atlas and gazeteer of the Isle of Man, published in 1867. This consists of seventeen maps describing the civil and ecclesiastical boundaries of each parish, and the boundaries of the several baronies, freeholds and quarterlands, as well as the several farms as they were then held. It has reference tables showing proprietors of land with the manorial description and extent of land held. On the atlas, land areas are colour coded; quarterland for example is red. The atlas records a number for individual parcels of land and the accompanying parish index gives the name of the proprietor of the land or property, relating to individual numbers. Thus from *Wood's Atlas*, researchers can find the parish, the treen, the quarterland (or intack), the owner and the extent of a land holding, as at 1867, from which a search of Manorial records may then be commenced. The Atlas has been microfilmed by the Genealogical Society of Utah, and is now available in digital format. It will also be provided through the iMuseum in due course. It should be noted that the atlas does not cover land in the towns; a useful explanatory article about *Wood's Atlas* by Nigel Crowe appeared in IOMNHAS *Proceedings*, Volume 10, 373–9.

Tithe Plans

These excellent reference aids are based on individual parishes and were produced as a result of the Tithe Commutation Act, 1841 which converted church tithes of kind (oats, hay, pigs, cattle, etc.) into money payments. These plans have been microfilmed and are available on microfiche in the MNH library. They give full details of each land holding as it existed during the period around 1840, though buildings are only shown as basic outlines.

Asylum Plans

These are similar to tithe plans. They were prepared in order to assess a rate or rateable value on properties to finance the building of the lunatic asylum at Ballamona between 1860 and 1864. They were published in summary form in *Wood's Atlas*. Originals are held in the MNH Library.

Development Control Plans

The Town and Country Planning Act, 1934, introduced 'Development Control' to the Isle of Man. Thereafter, individual planning applications were scrutinised. IOMPRO holds the original applications, which include architect's drawings and detailed plans, whilst MNH holds microfilm copies for the period 1934 to 1974.

Registered Plans

These are held by IOMPRO and include plans deposited at the Rolls Office and General Registry between 1833 and 1982. They cover plans of towns (valuation, boundaries and improvements), railways, tramways, harbours, gasworks, electric power and light, rivers, waterworks, water supply and drainage districts. Later plans can be found within the Third Division Staff of Government (3DS) records, a name given to a miscellaneous collection of official material (the other two being First and Second Division).

Other Maps and Plans

As well as those mentioned earlier, MNH has a collection that includes commercially published maps, archaeological site plans, nautical charts, building plans and drawings and estate maps. Mining, railway development and land divisions are some of the topics well covered in the collections. These are listed in card indexes which are arranged by subject/place or cartographer/publisher. Each card describes a map or plan and gives its size and format together with a library reference which is explained as follows:

    p.BN.1.L = printed map/plan. Braddan. number 1. large sequence
    LO.2.M = map/plan. Lonan. number 2. medium sequence

These plans are a useful source as an alternative to Ordnance Survey maps, for example, in showing the growth of Douglas. When looking in this index under place, it is important to remember to check under parish first. So for 'Cronkbourne', for example, one needs to look up 'Braddan, Cronkbourne'.

Aerial Photography

The MNH Library and Archive Service also holds a very good series of aerial photographs, created by the RAF between 1945 and 1946. MNH also holds a series of aerial photographs taken in August 2000, showing just coastal areas. The scale is 1:7500 and these are in colour. The MNH reference is PG 7304.

Isle of Man Survey Current Mapping

The Isle of Man Government has responsibility for current mapping of the Island. This mapping was formerly referred to as 'DOLGE' mapping (after the former Government department), 'CLARE Plans' (after the maps provided by the Land Registry) or 'OS', but the correct term is Isle of Man Survey mapping.

The Isle of Man Survey's main task is to act as custodians of the large-scale mapping of the Island, and is charged with developing, licensing and promoting this mapping and derived small-scale products. As well as undertaking survey management, data development, licensing and commercial activities, the Survey also acts as technical advisor to the Island's Government mapping and GIS user group, MANNGIS.

Since 1996, the Island's large-scale mapping has been provided to customers electronically or as hard-copy plots, and mapping is offered at the following scales:

- Large-scale vector @ 1:1250 for the main towns and 1:2500 for the rest of the Island
- Medium-scale vector @1:10,000 scale
- Small-scale raster 1:50,000 basic topographic map
- Terrain modelling and aerial ortho-photography are also available
- Tourist mapping: 1:25,000 scale Outdoor Leisure Map and 1:100,000 scale.

Road maps are available from retailers around the Island. The Ordnance Survey also produce the 1:50,000 scale Landranger map of the Isle of Man (LR95) with the help of the mapping service. The Isle of Man Survey has an extensive archive of mapping and aerial photography and offers a site-specific historical facility. For any given site the following data can be provided either electronically or in hard copy:

Mapping
- 1868/70 1st Series mapping – 1:2500 scale approx. (geo-referenced TIFF format or hard-copy reproduction)
- 1950s 6in scale mapping – 1:10,000 scale approx. (non geo-referenced PDF or hard-copy reproduction)
- 1970s 6in scale mapping – 1:10,000 scale approx. (non geo-referenced PDF or hard-copy reproduction)
- 1980s 1:1250 or 1:2500 scale mapping for the main towns (non geo-referenced PDF or hard-copy reproduction).

Aerial Photography
- 1964 monochrome (PDF scan or hard-copy reproduction/enlargement)
- 1972 monochrome (PDF scan or hard-copy reproduction/enlargement)
- 2001 colour – 20cm resolution (geo-referenced MRSID or TIFF formats)
- 2006 colour – 10 and 20cm resolution (geo-referenced MRSID or TIFF formats)
- 2009 colour – 18cm resolution (geo-referenced MRSID or TIFF formats).

Contact Details for the Mapping Service

Isle of Man Survey Mapping Service
Department of Infrastructure
Murray House
Mount Havelock
Douglas
Isle of Man
IM1 2SF

Telephone: 01624 685924
Email: mapping@gov.im
Website: www.gov.im/transport/planning/cartography.xml.

The Mapping Service's website contains more information about current mapping activities and includes downloadable information sheets, price lists and educational maps.

MILITARY AND NAVAL RECORDS

The earliest military records relating to the Isle of Man are the Castle Rushen garrison rolls dating from 1428 (held by MNH as MS 09241). A transcript also exists for this roll, together with notes prepared by Ann Harrison, the former MNH archivist highlighting the value of this roll to family historians. A Manx Militia was in existence at the time of the English Civil War, as we know that it was commanded by William Christian (Illiam Dhone) but no musters or rolls from this formation appear to have survived. Slightly later than this, eight muster lists for the Peel Castle garrison, compiled monthly between 1659 and 1660, have survived amongst the Castle Rushen papers. Transcripts of two of these were published in the *Journal of Manx Museum* (Volume III, 222, and Volume IV, 130), and these also appear on Frances Coakley's Manx Note Book website (www.isle-of-man.com/manxnotebook). At the time of the Napoleonic Wars, the Isle of Man raised a number of Fencible (derived from the word 'defencible'), yeomanry and volunteer units. Some of these units were very short-lived, whilst others were in existence for considerably longer. A good summary guide to these formations is to be found in Bertram Sergeaunt's *A Military History of the Isle of Man* (1949), together with some nominal rolls of officers.

Ensign Daniel Callow of the Douglas Volunteers. The unit existed only between 1799 and 1802, but a roll of officers appears in Sargeaunt's *Military History of the Isle of Man*. (1954-1376)

During the Napoleonic Wars the Isle of Man raised its own corps of Fencibles. Fencible Infantry were intended to replace regular troops in home garrisons whilst they were away fighting abroad. Four corps of Manx Fencibles were raised, but only one was ever in existence at a given time. The records held by MNH in relation to the Manx Fencibles are extensive. Some of this material includes standing orders and monthly and fortnightly returns (MS 06318). In addition, there are punishment books and daily ledgers, and a number of description books that record personal details of recruits (MS 06810, MS 00780 and MS 00781). The description books are of enormous value to the family historian, and they are specifically discussed in this context in the *Journal of Manx Museum* (Volume VII, 28). In addition, in this series there are court martial records, and these are also discussed in the *Journal*, in Volume VII, 36. It is also worth mentioning that whilst the Fencibles were nominally drawn from the people of the Isle of Man, at times there were difficulties in fulfilling the quota of recruits from within the Manx population, and significant numbers of recruits were obtained in London and elsewhere.

In addition to those of the Manx Fencibles, MNH holds a number of records relating to the Volunteer corps raised during the Napoleonic Wars. Some formations, such as the Douglas Volunteers, were very short-lived, but the two main corps, the Southern Manx Volunteers and the Northern Manx Volunteers, were in existence for a number of years. Of particular interest to family historians will be paylists, such as MS 04014, that of Captain Watson's Company of the Southern Manx Volunteers, showing the names of all the enlisted men, between December 1808 and June 1809. Other paylists for the southern regiment, organised by companies, are held at MS 04018 to MS 04027. As with many military records of this period, there is always more information available in regard to officers than with other ranks. If a forebear held a commission in either the Fencibles or Volunteers then it may well be possible to find a document relating to his appointment in this series.

The main records relating to the Manx Yeomanry Cavalry are not held on the Island but instead form part of the collections of TNA. The Manx Yeomanry was in part raised by George Quayle of Castletown. In common with other parts of the British Isles, in the Isle of Man at the end of the Napoleonic Wars the infantry volunteers were disbanded, whilst the yeomanry was retained into the 1820s. This was in the expectation of horsed soldiers being needed in situations of public unrest and disorder. The records of the Manx Yeomanry Cavalry are held at TNA under WO 13/4016 and in the main comprise muster books and paylists. These records are well written up in the *Journal of Manx Museum* (Volume III, 167–9). The *Journal* also contains information regarding Manx POWs in France in 1811 (Volume III, 55). The article states that the men were serving in the Army at the time and lists them by name together with the location in which they were held.

Large numbers of Manxmen were recruited into the Royal Navy during the Napoleonic Wars, either willingly or unwillingly. The most famous of these was Captain John Quilliam, who served aboard HMS *Victory* at Trafalgar. Oblique references to naval personnel in this era may be found in parish registers, memorial inscriptions and such like, but again the main source of information on men such as Quilliam is likely to be TNA. TNA hold the service papers of naval officers from this period, and these often contain a baptismal certificate – a transcript from the parish register signed by the clergyman. For men who served below decks in the Royal Navy between 1802 and 1894, it may be worth checking the certificates of service (for example, if they went on to apply for a pension). These certificates of service are held at TNA in the series ADM 29/1-96. Many of these records can be searched by name using TNA catalogue at: www.nationalarchives.gov.uk.

From 1861 onwards, Royal Navy officers and sailors were recorded in the census on special naval schedules, recording servicemen and any passengers. Vessels were enumerated in home and foreign waters. The schedules note the name, rank or rating, marital status, age and birthplace, as well as location at the time of the census. In the later schedules of 1891 and 1901 name, relation to vessel (whether a member of the crew, etc.), marital status, age last birthday, occupation, birthplace and 'whether blind, deaf or dumb' were noted, along with the location.

Manxmen continued to serve in the Royal Navy throughout the nineteenth century and did so in large numbers during the two world wars of the twentieth century. When researching sailors or naval history it is important to remember that the line between the Merchant Marine and the Royal Navy was often somewhat blurred. Many Merchant Mariners serving with the IOMSPCo or other lines could also be members of the Royal Naval Reserve, Royal Fleet Reserve or Mercantile Marine Reserve. In wartime they could be called upon to serve with the Royal Navy, and one of the first indications that the First World War was imminent came when fifty naval reservists were called up and left the Isle of Man for active service in August 1914.

No Royal Navy or Royal Marines service records are held on the Isle of Man. On TNA's DocumentsOnline website it is possible to search and download over 600,000 service records for most ratings who joined the Royal Navy between 1853 and 1923, in the Registers of Seamen's Services (ADM 188) and the Continuous Service engagement books (ADM 139).These records contain details of a sailor's year of birth, their physical appearance, their occupation and which ship(s) they served on. Details of service are recorded up to 1928. If a rating joined the Royal Navy before 1873 and continued service after 1873, he might have a service record in both the ADM 139 and ADM 188 series. Also, some men may appear to have two accounts of service within ADM 188; firstly in the register and then continued in the Continuation Books ('new register'). In these cases both records have been linked together, so both are attached to the same man's online entry.

The records of seamen who entered the Royal Navy after 1923 are not yet publicly available. For details of a sailor's service between 1928 and 1938 a request must be made to:

One of the first indications in the Isle of Man that war was imminent in 1914 was the call-up of Manx members of the Royal Naval Reserve. These men left Douglas on 2 August 1914, and many of them went on to serve aboard the obsolete battleship HMS *Goliath* in the Dardanelles. HMS *Goliath* was torpedoed and sank on the night of 12–13 May 1915, in Morto Bay. Some 570 members of her 700-man crew perished in the incident, and given the strong Manx presence on board, the tragedy was widely reported in the newspapers of the Isle of Man. One of those who survived the sinking was William Henry Moore, who later became Harbourmaster of Douglas. In his obituary, published in the *Isle of Man Examiner* in 1938, a comrade who was with him recalled that Moore had dived into the water as the ship sank but was pulled under by the suction, and he was severely injured. 'His head was opened up like an oyster and blood was pouring from it', remembered his comrade, but in spite of his injuries Moore, who was a strong swimmer, reached a log to which other Manxmen were clinging and for over an hour he held it steady for them until help arrived. His Royal Naval Reserve service record from the Fleet Air Arm Museum confirms his home address, the names of his parents, his Three Legs of Man tattoo on his arm, and the head injury which he sustained in the *Goliath* incident.

The Royal Naval Reserve service record of William Henry Moore, of Douglas, who was aboard HMS *Goliath* when she was torpedoed. (Courtesy of the Fleet Air Arm Museum)

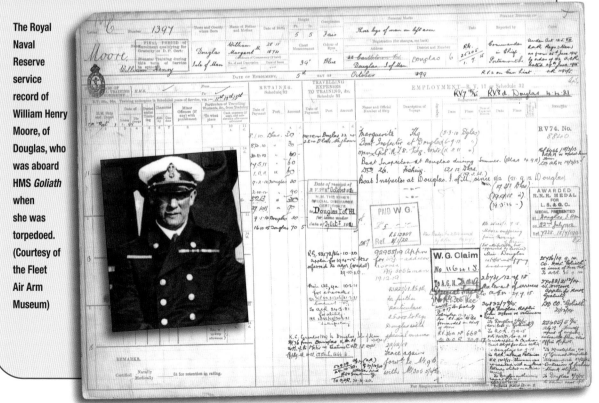

The Directorate of Personnel Support (Navy)
Navy Search
TNT Archive Services
Tetron Point
William Nadin Way
Swadlincote
Derbyshire DE11 0BB

Telephone: 01283 227913
Fax: 01283 227942
Email: navysearchpgrc@tnt.co.uk

For service after 1938, the request must be made to:

Data Protection Cell (Navy)
Victory View
Building 1/152
HM Naval Base
Portsmouth PO1 3PX

Some Royal Naval Reserve ratings' service records are held at TNA under BT 164, however this is only a representative sample. If a record cannot be located it could be possible that it is not amongst the selected sample. Records of service between 1919 and 1922 are held on microfiche in the series BT 377. Name indexes are available within the same series on microfilm covering the period back to 1860. It may also be worthwhile checking the service records of merchant seamen for the war period, covered elsewhere in this book.

For Royal Naval Reserve service records from 1922–39 and after 1945 it is necessary to contact:

PPPA (Pay, Pensions, Personnel, Administration)
Centurion Building
Grange Road
Gosport
Hampshire O13 9XA

The Fleet Air Arm Museum holds the original records for Royal Naval Reserve ratings from 1908 to 1955. The museum can supply copies of service records following a written request, and payment of a fee, to:

Fleet Air Arm Museum
RNAS Yeovilton
Ilchester
Somerset BA22 8HT

Website: www.fleetairarm.com/en-GB/default.aspx

One Manx war writer who might well have made a name for himself was John McCauley. Writing in the 1930s, his work might have reached a wider audience, but the war memoir 'craze' was at its height and the market was simply flooded. The opening paragraphs of McCauley's memoir run as follows:

The World War was a fortnight old when my employer came up to me in the workshop and said, 'Well John, England is at war, you know; she badly needs young men like you today.' He knew that I had served in the special reserve before the outbreak of war. Perhaps that knowledge gave him the courage to ask me to go, for after all, it needs a little courage to ask a young man to go out and face death, even for his country's sake. My only reflections then were: 'How romantic it will be, what can war be like?' I might just be in time to see the end if I join up at once ... How pleased he was. Perhaps he thought he had done his bit. My decision seemed to give pleasure to my workmates, too. Why it was so, I never could tell, but they shook me by the hand, clapped me on the back, and wished me good luck and a safe return. I too began to feel quite pleased with myself. I was already getting elated at the promise of the great adventure. There was a grim awakening in store for me.

John McCauley, who served with the Border Regiment in the First World War. (Pg7058/3)

The Royal Marines are the Navy's soldiers and as their motto (*Per Mare Per Terram*) suggests are equipped to fight on land or sea. The Royal Marines were raised in 1755, and in 1855 the Royal Marine Light Infantry (RMLI) was formed, followed by the Royal Marine Artillery (RMA) in 1859. During the First World War a Royal Marines Medical Unit and Royal Marines Labour Corps (to undertake dock labouring work) were also created, but they were disbanded at the close of hostilities. The RMLI and RMA merged in 1923 to form a single Corps of Royal Marines.

TNA holds Royal Marines service records in the series ADM 159, which was begun in 1884. A record was created retrospectively for anyone who had joined earlier and was still serving in 1884. The DocumentsOnline website allows Royal Marine service records between this date and 1925 to be searched. Records relating to enlistments after 1925 are still held by the Ministry of Defence. If the Marine in question had left the service by 1884, it is necessary to search the records in ADM 157, which are not available online. However, it is possible to search the index to records ADM 157/1-1251 for the Marine's name, using TNA's online catalogue at: www.nationalarchives.gov.uk/catalogue/default.asp.

For regular soldiers who enlisted in any British regiment in the Victorian period and up to 1913, the primary source of information is the WO 97 series at TNA. For the first half of the nineteenth century this series effectively only covers those soldiers who served long enough to receive a pension. For the latter half of the century, coverage is better. Records of soldiers discharged between 1913 and 1920 are held in the 'burnt' and 'unburnt' series at Kew (also available through www.ancestry.co.uk). This effectively covers most of the soldiers who served in the First World War.

From the 1860s until the end of the First World War the Isle of Man also maintained a Volunteer battalion, which for the last forty or so years of its existence was affiliated to the King's Liverpool Regiment as the 7th (Isle of Man) Volunteer battalion. MNH holds a series of records relating to the unit, originally produced by Government Office. These records are mainly administrative and largely document wrangles with the War Office over who should cover the costs. A muster roll for the Volunteers does survive and covers the years 1864 to around 1918. The entries consist of the soldier's name, home address, number, the date he enrolled and the date he resigned. Some names are annotated 'Served with Volunteer Service Company King's Liverpool Regiment in South Africa', indicating service in the Boer War. Other entries during the First World War are equally detailed and also record the other units that members of the Volunteers might have served with in France. This roll is microfilmed and is available in the MNH Reading Room (MS 00789c). Two other nominal rolls are held by MNH, one each for the 1st and 2nd Manx Service Companies (which comprised those men who had volunteered for overseas service in 1915). These are held at MS 00887 and MS 09568. An additional series of documents, covering Douglas soldiers only, is held at MS

William S. Cain was born in Castletown in 1836. In 1855 he left for the United States, and was soon followed there by his father and the other members of his family. They took up residence in Kansas, where they farmed. When the Civil War broke out, William Cain joined the Union Army. He enlisted in the 8th Kansas Infantry, and in that regiment rose from the rank of private to second lieutenant. He was then transferred to the 1st Regiment U.S. Colored Infantry, and subsequently to the 12th Regiment U.S. Colored Infantry, ultimately gaining the rank of captain. In his autobiography, published in 1908, Cain writes:

WILLIAM STEPHEN CAIN,
Late Captain 12th Regiment U. S. Colored Infantry.
Farmer, Merchant.

William S. Cain was born at Castletown, but like numbers of other Manxmen, he served in the American Civil War.

We were put on board the transport Lancaster No 3 and sent up the Cumberland River. Landed at Fort Donelson to repel a threatened attack, but were soon sent on to Nashville, Tenn., where we remained until the forward movement in June, against Bragg's army. We took part in the Battle of Hoover's Gap, the taking of Tullahoma, the crossing of Elk river and the taking of Winchester, Tenn. . . . It was at Hoover's Gap that I first saw a little of the horrors of war. Some Ohio and Indiana troops had charged a battery and captured a section of it that interfered with our advance. We were sent forward double quick to sustain and hold the position, and saw the ambulance corps carrying the wounded men to the rear. It looked awful to me. There is very little to make any sane man love actual war, but it is the last resort, and every man should be ready to sustain his government in conflict if so ordered.

10003. This takes the form of a register listing soldiers by surname, initial, regiment and number (when known). There are various comments added about the personal circumstances of each soldier and it appears the records were created for the purpose of administering charitable funds. It is believed that the author may have been Canon Kermode of St George's Church, but this is by no means certain. These records should all be used in conjunction with the Medal Index Cards, which are held by the TNA and which are available online via the DocumentsOnline website. A series of better quality images of the same cards are also available via www.ancestry.co.uk. As the index cards list virtually every soldier who went overseas, they are useful for corroborating information held in other sources.

No significant published personal memoir from a Manxman who served in the First World War exists, nor is there a published history of the Manx Service Company. However, Bertram Sargeaunt's *Isle of Man and the Great War* (1920) does include a chapter on how the Service Company was raised and its experiences in Salonika fighting against the Bulgarian army.

In the 1920s and 1930s Manxmen wishing to join the Regular Army would have enlisted, as they had prior to the First World War, into the regiments of the closest English counties, usually the Cheshire Regiment and the King's Liverpool Regiment. However, in 1938, the Isle of Man raised its first Territorial Army formation, the 15th Light Anti Aircraft Regiment, Royal Artillery, known as the Manx Regiment. MNH holds some records relating to this formation under MS 08261, including material from the Old Comrades Association, and research material gathered by the author Curwen Clague when preparing his published history of the regiment *Ack Ack* (1981). The museum of the Manx Regiment is housed within the Manx Aviation Preservation Society Museum at the Isle of Man's Ronaldsway airport. Whilst this museum does not hold service records of personnel, its archives do include a considerable number of personal memoirs compiled by former members of the regiment, ephemera and photographs. The contact details for the museum are:

Manx Aviation and Military Museum
Ronaldsway Airport
Ballasalla
Isle of Man

Telephone: 01624 829294
Email: webmaster.maps@iofm.net.

Many soldiers of the Manx Regiment were taken as POWs, when one battery was lost on Crete in May 1941. A little-known series of records sheds light on some of these men, because MI9 (the branch of Military Intelligence that dealt with POWs) requested that ex-prisoners fill in a questionnaire upon repatriation in 1945. The questions asked for personal details such as home address, and also details of the circumstances of capture and POW camp conditions. The extent of the answers vary from individual to individual, but this series of records are now available for consultation at TNA under WO 344.

Personnel records for both Territorial and Regular Army soldiers discharged after 1920 are still held by the UK Ministry of Defence (MOD). Similarly no naval or Royal Air Force personnel records are held on the Isle of Man. Applications to view such records may be made by the next of kin or, if it can be proved that the person in question has been dead for more than twenty-five years, by any third party. There is normally a charge levied by the MOD for this service. Details of how to make such an application are available from the MOD website at:

www.veterans-uk.info/pdfs/service_records/army_pack.pdf.

However, MNH does hold information relating to individuals called up under the 1939 National Service (Armed Forces) Act (MS 09871). These records were created by the Government Office Military Service Division and consist of call-up papers and medical records of every individual on the Isle of Man who was conscripted between 1939 and the 1960s (the end probably coincides with the abolition of National Service in Britain in 1960–2). The information in these files would clearly be of tremendous value to family history researchers, but at the moment it must be stressed that the records are closed under similar terms to those held in Britain, under the seventy-year rule. MNH also holds records relating to the Manx Home Guard in the Second World War (MS 11320 and MS 08387), but these are incomplete. Records for certain companies appear to have survived largely intact, whereas for others there are no surviving records at all.

The careers of Army, Navy and RAF officers from the two world wars (and earlier in the cases of the Army and Navy) are most easily traced by means of either the monthly lists produced by each branch of the service, or the *London Gazette*. Army, Navy and RAF lists are usually only held by large reference libraries, though the MNH Library and Archive Service does hold copies of the *Army List* for 1840, 1860, 1885 and 1914. The *London Gazette* has the advantage that it is available online and is searchable. In addition, the *Gazette* carries details of decorations awarded to military personnel of all ranks and across all three services. Copies can be searched via www.gazettes-online.co.uk.

Service papers of officers of the three branches, dating from the First World War and earlier are held by TNA, but presently these are not available online.

Photographic evidence in relation to the RAF bases at Andreas and Jurby is held by MNH, and additional information about the Royal Naval Air Station at

Ronaldsway is held by the Fleet Air Arm Museum at Yeovil. Once again material relating to individual personnel in Royal Naval or RAF service at these establishments is still held by the MOD. An important series of published works are Paul Francis' five volumes entitled *Isle of Man 20th Century Military Archaeology* (2006), held by MNH as M 27787 to M 27791. Francis covers the surviving structures at Ronaldsway, Andreas, Jurby and other lesser known installations such as the Chain Home radar station at Niarbyl.

Before leaving the subject of military records it is worthwhile discussing those records held outside of the British Isles which might hold information pertaining to a Manx relative. As noted elsewhere, large numbers of Manx people emigrated to the United States in the 1840s. Manxmen fought on both sides during the American Civil War of 1861 to 1865, and quite detailed personnel and muster roll records are held at state level in the United States, usually in the state library or archive. Many of these records are available online. One of the most detailed series is held by the state of Illinois and can be accessed at: www.ilsos.gov/genealogy/.

Inputting the name Corlett into the Illinois database, for example, brings up four records, three of which give the soldier's place of birth as Isle of Man. Daniel Corlett died at Lexington, Kentucky in 1863, John Corlett, who may have been his brother, was discharged due to disability in Illinois, whilst Thomas Corlett died at Midgeville, Kentucky, also in 1863. Soldiers of Manx birth may also be found in records of the 1917–18 draft for the US Army, which can be found at www.ancestry.co.uk. Emigration in the later nineteenth century was often to the countries of the British Commonwealth and the online records of Australian and Canadian armies in the First World War contain many recently emigrated Manxmen. Unlike their British counterparts, these series are complete so if it is known that an ancestor served in the Australian or Canadian armies finding their details should be relatively straightforward.

MINING RECORDS

Anyone who has traced their forebears to Laxey, Lonan or Foxdale in the nineteenth or early twentieth centuries will almost certainly at some point discover an association with the mining industry. A cursory perusal of, for example, the 1881 census for Lonan shows that almost every household was dependent upon an income from one of the mines operating in Glen Mooar. Rich veins of lead and zinc ore are to be found amidst the rock strata of the Isle of Man, and from the mid-nineteenth century onwards, the extraction of these metal ores became one of the Island's key economic areas. Indeed, by the late nineteenth century the Great Laxey Mine was the single largest producer of zinc in the British Isles.

The MNH website provides a useful introduction to this subject at; www.gov.im/mnh/education/curricularresources/mining.xml. MNH also holds extensive

The Great Laxey Wheel, the Isle of Man's greatest industrial monument. (Pg0908)

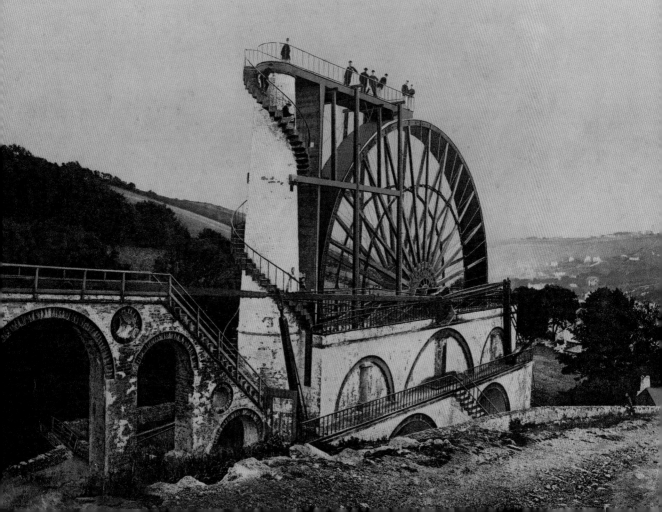

This Nomination Book entry from 1911 shows that William Joseph Scarffe, a foreman washer of Dumbells Row, Laxey, left his Co-operative shares to his daughter Mary Anna.

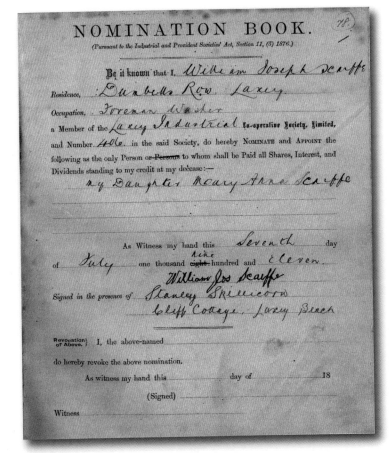

records relating to the Kirk Lonan Mining Association, the Great Laxey Mining Company and its successor, Great Laxey Limited. So extensive are these records that at the time of writing a large percentage has yet to be fully indexed and thus may not be readily available for public consultation. Probably of greatest interest to the family historian are the Setting Books which cover the period 1852 to 1896, with some gaps. These books record the 'bargains' or patches of ore granted to particular groups of miners. These records must be treated with caution when attempting to build genealogies and writing up family trees. With the wages and day books, there is a common problem throughout. Often, the miners and labourers worked in a group called a pitch. All these records appear only to list the 'bargainman' who was in charge of the pitch. The descriptions are thus 'Robert Kelly and six men' or 'John Corkish plus three miners and two labourers'. One such pass book has been noted in which there were thirteen men in the pitch, but only the bargainman's name was mentioned. It should also be noted that many of the names given would have been common in the Isle of Man at the time, for example, Robert Kelly. Rarely have any records been noted that show details of an employee's place of residence.

There are also underground labourers' pay books, surface labourers' pay books and washers' pay books. These record payments made to individuals between roughly the late 1850s to the early 1900s. Again it must be stressed that groups of records are non sequential and there are considerable gaps, though some of the records for pay to surface workers do at least record the subject's age. Much of the material, though not specific to individual miners, nevertheless gives useful background on the conditions under which the miners and their families lived. These include shareholders' reports, managers' reports, literature pertaining to strikes and the strikers' demands. Newspapers are also useful for contemporary reports on the state of the Island's mining industry, and a parallel but related series of records are those of the Laxey Industrial Co-operative Society, held by the MNH Library and Archive Service at MS 08574. The society was set up by the miners themselves, who because of the nature of their payments needed to be able to obtain goods on credit, at fair and equitable rates. Of particular interest will be the share ledgers (c. 1878 to the 1960s) and the Nomination Book (MS 08574/3), which runs from 1900 to 1954. Typical information included is the name of the shareholder, his address, occupation and person nominated to receive his dividend in the event of his death. This is usually a relative, so this is also useful for confirming family relationships.

The best published source for the Laxey Mine is undoubtedly Andrew Scarffe's *The Great Laxey Mine* (2004). Sadly nothing comparative exists (as yet) for the Foxdale mines. In 1963 the Isle of Man Government commissioned MacKay & Schnellmann Ltd to produce a survey detailing all known mines on the Island. Their report, *The Mines and Minerals of the Isle of Man* (1963), remains a useful overview of this subject.

See also:
✿ Census Records
✿ Dissolved Registered Company Files

In the Sound Archives of MNH is an interview with Bobby Kelly, a Laxey miner before the First World War. He recalled an incident when he was injured, and relied upon the Rechabites:

I remember the day I got hurt . . . there was a chap in the mines the [previous] night . . . and he broke his leg and he got brought up. This day, I had a feeling, I didn't want to go . . . I said 'I think I'll go home'. Anyway, I went, but I weren't long at work till I was brought up in the box, what they call the dead-box . . . I just went down into this hole, when a lump of rock slipped off the hanging, and fell and caught me leg . . . Well I was off, oh I was off for months, and the Captain of the Mines come to see me, and he said, 'You know Robert,' he said, 'We can't give you no compensation. Can't give you anything.' He said, 'You're a member of that Club,' and he said that'll have to keep you.'

NEWSPAPERS

The oldest known Manx newspaper is the Manks Mercury, first published in 1792.

Leaving aside the *Cumberland Packet*, which carried some Manx news, the earliest known Manx newspaper is the *Manks Mercury*, which was published between 1792 and 1795. Copies of virtually every newspaper title published on the Isle of Man since then are held in the MNH Library, though not every run is complete. The collection holds more than seventy titles, though many are of a specialist nature and include titles produced in German in internment camps, or produced only at certain times of the year in connection with the TT races. More details are available from the MNH Library, but the chief titles of interest to family historians are likely to be: *Manks Advertiser* (1801–42), *Manx Rising Sun*, later *Manx Sun* (1824–1906), *Mona's Herald* (1833–1975), *Isle of Man Times*, later *Weekly Times* (1867–1987), *Isle of Man Examiner* (1880–present), *Ramsey Courier*, later *Isle of Man Courier* (1884–present), *Peel City Guardian* (1882–present).

A flagship part of the iMuseum project has been the digitisation of all the main newspaper titles from 1792 to 1960, along with Optical Character Recognition indexing. This allows free text searching of an incredible 400,000 pages of newsprint, with various keyword search options, limits on title and date range. The software also ranks results in order of relevance to the search terms. This service is now available in the iMuseum building and is planned to be accessible online through subscription by the end of 2011.

All the main titles are also on microfilm in the Reading Room and it is necessary to consult these for the period from 1960 to the present. In most cases original newspapers will not now be produced for the public, due to their fragile nature. A card index (which includes biographical entries) from 1957–94 is held in the Reading Room. Card indexes relating to the eighteenth and nineteenth centuries are also held in the Reading Room. Entries include obituaries, awards and significant events affecting individuals. Family announcements are not usually indexed but this latter

The staff of the Manx Sun newspaper. As well as journalists, many would be compositors working with lead typeface in the composition room.

index has been largely rendered redundant by digitisation. For off-Island researchers, as of 2011 copies of Manx newspapers are also available at the:

British Library Newspaper Library
Boston Spa
Wetherby
West Yorkshire
LS23 7BQ

Telephone: 08432 081144
Email: newspaper@bl.uk
Website: www.bl.uk

Newspapers offer tremendous scope for research in a number of areas, the most obvious being obituary notices, notices of the sale or rental of properties, and reports of major events and tragedies, such as the Snaefell Mine disaster of 1897. There are also frequent reports of Manx involvement in the major events of the twentieth century such as the Boer War, First World War and Second World War. Theatre and cinema performances are advertised, as are movements of shipping in and out of Manx ports. It is no exaggeration to say that the scope for research now offered by newspapers in the iMuseum is tremendous, and cuts across almost all areas of interest.

Before leaving the subject of newspapers it is also worth commenting upon the *Isle of Man Examiner Annual Yearbooks*. Each one is a compendium of useful information containing details of local clergymen, Members of the House of Keys, local commissioners, members of Government boards and so on. Those volumes covering the First World War are particularly useful in that they contain a significant series of portrait photographs of local casualties and of those decorated for bravery. The 1915 *Yearbook* also contains a useful 'Manx Roll of honour' listing all those men from the Island who were known to have joined the Army or Navy up to that point, together with their unit. Akin to these are the *Norris Modern Press Yearbooks*. Of a similar nature to those produced by the *Examiner*, they none the less contain complementary information, for example, statistical information about the amount of land under agriculture each year, the type of crops being grown, and the number of crimes being reported year on year. Some editions prior to the First World War contain listings of all private car and motorcycle registration numbers in use on the Isle of Man at that time, and details of who the vehicle was registered to. The *Yearbooks* are held in the MNH Reading Room, with some information from them available via the Manx Notebook website.

See also:
✿ Directories

PARISH RECORDS

Parish records include (but are not exclusively) parish registers. Other components of parish records (such as burial plot transfers) are discussed elsewhere in this book. The earliest surviving parish register is that for Ballaugh, which commences in 1598 with the burial of Averick Steane, daughter of Thomas Steane on 17 June of that year. Registers continue into the early twenty-first century, and in most cases have been microfilmed up to 1883. In 1910 all Manx parish registers were passed temporarily to the General Registry, in order that handwritten copies could be made by Government staff of all records prior to 1849. These copies together with original registers spanning 1849 to 1883 were microfilmed, beginning in the 1940s, by the Genealogical Society of Utah. Together with indexes arranged by parish for baptism and marriage entries, they are available for family history use in the MNH Reading Room. The IOMFHS has produced detailed transcripts of burial registers, which again are available in the Reading Room. Recently, the latest volumes of parish registers from across the Isle of Man were deposited with MNH for photography and, together with the earliest registers, these are gradually being released in digital format through the iMuseum. In the future this will include for the first time images of original register entries rather than copies, and at the time of writing indexes to baptism registers for the period 1800 to 1878 are available in the iMuseum.

Since 2009 MNH with the help of a team of dedicated volunteers has been constructing a database formed from the information contained within the parish registers. It is envisaged that the project will ultimately include all parish registers known to exist. The project has revealed a wealth of information. Many of the entries are surprisingly detailed and, for example, for burials contain information about the cause of death, the circumstances in which a body was discovered and so on. The burial register for Malew contains a detailed

The burial register of St George's, Douglas records the interment of Sir William Hillary, founder of the Royal National Lifeboat Institution.

description of the fate of William Christian (Illiam Dhone), as described in the introduction to this book. The volumes of baptisms for Castletown contain many references to soldiers, members of the garrison of the Island, whilst those from Lonan naturally contain many references to miners.

An example from Lonan in May 1834 records Joseph Millican, a miner, 'who was killed by an unexpected explosion of powder in the mining shaft'. From 1819 we find Daniel Cowill of Bride 'supposed to be killed by a stone being cast at him on the night of Kirk Andreas fair on Wm. Tear's street. The jury's verdict was:- That the blow was the occasion of his death.' Even more intriguing is this reference from Santon, dated 28 February 1728: 'Katherine alias BRIDSON, wife of Robert BREW of Ballaquackin, who was shot in her Bed by a Gun that accidently hung over her where she lay.'

The level of detail, particularly with early registers, varies enormously and to a large extent relies upon how much the clergyman concerned could be bothered to write. One intriguing example comes from Lonan in the 1840s, when the Reverend Joseph Qualtrough had clearly misunderstood the meaning of the term 'condition' in the marriage register. Whilst it is usually taken to mean bachelor, spinster or widow, Qualtrough seems to have thought it referred to a person's status. Thus he used this column to make reference to whether the bridegroom was 'humble' or 'moderate'! When using parish registers it is important to remember that dates recorded prior to 1751 were based on the year being from 25 March to 24 March, rather than 1 January to 30 December, with which we are familiar today. Thus a burial recorded as occurring in January 1729 would be 1730 by our modern calendar. In these situations, data that has been digitally captured will be indexed using the old-style date as it appears in the original documents. In addition to details of baptisms, marriages and burials, parish registers often record significant events within the parish, for instance that for Ballaugh records:'1648: In this year there was great scarcity of corne.' This is significant, because it tallies with reports of poor weather leading to famine and hardship in other parts of Britain at this time. However, the information that registers hold cannot always be considered a complete record of family events within a parish. Baptisms it seems frequently went unrecorded. The Malew parish register states:

If there should be any child not Registered in this book prior to the year of Our Lord 1817, this error is owing to the neglect of sponsors and parents who would not attend to give the Vicar and Clerk after divine service the name of the parents and children. The Vicar gave public notice for this purpose repeatedly.

The Reverend Edward (Ned) Caine of Onchan church also seems to have been rather remiss in recording baptisms in the 1840s.

Finally, it should be remembered that these are the records of the Established Church, and as such will not in most cases record the marriages or baptisms of Quakers or other dissenters. Nor will they reflect the growing numbers of Nonconformists and Catholics living in the Isle of Man in the nineteenth century.

See also:
✿ Church Records
✿ Civil Registration

PAUPERS AND RECORDS OF THE POOR

There was no equivalent of the English Poor Law in the Isle of Man. The Island had traditionally looked after the poor through collections raised in churches and distributed amongst the needy of the parish. In some cases records exist within parish registers detailing the monies that were collected and to whom they were distributed. The publication *The Isle of Man Charities* (1831) sheds much light on how the system worked.

Two very good sets of records cover the special Sunday collections at Jurby, held within the parish records and covering the years 1749–90 (MNH archive reference MS 09321/1/2). Bride parish register contains similar details for 1744–57 and 1791 (MS 11380/1). The parish registers for these dates are microfilmed and researchers would normally be referred to these rather than the original documents, which are somewhat fragile. The records of Douglas chapel contain details of monies distributed by Mr Thompson's charity in 1730 (MS 01610). The records of the parish of German contain accounts for the distribution of money to the poor of the parish. Particularly useful in this respect is a list of paupers in German between 1841 and 1845 (MNH archive reference MS 10974/8/1-2). This includes notes of nicknames and means of identification. Similarly, the deposit contains a list of paupers in Peel receiving aid from the parish between 1864 and 1886. Several churchwardens' account books, listing those claiming poor relief in Ballaugh, were passed by Ballaugh church to MNH. The earliest of these, dating from 1838, is held as MS 10457/13. The MNH Library and Archive Service also holds a Poor Accounts book from St Matthew's charity which covers the poor of Douglas in the years 1814–17 (MS 09888/3/10). This fascinating document provides a great deal of detail about individual family circumstances. A typical entry from this book describes the

Agnes Hanson, recorded in the 1911 census as living in the Widows' House, Douglas, a charitable home for poor and elderly women. (Pg7127/11)

condition of Catherine Kermode, a widow aged 76 whose place of residence is shown as Big Well Street. Her family consisted of her daughter and two grandchildren, the daughter's husband being away on board a man-of-war, though they received money from his wages. They had been in the town of Douglas for seven years and the two children, a boy and a girl, attended both daily and Sunday schools.

This method of parish-based provision for the poor had usually been sufficient in the rural areas where there was a degree of family support for those who were infirm and unable to work. This was true to a lesser extent in Douglas, due to its large itinerant population, and reduced level of family support for those in poverty. There was a rapid decline in the living standards of the poorest elements of the lower classes at the end of the Napoleonic Wars, with many discharged soldiers and sailors flooding onto the labour market. A *Report of the Committee of the Institution for Bettering the Condition of the Poor* (1818) contains some 204 names of those considered for contributions in Douglas, and notes whether they were rejected or a grant made. This can be found under the MNH Library reference D50/2. It is also worth noting that Manx newspapers around this time sometimes published lists of those of the poor who received money from charitable funds. Newspapers from 1792 to 1960 can be searched electronically through the iMuseum, or online from late 2011. Microfilm copies are available in the MNH Reading Room at the Manx Museum.

In 1869 High Bailiff Robert J. Moore circulated a questionnaire among the clergy of the west of the Island seeking information about how many people in each parish in that area were in receipt of poor relief. Not all of the clergy were co-operative but some did provide details, including in a number of cases lists of names. Other High Bailiffs collected information about the situation in their parts of the Island, for instance High Bailiff Harris recorded the names of residents in the Douglas house of industry. The names of those in receipt of poor relief collated by Moore are listed on the Manx Note Book website at: www.isle-of-man.com/manxnotebook.

From 1889, Boards of Guardians administered poor relief, such as it was. The minute books of the boards name the members, and also in many cases name the individuals requesting poor relief and describe the circumstances under which they were claiming. The records extend at least into the 1930s (probably up to the creation of the welfare state after the Second World War), although many of the later volumes will still be subject to closure.

The MNH Library holds the annual reports of the house of industry on Kingswood Grove in Douglas (now the Ellan Vannin old people's home), which was established in 1834 as a charitable institution to provide shelter for those in poverty. The reports include the names and ages of those who were resident within the home at the close of each year and also name those who died within the home in the preceding year. These records are held under Library reference D50/2 and cover the years 1857 to 1953, though it should be noted that the records for later years carry less detail than earlier

In the nineteenth century there was a large population of itinerant rural poor; beggars who wandered the Island. George Quayle in *Legends of a Lifetime* (1973) states that:

Up to fifty years ago the Island supported an army of vagrants. They went round with a bag carrying smaller bags to carry the meals and other commodities which they collected from the people. It was the custom to let them sleep in the barns, but on some of the bigger farms a special house was often built for them, a kind of doss-house, where they could sleep and prepare a meal. The remains of these houses can still be seen. Most houses, too had a small basin, known as 'the beggar's bowl', used to measure out flour or meal. This was given grudgingly and under silent protest, for with these thugs of the road people had no choice. It had been proved wiser to give than to run the risk of having the haggard or the house going up in smoke. Perhaps I have destroyed another romantic belief, namely that this charity was given out of pity or kindliness.

The Beggars' House at Ballamoar, Rushen, by A.C. Quayle. (2005-0160)

ones. The later nineteenth-century directories are sometimes worth consulting, as the occupants of charitable dwellings for the poor (for example, the Widows' House on Big Well Street in Douglas) are sometimes listed by name.

The IOMFHS holds indexes covering the many sources of information for poor relief or its equivalents, and this has also been the subject of a number of articles in the Society's newsletter *Fraueyn as Banglaneyn (Roots and Branches)*. Finally, it is also worth checking the Poor Law records of Scottish and English districts bordering the Irish Sea in search of Manx ancestors. One entry from the 1818 report referred to above concerns a Margaret Tear who was 'sent to Whitehaven to her husband', whilst Strathclyde Regional Archives Poor Law database contains the names of some eighty people claiming poor relief in that area, who gave their birthplace as the Isle of Man.

PERIODICALS

A number of periodicals held within the collections of MNH will be of particular interest to family historians. Perhaps the most obvious one to start with is the *Journal of Manx Museum*, which was published up to 1980. Its pages contain numerous articles of interest to those researching the general history of the Isle of Man, but certain articles in particular will be of great help to family historians, highlighting as they do unpublished documents within the MNH archives, or drawing attention to particular sets of documents, for example, the Manx Fencibles records. The *Manx Quarterly*, published between 1907 and 1922, is also worthy of special mention, containing as it does many detailed obituaries, and historical articles and accounts, together with reports from overseas Manx societies. The *Manx Quarterly* is indexed in Cubbon's bibliography, discussed elsewhere in this book, as are a number of other early periodicals.

A selection of periodicals that may be of use to family and local historians includes:

- *Barrovian* – the magazine of King William's College, 1879–present
- *Buchan School Magazine*
- *Cushag* – Douglas secondary schools' magazine, 1906–41
- *Crusader* – Castle Rushen High School magazine, 1950–63
- *Ellan Vannin* – World Manx Association magazine, 1923–8
- *Fraueyn as Banglaneyn* – IOMFHS journal, 1979–present
- *Irree Laa* – Douglas High School for Girls magazine, 1947–69
- *Isle of Man Victorian Society Newsletter*, 1980–present
- *Journal of Manx Museum*, 1924–80
- *Mannin* – journal of Yn Cheshaght Gailckagh, Nos 1–9, 1913–17
- *Manx Catholic Magazine*, 1895–present
- *Manx Church Magazine*, 1891–1975
- *Manx Life*, 1971–96
- *Manx Note Book* – Volumes 1–3, ed. A.W. Moore, 1885–7
- *Manx Pictorial* – not so much a periodical but a yearbook, 1934, 1937, 1938, 1957, 1958–9
- *Manx Quarterly*, 1907–22
- *Manx Tails* – includes some biographical detail, 1982–present
- *Manx Wesleyan Church Record*, 1893–1932
- *North American Manx Association Bulletin*, 1928–present
- *Ramsey Church Monthly*, 1889–1901 as *Ramsey Church Magazine*
- *Manxman*, ed T.E. Edwards, 1911–14
- *Unemployed Boys Magazine*, 1934–9
- *Viking* – Douglas High School for Boys magazine, 1948–63
- *Wilsonian* – Bishop Wilson Theological College magazine, 1927–31
- *Y Feeagh* – Ramsey Grammar School magazine, 1926–2000.

PERSONAL MEMOIRS

See also:
✿ Folk Life
Survey

Personal recollections can be an invaluable resource for invoking the feeling or atmosphere of a bygone time and place. A hundred or more years ago such memoirs would only be written by the great and the good. Apart from the fact that only people of some social status were likely to be literate, it was also generally accepted that only persons of high birth were likely to have done anything significant in their lives. Fortunately, since the 1960s and 70s the growing interest in working class history, and history 'from below', coupled with advances in publishing, have encouraged the growth of personal memoirs. Many such volumes are held under G88 in the MNH library, and they shed an enormous amount of light on what life was like for ordinary people at various times during the twentieth century. George Quayle's *Legends of a Lifetime* (1973) mixes personal recollections with Manx folklore and is an excellent memoir of rural life in the north of the Island around the time of the First World War. Pat Skillicorn's *Wave to Your Daddy* (2006) mixes personal memoir with family history. Another good example of the genre is Ivy Barry's *Something Different* (1993). The *Our Heritage* series of books published by Kate Rogers in the 1980s and 90s contain a quantity of personal recollections and snippets of detail particularly relating to Rushen in the early twentieth century.

> In Ivy Barry's memoir *Something Different* she recalls many of the Douglas characters and street traders of the pre-Second World War years:
> *There was Mr Wade, a blind man who sat on a stool on the North Quay. He played popular tunes and hymns on his concertina and hopefully, expected that passers-by would drop coins into his cup which hung on a strap around his neck. The money was his only means of livelihood, there being no Social security at that time . . . Some interesting street traders were seen, such as Billy Kelly, a well known pedlar – who lived in Douglas, he had a knife grinding machine which he himself had made and as he went along he called out 'Knives and scissors to grind!' This machine consisted of a large wheel to which a belt was attached, this was in turn connected to a foot treadle, and when the treadle was worked up and down, the wheel was set in motion. On top of this wheel was a grinding stone on which the scissors and knives were sharpened.*

PERSONAL NAMES

The three key works on personal names are A.W. Moore's *Manx Names* (1906, first published 1890), J.J. Kneen's *Personal Names of the Isle of Man* (1937) and Leslie Quilliam's *Surnames of the Manks: a review* (1989). Kneen dealt with the earliest recorded personal names which appear in Ogham and runic scripts on the Island's ancient monuments, through the earliest known volumes of the Manorial Roll of the Isle of Man of 1511 to 1515, which listed the Lord's tenants (and which in 1924 was translated from the Latin into English for the first time.) Kneen continued searching through parish registers and other sources down to about 1830 when, he concluded, 'There is a great influx of surnames from the surrounding countries, the inclusion of which would have overburdened the text and would not have added materially to its historical value.'

Kneen's work illustrates the way in which in many cases, personal names developed into surnames (through prefixes meaning 'son of'), and these in turn became place names. Some of the earliest Manx names are found in the *Chronicles of Man*, the oldest known history of the Island, widely believed to have been compiled by the monks of Rushen Abbey. The *Chronicles* are held by the British Library and amongst the names recorded are Macmaras (1098); Maclotlen (1166); Mackerthac (1238); Mactoryn (1293) and Macdowal (1313). Macdowal, who defended Castle Rushen against Robert the Bruce, gave his name to Balladoole (farm of Dowal).

With regard to the use of the 'Mac' prefix, which survives in modern Manx surnames as the hard letter 'C' at the beginning of names such as Christian, Cubbon, Kerruish, Kermode and the 'Q' as in Quilliam and so on, Kneen notes that although similar surnames can be found in Scotland, the Manx use can be shown to be considerably earlier, so the names originated on the Isle of Man, though they probably reflect a process that began in Ireland. The Manorial Roll gives only four individuals without surnames, and even if these had not yet fully crystallised, their usage in the Isle of Man predates that in many other parts of Europe.

An interesting aspect of the development of Manx surnames are the fusion of Celtic and Norse influences, the latter arriving on the Isle of Man in the tenth century, and rather than any military conquest, seem to have taken control of the Island through inter-marriage with the local ruling families. On the Manx runic crosses we find Norse personal names indiscriminately mixed with Celtic names. Over time the Norsemen seem to have added Mac to their own personal names, and a hybrid series of surnames has developed from this blending of cultures.

Kneen gives the following examples:

See also:
✿ Place
Names

Modern Manx Surname	Older Surname	Norse First Name
Callow	Mac Calo	Olafr
Christian	Mac Cristin	Kristinn
Corkill	Mac Corkell	Thorketill
Costain	Mac Austeyn	Thorsteinn
Cowley	Mac Auley	Olafr
Crennell	Mac Reynylt	Rognvaldr
Quine	Mac Quyn	Sveinn

Kneen goes on to discuss the greater occurrence of certain surnames in particular parts of the Isle of Man, and the earliest recorded uses of them. Quilliam's work also analyses both the relative rarity and the distribution of Manx surnames. He attempts to establish if the traditional northside and southside divide in the Isle of Man is reflected in its surnames, with some occurring more frequently in one side or the other. All of the books mentioned in this section are available in the MNH Reading Room.

PHOTOGRAPHIC COLLECTIONS

MNH holds extensive photographic collections including a large number of individual portraits, and these will form one of the largest components of the iMuseum. In particular, MNH holds the archive of the Douglas photographer W.H. Warburton. Over 4,000 glass plates from his studio have been digitised, and will be made available through the iMuseum. All of the subjects in this collection are identified by name, and apart from the obvious family history interest they provide much information on nineteenth- and early twentieth-century costume. The approximate dates of coverage are 1860 to 1918.

An additional series of over 3,000 glass negatives contains mainly portraits of internees and guards in the Douglas and Knockaloe internment camps between 1915 and 1918. It is not known who took these photographs, as the negatives were received from the Isle of Man Government following the closure of the internment camps in the early 1920s. The subjects are largely anonymous. However, some internees were photographed alongside a number board bearing their internee number, so it is possible by cross referencing with other sources to identify some of the subjects at least. These have also been digitised and are being made available for public access through the iMuseum.

The photographic collections of J.J. Frowde are also worthy of note. Frowde was an antiquarian and historian, active in the 1930s. He made several photographic tours of Douglas, recording the slums and other old buildings that at that time were in the process of being cleared. Copious notes accompany each photo, often recording details that Frowde gathered orally about former occupants of the buildings in question. Aside from his photographic work, Frowde was an avid local historian, and gathered information from many obscure sources on topics that interested him, as well as writing about his own memories of childhood on the Isle of Man in the 1870s. Frowde's papers are held by MNH at MS 05929, and his photographic collection is being made available through the iMuseum from late 2011.

Other photographs from disparate sources are held in the MNH photographic archive 'People' boxes, organised by surname. Many prominent local families are represented in some strength here, for example, the Quayle family of Bridge House in Castletown. Other photographs are organised by location, or by theme, for example, 'Events'. These have also been digitised, bringing the total number of images being made available through the iMuseum in the next 2–3 years to around 20,000, with many tens of thousands still remaining for future digitisation projects.

Another photographic resource worth highlighting is the Bill Peters/Manx Press Pictures archive (PG/13633), which the MNH Library holds in its entirety. The coverage spans the late 1950s to about 1980 and although the collection is not indexed by subject, it is organised in basic date order. If a forebear took part in an event that was in any way newsworthy during these years, there is a reasonable chance that it will be covered. However, it should also be noted that 99 per cent of this collection is in negative format, so searching can be laborious. Bill Peters was also a wedding

photographer and the Library holds his negative archive of wedding photographs. The date span is 1959–86 and the negatives are organised chronologically by year and then by month and surname.

Family photographs can also be a good source of information. Victorian cartes de visite and cabinet cards often carry the name and address of the photographer. Research into the photographers who took these photographs can also yield valuable clues for family historians. Some photographers were in business for only a relatively short space of time, and research into directories can also prove useful in this respect. Military photographs from the First World War and earlier are also worth scrutinising carefully in order to reveal details such as cap badges, etc., which can be pointers to a forebear's regiment and the date at which he served.

J.J. Frowde meticulously recorded the demolition of the Fairy Ground area, including Smagg's House on Seneschal Lane. Frederick Smagg was a grate setter, who would read his newspaper by the light of the gas lamp outside his bedroom window! (Pg8224/5)

See also:
✿ Personal
Names

PLACE NAMES

The most recent and comprehensive study of Manx place names has been Dr George Broderick's seven-volume study *Placenames of the Isle of Man*, published between 1994 and 2005, which follows on from the work of J.J. Kneen and Professor Carl Marstrander in the early twentieth century. Much of the debate surrounding place names centres on the dominance or otherwise of Old Norse over the Manx language during the era of Scandinavian rule. Study of place-name etymology provides a useful background to the understanding of the Manx system of land tenure as discussed elsewhere in this book. Although many place names comprise a personal name element (for example, Knockaloe = Knock Callow, the hill of Callow), this cannot be taken to have a direct link to family history research. Broderick's work is useful in understanding the construction of Manx placenames and which elements of them derive from either the Old Norse or Gaelic languages. Broderick states:

With perhaps the exception of three or four names, the Gaelic place-names of the Isle of Man (which constitute the vast majority) can be shown to be largely post-Scandinavian, i.e formed since the end of the Scandinavian period in the 13th century . . . in the formation of Manx place-names common elements occur again and again, as dictated by the geography, vegetation and environment.

Common Gaelic elements include:

- Balley = farm, village, town (in its anglicised form 'Balla')
- Creg = rock
- Cronk = hill
- Purt = harbour

Scandinavian elements include:

- Ey = river (Laxey, Ramsey)
- By = farm, settlement
- Fell = mountain
- Howe = hill (often a burial mound or barrow)
- Wick = cove, bay.

POLICE RECORDS

Police records fall into two categories, the first being records *of* the police themselves, for example, personnel records, and the second being records generated *by* the police, for example, mugshot books and crime reports. Extensive records are held by MNH, under reference MS 09310, and it must be stated that due to the quantity of this material it has not yet been indexed or sorted to any great extent. Nevertheless, it is possible to provide here a very brief overview of the types of material held within this deposit. Those researchers who have an ancestor who served with the Manx police (or perhaps have an ancestor who was known to the police!) can contact the MNH Library and Archives staff with specific enquiries.

The Isle of Man Constabulary maintained a Register of Officers and Constables. The approximate dates of coverage are 1874 to the late 1940s. A typical entry contains details of a constable's date and place of birth, his height, marital status, previous occupation before joining the force, where he was stationed, his promotions, conduct (as in any walk of life, not always perfect!) and any military service undertaken during wartime and so on. There are also files listing cadets and constables aged 19 to 29 eligible for service in HM forces in 1939, together with their date of birth, a list of police officers still awaiting return from active service in 1945 and extensive records relating to the Isle of Man Special Constabulary including Specials listed by division (in some cases also with their home address). Records relating to those awarded the Police Long Service and

Mrs Louisa Cannell and Miss Margaret Lewin, the first two female Manx police officers, in 1917. Their oaths, signed upon joining the force, are held by IOMPRO. (Ms09310)

Good Conduct Medal are held as recently as the 1980s. These records should be used in conjunction with the registers of Police Constables' oaths, held by IOMPRO.

From the other side of the fence, police records in MS 09310 offer a fascinating glimpse into the darker side of life on the Isle of Man in the nineteenth and early twentieth centuries. The Island's booming tourist industry gained it a reputation in some quarters which was not far removed from that which some of the less salubrious Mediterranean resorts enjoy today, and the vast crowds of holidaymakers with money to spend drew in a motley assortment of pickpockets, card sharps and prostitutes. There were also home-grown criminals and charges of vagrancy, abandonment of children and housebreaking are all to be found. Records in this series also include Alien Registration Cards, lock-up charge books, details of habitual offenders, commendations, mugshot books and crime reports. An Isle of Man Constabulary register of criminals from the 1880s to 1914 is held at MS 10973. There is also another early mugshot book, being a register of convicted criminals with details of their offences and photographs, held separately as MS 10521.

Police licensing files from the 1920s and 30s contain applications to run licensed premises, together with statements from those willing to support the application. There is also a register of public houses from 1912–42 giving details of the licence holder year on year. Not surprisingly for the Isle of Man, many of these premises are actually hotels. Finally, the diaries of the Chief Constable from 1911 to 1924 offer an overview of police activity during these years. The diaries are often detailed, and mention the activities of individual policemen, as well as particular arrests and court cases.

Many of these records are closed to general researchers for seventy-five years, but if you have a specific enquiry about a particular individual, staff may be able to assist in providing limited information if a lengthy search is not required. Digitised newspapers

> **Arthur C. Underhill writes in *A Policeman's Lot* (1993) about a police officer named Kinrade for whom:**
>
> *. . . report writing and spelling were not his strong point ... Long before I joined the Police Force, the area where the Douglas Bus Station [was] situated was a mass of narrow streets and an extraordinary large number of public houses! A character called Harry Winter was a travelling purveyor of fruit and vegetables, his cart being drawn by a donkey. The donkey collapsed and died in Seneschal Lane, one of the side streets. The aforementioned officer was called and realising he would have to write a report on the incident and doubting his ability to ensure the correct spelling of the venue, he dragged the donkey into Fort Street!!*

available in the iMuseum contain numerous reports about incidents involving the police. In many cases, individual police officers who performed an arrest are named (particularly if a case came to court). George Turnbull's published *History of the Isle of Man Constabulary* (1984) provides a useful background to the development of the Island's police force, and also includes a nominal roll of Manx police officers with their dates of service, whilst Arthur C. Underhill's *A Policeman's Lot* (1993) is a personal memoir of service in the Isle of Man Constabulary either side of the Second World War. *Manx Quarterly*, Number 5 (1908) contains an interesting article on the formation of the Manx police force seventy-five years earlier.

See also:
- ✿ Castle Rushen (Prison) Records
- ✿ Court Records
- ✿ Prison Records

'Peg Leg Caley' was a notorious criminal and bane of the Douglas police. This is his police record. (Ms09310)

POLITICAL HISTORY

Allowing for breaks, for periods of martial conflict or temporarily successful attempts at despotism, the Isle of Man's Tynwald Court is probably older than the Althing, which was founded in Iceland in the year 930, though 979 is sometimes taken as the date from which the continuous Manx parliament dates. It had met from time to time to 'declare' the laws, which in practice often meant making judgments developing the law, and making it clear and effective for the first time since the Norsemen had first settled in the Island. At the time of the extended Kingdom of Mann and the Isles, the House of Keys had thirty-two members but since about 1156 it has had a constant membership of twenty-four. Tynwald as a law-making body, a body permanently constituted and not summoned for special occasions, crystallised at the end of the sixteenth century. The Keys originally functioned as a jury, to serve in cases of treason and felony, and to assist the Deemsters in resolving 'great and high points of law'. Until 1825 they were part of the Court of General Gaol Delivery, and until 1866 they were a court of appeal in certain civil cases.

Deemster John Parr, in the abstract of the laws of the Isle of Man which he compiled towards the end of the seventeenth century (republished by the Manx

Tynwald Fair at St John's in 1795, painted by John Warwick Smith. (1954-7220)

Society in 1867, and held by the MNH Library and Archive Service under F64/48), stated 'The Keys are called the representatives of the country'. In the heading to certain Acts passed in 1645 and at various dates for another eighty years the Keys are described as 'the representative body' or 'the representatives' of the Island. The word 'representative' can have two meanings. As a noun it means a person chosen by another to speak for him; as an adjective it means, amongst other things, typical, a sample of, 'presenting the full character of a class'. The Keys, in the

Alfred Teare was first elected to the House of Keys in 1919, and Ramsey Johnson described him at that time as the most powerful figure in the Isle of Man, having the previous year led the workers in a general strike that had humbled the Manx Government. He was re-elected in 1924, 1929, 1934 and 1946. In 1951 he was elected by the Keys to the Legislative Council, and served a remarkable forty-three years in Tynwald. In *Reminiscences of the Manx Labour Party* (1962) he wrote:

One thing which stands out prominently in my memory is the fact that the founders of the Labour movement in the Island fifty to sixty years ago were men of high Christian principles – many of them 'local' preachers – who sought to apply to industry and social conditions the teachings of Christ. It was a revolt against the appalling social injustices as they existed at that time. The misery, poverty, cruelty and inefficiency of society drew forth a protest and led to the formation of a new movement dedicated to the task of building a new society. Its ideals were simple and compelling. They believed in the brotherhood of all men, and in the ideal of service, and in the doctrine that the resources of the community should be used for the benefit of all. 'Converts' to the movement spread their propaganda by linking up with others of progressive views by joining debating societies which were a feature of church life at that time. When we could afford it, we rented a hall; at other times our platform was the market place or street corner.

Alfred Teare, Manx Labour leader and in 1919 the most powerful figure in the Isle of Man. (Pg7376/3)

earlier part of their history, were not elected by the people, but like a jury, they represented their peers, the body of people within the country who mattered.

Until the House of Keys was reformed, the membership was a self-perpetuating oligarchy, drawn from the foremost families on the Island. One of these families was the Quayles of Bridge House, Castletown. George Quayle was a member of the Keys for fifty-one years. His father John Quayle was Clerk of the Rolls, and both his grandfather and brother were members of the Keys also. The Quayles of Bridge House Papers (effectively the records of the Quayle family) are held by MNH under a number of manuscript references. It is interesting to observe how this self-appointed political class worked, in the case of Captain John Quilliam. Having returned from the Napoleonic Wars as a rich and powerful man, he was deemed to be suitable for membership and was invited to join, in spite of the fact he was of humble birth. The House of Keys became a directly elected body for the first time in 1866, in exchange for a greater degree of control of revenue.

MNH holds a considerable quantity of political literature from this era onwards, including leaflets, manifestos and related material. Even if a forebear did not actually manage to gain election to the Keys, he or she may well be represented in the collections as there is an equal quantity of literature relating to unsuccessful candidates. A full list of members of the Keys (or at least as full as it is possible to compile for such an ancient institution) is available on the Tynwald website (www.tynwald.org.im), and includes the names of members as far back as 1417.

Debates in the Manx legislature were reprinted in book form from reports in the *Isle of Man Times* between 1887 and 1923. The *Times* continued to print the debates as bound volumes until the early 1970s, when the *Reports of the Proceedings of Tynwald Court, the Legislative Council and the House of Keys* were published by Hansard. Hansard may now be accessed via the Tynwald website or in hard-copy form in the Tynwald Library, or in the MNH Reading Room under D152. Early records of the House of Keys, from 1422 to 1934, are held by MNH as MS 09191.

A forebear might equally well have served as a local commissioner or as a member of Douglas Borough Council. Douglas is the only local council resembling an English model on the Isle of Man, and is similar to an urban district council in size and scope. MNH holds the minutes of the proceedings of Douglas Borough Council from 1903 onwards. A description by Alderman Corlett of open voting for Douglas Town Commissioners is held at MS 01635/1. In other parts of the Island local services are administered by parish commissioners. MNH holds some records relating to other local authorities, for example, the Maughold Commissioners' minutes from 1894 to 1970.

From the formation of the local authorities on the Isle of Man, properties in their districts had to pay an annual rate (as they still do today) in order to fund that authority. Most local authorities still retain their old rate books and this may contain information of use to family historians. For those interested in a particular property, the year in which it was first rated may indicate the year in which it was built. This information is only available from certain local authorities, usually by prior appointment.

Other local authority records are held by IOMPRO, including:

- Douglas Borough Corporation (town plans, minutes and correspondence) from the nineteenth and twentieth centuries
- Castletown Commissioners (minutes) from the nineteenth and twentieth centuries
- Castletown Commissioners Records, Correspondence, etc. from 1920s–70s
- Port Erin Commissioners (minutes, accounts and correspondence) from the nineteenth and twentieth centuries
- Peel Town Commissioners (plans and accounts) from the twentieth century
- Marown Commissioners (minutes) from the nineteenth and twentieth centuries
- Malew Commissioners (minutes) from the nineteenth and twentieth centuries
- Arbory Commissioners (minutes) from the twentieth centuries.

The *Examiner* and *Norris Modern Press Yearbooks* often provide biographical (and sometimes photographic) portraits of MHKs and other public figures, particularly if they became a mayor or alderman. Dollin Kelly's *New Manx Worthies* (2006) contains information about many Manx political figures of the twentieth century. *No Man is an Island* (2009) by Roger Rawcliffe is an interesting discussion of the inter-relationship of banking and finance, politics and architecture in the Isle of Man. In particular, it includes coverage of the FSFO political campaign of the 1980s. D.G. Kermode's *Offshore Island Politics* (2001) covers the constitutional and political development of the Isle of Man in the twentieth century.

Political autobiographies and memoirs are relatively uncommon in the Isle of Man. Sir Charles Kerruish, arguably the most significant politician of the second half of the twentieth century, left no memoirs. Neither did his great adversary Victor Kneale, nor his contemporary Clifford Irving. One has to go back to an earlier generation to find first-hand accounts of political life in the Isle of Man, with Alfred Teare's *Reminiscences of the Manx Labour Party* (1962) and Samuel Norris's *Manx Memories and Movements* (1938).

See also:
✿ Electoral Rolls

PRISON RECORDS

HM Prison Victoria Road, Douglas was built in 1891 in order to provide a much-needed replacement for Castle Rushen. The castle by that time had outlived its usefulness as a prison. Victoria Road gaol served as the Island's penitentiary until the opening of the newly constructed HMP Jurby in 2008, when all prisoners were transferred to the new prison.

Victoria Road was a classic Victorian prison, built along the lines suggested by social reformers, which were also used as the model for prisons of a similar era in England. Anyone who has seen the 1970s TV series *Porridge* will be familiar with the style of its brick-built wings with iron landings and staircases, leading up to a second tier of cells. The cells were originally designed for one prisoner,

The imposing architecture of the former Isle of Man Prison, on Victoria Road in Douglas.

and problems with overcrowding in the 1980s and 90s led to the eventual abandonment of the prison in favour of a new build. As it was originally constructed, Victoria Road prison consisted of a gatehouse and prison officer's house and two identical wings, one each for males and females.

The prison was designed by the Manx architect James Cowle and at the beginning of the twentieth century it received a glowing report from Major Darnell, the HM Inspector of Prisons: 'The present accommodation consists of 21 cells in the male and eight cells in the female prison. The cells are light and airy, and well ventilated and compare quite favourably with those in the best English prisons — boarded floors, clear glass in the windows and external gas boxes. They were uniformly clean and well kept.'

Records of HM Prison Victoria Road are held by MNH under MS 09672. These comprise warrants, correspondence, the gatekeeper's daily occurrence books, the Gaoler's journal and the Chaplain's journal. Most interesting for family historians are the registers of prisoners. MS 09672/6/1/1 begins in 1891 and runs to 1896. It lists the name of the prisoner, place of birth, offence and other details. Subsequent volumes run to 1957, though these latter volumes will be subject to seventy-five-year closure rules. Likewise, MS 09672/12/1-2 are albums of prisoners' photographs. These are a piece of social history in their own right, showing details of the prisoner's costume (usually the clothes in which they arrived at the prison) and the rooms and surroundings in which they were photographed. In some cases prison warders are also visible in the photographs, as some prisoners required coercion to sit still long enough for the photographer to take their pictures. The series runs from 1893 to 1916. A subsequent series of prisoner mugshots runs to 1948, but as with the registers, these later volumes will be subject to a seventy-five-year closure.

The volumes covering 1914 to 1918 are particularly interesting as they contain large numbers of internees from Douglas and Knockaloe Camps, arrested for a variety of offences, including forgery and absconding from work parties, and also, surprisingly, numbers of guards, often arrested for offences involving alcohol. Norman Quilliam's book *Keys and Cuffs* (2009) provides a history of the prison service on the Isle of Man from the perspective of a retired prison officer.

See also:
✿ Castle Rushen (Prison) Records

RAILWAY RECORDS

IOMPRO holds a variety of railway records, including maps, plans, drawings, minute books and other items pertaining to the Isle of Man Railway, Manx Electric Railway and Snaefell Mountain Railway from the nineteenth and twentieth centuries.

MNH also holds extensive records relating to the Isle of Man Railway Company under MS 09563. The vast majority of the records concern traffic but significantly there are also large quantities of documents relating to land purchases, including deeds and mortgages. There are also records of major shareholders in the company, who were entitled to carry a gold fob allowing them free travel on the railways. The records also cover the IMR's subsidiaries, including Isle of Man Road Services which operated buses from the 1930s. Isle of Man Road Services' minute books go up to 1976 when the company was wound up. There are also detailed fleet lists (for those interested in the types of vehicles operated) and perhaps most significant the wages books contain the names of employees from approximately the 1930s to 1960s.

Douglas railway station, c. 1900. Stationmaster G.H.Wood stands in the foreground.

Further subsidiary companies included the Foxdale Railway Company and a ledger of shareholders in this company exists. The Isle of Man Railway subsumed the Manx Northern Railway in 1905 and again the records of this company make up a significant portion of the holdings. There are records of land purchases by the Manx Northern Railway in Ballaugh, Michael, Lezayre and German, but perhaps of greatest importance are the shareholders' ledgers. More than any other part of the company the shareholders in this branch were overwhelmingly local and a scan down the list of names and details reveals grocers, joiners and even the Bishop! All are shown with their address, occupation and shareholding.

It would not be proper to leave the archives of the Isle of Man Railways without also making reference to the five boxes of Home Guard papers contained within the railway company records. It appears that 'D' (Railway) section made up part of the 1st Manx Battalion of the Home Guard. Amongst the boxes are included rolls of members present on parade, routine orders, practice exercises and so on from 1940 onwards. Other railway records include a ledger of the Douglas and Peel Railway (held at MS 01615/14), and of course there are extensive maps and plans created by the railway companies, discussed elsewhere in this book. The personal papers of J.D. Clucas are held by MNH as MS 10038. Clucas was Director and Chairman of Manx Northern Railway Company and his papers include deeds, accounts and correspondence with IMR personnel.

Denwyn Dobby has written about the MNR level crossings manually operated by gatehouse keepers:

The gatehouses were attractively designed and erected on contract by J. and W. Grainger of Glasgow . . . They were stone-built, with slate roofs, with two bedrooms and a living room with [an] iron range for cooking and heating water, but with no other amenities, not even piped water . . . The cottages, meagre as the amenities were, at least came rent-free and the gatekeeper, who was traditionally the wife, the father earning a living elsewhere, was paid 10/- a week until 1945 . . . the day to day (and night) routine for a gatekeeper was to open the two main gates on each side of the track, then hang on a pole a white flag to say that all was clear, or a red for an emergency, while at night an ordinary paraffin-lantern showed white for all clear and red for an emergency. She also had to use her discretion whether to let a pedestrian through the small wicket gate when the main gates were closed . . . Although this work meant continual vigilance and no time off unless the children were old enough to take a turn looking after the gates, the position was in demand as it meant rent-free living . . .

See also:
❀ Mapping
❀ Buildings as
   Historical
   Evidence

Extracts from the diary of G.H. Wood, the Douglas station master, are held under MS 08095. Denwyn Dobby has written about the history of the Ballacrye level crossing (MS 09353), whilst the memoirs of J.E. Kneale include work on the Manx railways in the 1920s (MS 10932).

The standard published work on this subject is James Boyd's three-volume *The Isle of Man Railway* (1993–6). Barry Edwards has also written prolifically on Manx transport matters, and has produced registers of rolling stock and other monographs. *Steam Railway News*, a run of which from 1968 to the present is held by the MNH Library and Archive Service, is an invaluable source of information about railway history. The early editions contain first-hand memories of the railways from as far back as the 1920s, and the more recent editions frequently contain archive images from the steam railway network. Likewise, *Manx Transport Review* covers all aspects of Manx transport, though it is published by the MER Society.

The MNH photographic archive also contains many photographs of the Isle of Man rail network, including rolling stock, travellers and rail employees.

A director's or major shareholder's watch fob, which entitled the holder to free travel on the Manx Electric Railway. (1954-6564)

ROLLS OFFICE RECORDS

The Rolls Office was for many years effectively the record office of the Isle of Man Government. The records of the Rolls Office held by MNH were deposited by the General Registry and are held under MS 09862. There are also records created by the General Registry held at MS 09862 (GR) and it is worth noting that there is also some overlap with the Castle Rushen papers held by MNH (MS 09782).

The records are not indexed by name but are organised chronologically and contain a wealth of information valuable to family and local historians. They refer to such diverse subjects as payments of the Dog Tax (1777 to 1808), applications for Public House Licences, Peddlers Licences and Brewers Licences, all of which contain the names of individuals and which may be useful for family history research.

The Dog Tax is particularly interesting and almost a study in itself. The story begins in 1763 with the Highway Act, the preamble of which, as well as noting the lamentable state of the Island's roads, identified the nuisance of 'useless dogs' kept by the public which were free to roam at will, terrorising both travellers and livestock. An attempt was made to solve both problems by imposing a tax on the animals. There were however numerous exemptions and a new Act of 1776 made all persons without exception liable for the tax, as well as introducing different classes for sporting and working dogs. Records of who was liable for the tax were kept by parochial surveyors and presented to the Clerk of the Rolls. The detail and accuracy of these rolls varies from surveyor to surveyor, but Thomas Corkill, surveyor of Braddan, for the period 1776 to 1777 set out a highly efficient, 'true and regular account of the dogs within the parish of Braddan and the sums received for the repairs of the highways'. Corkill usefully noted the names and property of the owners of the dogs and his first entry, quite properly, is for the Nunnery (perhaps the finest private house on the Isle of Man), of which he writes:

Mr Durie for 1 house dog and 2 lap dogs	*1*	*6*
Tho. Quayle (Miller) for 1 greyhound	*6*	*0*
Geo. Redfern for a beagle and a house dog and a greyhound	*9*	*6*
Wm. Reed for a common dog and John Clague for do.	*1*	*0*
Dal. Teare for 1 dog and Tho. Collier for do.	*1*	*0*
Paul Quirk for a common dog		*6*

The Castle Rushen papers are effectively the records of the Isle of Man Government from the period in which the castle was used as a repository for these documents. Of particular note amongst these are the highways records and parochial labour lists.

Following an Act of Tynwald in 1819, people were required to do a certain amount of work each year to maintain the highways. These records are organised by parish and contain the name and residence and the type of work undertaken of everyone liable for this service. These records are held under MS 09782 and cover the 1820s to at least the 1840s, with occasional gaps. They are particularly useful for catching individuals between the census years.

The Castle Rushen papers at MS 09782 include the records of the Chancery Court, the general criminal and civil courts. The records are piecemeal but contain such things as Deemsters' records, jury lists and such like. Other material is held under MS 10071 (discussed under **Court Records** in this book). Another subsection of the Castle Rushen papers are the minutes of the Harbour Commissioners (MS 09266). Whilst they do not contain extensive lists of names, such things as the appointment of Harbour Masters are noted in these minutes. Likewise, the customs records held at MS 10637 complement the Ingates and Outgates mentioned elsewhere. The records are for the dates 1703 to 1765 and cover goods entered at the various ports. They give an account of the goods carried by each ship and the name of its master.

A number of other records from the Rolls Office survive within the Quayles of Bridge House papers. John Quayle of Bridge House was Clerk of the Rolls around 1725, and made copies of a number of documents still extant at that point that have since been lost. Quayle compiled these as a *Book of Precedents* (held by MNH as MS 00510) in which he gave numerous examples of cases, for as he stated in his introduction, his purpose was: 'To Trace out the Antiquity or Origine of the antient Laws and Constitution of this Isle, or to know whether they have been introduced or borrowed from other Nations is a matter that admits of some difficulty, since we have no Records now Extant that might justify or Awarrant such an Essay or Undertakeing.' The cases that Quayle highlights provide fascinating glimpses into life in the Middle Ages on the Isle of Man generally, but also offer family historians clues to the nature of their forebear's way of life. One example reads:

Isle of Man AD 1417 Lord John Stanley, Lord of Man and the Isles.

At a Head Court holden there at the Castle on the 4th day of October in the year of Our Lord 1417 and the fourth of the Royalty of the Lord of Man, before John Litherland, Lieutenant, then in that place.

A presentement for trespasses in the Calfe Isle.

An inquisition was taken in the same Court concerning trespasses made in le Calfe, upon oath, &c., who say that Thomas de Yvenhow (20d) and Gilbert McWaddy keep 4 pigs, against the order, in le Calfe; and that Michael Shirlock has two horses, and that John Shirlock cut down a wood in the same place, therefore these men in fine.

The IOMPRO also holds related Isle of Man Government records including: Police Constables' Oaths and Commissions (1864–1978) and Oaths of Allegiance (1942–90). Libri Irrotulamentorum (Lib Irrot) covering Commissions, signed by the Governor and enrolled by the Clerk of the Rolls (1803–94) are held by IOMPRO but are on microfilm at MNH and are available in the Reading Room. Likewise, Libri Juramentorum (Lib Jura), the volumes containing the oaths taken by various officials when they receive their appointments and by the Governor or Clerk of the Rolls (1803–1980), are held at IOMPRO but are also on microfilm at MNH.

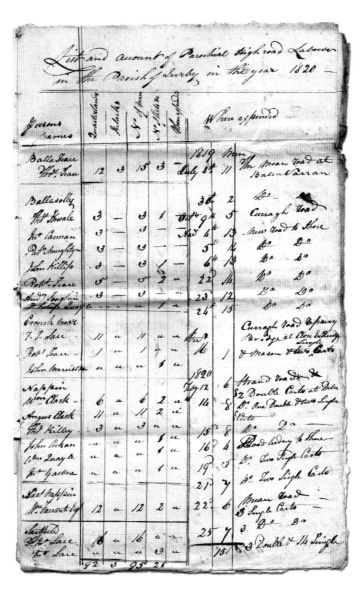

Jurby parochial labour list from 1820 pre-dates the earliest official census. (Ms09782)

IOMPRO holds the Statutes of the Isle of Man (1703–2007), records of Government Orders, and staff of Government 3rd Division (3DS) (1848–present). These include statutory documents, Government orders and circulars, resolutions of Tynwald, plans, appointments and swearing in of various officials.

See also:
♦ Court Records

SCHOOL RECORDS

For such a small and perhaps one might think parochial place, the Isle of Man has often shown a surprisingly advanced and enlightened attitude to education. In this respect it has often been many years in advance of its larger neighbours. In the eighteenth century, regulations concerning universal education (offered free to the poor) were incorporated in an Act of Tynwald. In the nineteenth century the Island embraced rate-assisted education in 1851, and in 1872 a further Act made elementary education compulsory, some eight years before similar legislation was enacted by the Westminster Parliament. In the twentieth century the Isle of Man was the first education authority in Britain to introduce a complete system of comprehensive education, in 1947.

Some educational records are held by MNH under MS 10092. Library and Archive staff at MNH receive frequent enquiries regarding school registers, and in the main these seem to have been destroyed. However, it is sometimes worth checking with individual schools. It is known, for example, that St Ninian's High School and Ramsey Grammar School hold school registers for the post-war years at least. A few examples do survive within MNH collections, and it is possible to list these here:

- Andreas Parochial School, 1873–88
- Baldwin School first class, 1918–19
- Ballasalla (boys), 1864
- Ballaugh Board School, 1888–1932
- Bride School, 1873–90, 1892–1946
- Cronk Y Voddy School, 1873–1927
- Dhoon Board School, 1879–1905
- Douglas Grammar School, 1895–1922
- Drumgold Street Girls School, 1888–98
- Kirk German Parochial School, 1870–1905
- Laxey Glen School, 1907–28
- Maughold Central School, 1872–1919
- Ramsey Albert Road School, 1911–20
- Ramsey Wesleyan School, 1874–91
- St John's School, 1905–77
- St Jude's School, 1895–1911
- Sulby School (1867–1912).

If you are fortunate enough to find a surviving register that includes a forebear, this can be a treasure trove of information. That for Kirk German records the date of birth of its pupils (something often hard to find before civil registration), information about where the pupil was living, and most significantly information about why a pupil left the school. If this was because the family had left the district there is often a note of where they went. For boys, the reason for leaving is often that they went into employment, and the nature of this employment is frequently given.

The most extensive surviving sources of information aside from the registers are the school log books, which record events of note and do include some names, usually if a child had an accident or was punished for any reason. In order to consult these you will need to know where a child went to school and when. The series tends to be for schools that have closed, whilst schools that are still in operation often seem to retain their log books.

The other main series relating to education contains the Minute Books of the individual school boards set up to govern each school. These boards, and the records produced by them, mainly predate the unified Board of Education which was set up

Some of the staff of Tynwald Street School, from a 1904 bazaar brochure.

by the Isle of Man Government after the First World War. These Minute Books include in some cases names and salaries of teachers upon their appointment or promotion. It is also worth examining the records held by IOMPRO created by the Department of Education and covering the nineteenth and twentieth centuries. These include the log books of Peel Clothworkers' School, HM Inspectors Reports, financial, administrative and staff records and minutes of various committees, including the Children's Committee and Welfare Committee. There is also a small selection of school admission and attendance registers.

There were in the nineteenth and early twentieth centuries a number of small private schools on the Island, many of which were charitable. These included a Home School for the Daughters of Gentlemen run by Mrs Christian, widow of William Bell Christian of Milntown, Catherine Halsall's school in Castletown, and private schools such as that at Rushen Abbey run by the Misses Stowell. A register of pupils from Mrs

Students at Bishop Wilson's Theological College, Bishopscourt, in the 1940s. (Pg6974/15)

Christian's school is held by the Milntown Trust at Ramsey, though it is not extensive. Other educational institutions included Castletown Grammar School, Douglas Collegiate School, a Navigation School and a Mathematical School, both in Peel. A number of records have survived from these smaller schools and are held by MNH, for example, the registers of Castletown Grammar School between 1880 and 1916 (MS 08137), and those of Douglas Collegiate School which are at MD 00236. Records for the Peel Mathematical School, which operated from approximately 1768 to 1892, form part of the Goldie-Taubman papers. A roll survives of pupils who had passed through the school up to 1784, and a transcript of this has been published in the *Journal of Manx Museum*, Volume VII, 212–16.

In the nineteenth century a theological college named after Bishop Wilson existed at Bishopscourt (the former seat of the Bishops of Sodor and Man) near Kirk Michael. Considerable numbers of Church of England clergymen were ordained here, and whilst no register exists from the college, ordinands' papers do survive and are held at MS 09756 and MS 09309. The date range is approximately 1880 to 1910.

By far the most significant single school on the Isle of Man however is King William's College at Castletown. It was founded in 1833 by Bishop William Ward and the then Lieutenant Governor Cornelius Smelt, who built a day and boarding school, funded by charitable funds left for the purpose by a previous primate, Bishop Barrow, and by public subscription. The institution took the form of an archetypal (if minor) English public school, and educated the sons of the gentry from across the British Isles and also those of the moderately well-to-do Manx middle classes. In particular, in the nineteenth century the school was noted for educating the sons of Army officers, and in turn produced a number of notable military figures, such as General Sir George White VC, in his day famous as the commander of the besieged town of Ladysmith during the Boer War.

The chief records relating to King William's College held by MNH are the school magazine, the *Barrovian* (L6/B1), and the register of former pupils, which is available for consultation in the Reading Room. This includes basic biographical details such as father's name, dates at the school and in many cases subsequent career details. The *Barrovian* was first published in 1879 and as well as information about what was happening in the school at the time, contains articles about former pupils. There are many obituaries, and the issues for the First World War years are particularly interesting, containing plate photographs of those former pupils who fell in action.

In 1991 a new co-educational day and boarding school was formed when the College amalgamated with its sister foundation, the Buchan School, founded for girls in 1875 by the generosity of Laura, Lady Buchan. The school is still flourishing in the twenty-first century and attracts students internationally. There is a strong interest in the history of the establishment both amongst current and former masters and pupils.

A fascinating book entitled *A Blessing to this Island, The Story of King William's College and The Buchan School,* was written by Michael Hoy MBE and published in 2006. It is available from the school shop. Further information about former pupils may be obtained from the King William's College Society, which maintains links between alumni. Its website can be accessed at: www.okwsociety.com/default.aspx.

The former Hanover Street School in Douglas is now occupied by the Isle of Man Office of Fair Trading. A website outlining the history of the building, and describing the social conditions in this poor part of Douglas during the nineteenth century, can be found at: www.gov.im/oft/About/History_Gov/.

Another useful web resource is Frances Coakley's Manx Note Book. The history of Manx education is covered in a dedicated section, with many quotations from rare or little known works.

Similar, though not related to school admission registers, are the registers of those children who attended Sunday schools. These were organised and run by various churches, so strictly speaking may be considered as church records, but they are none the less equally useful to a family history researcher. Again, the survival rate is somewhat erratic, but those held within the collections of MNH include:

- Agneash Primitive Methodist Sunday School, 1899–1960
- Arbory Street (Castletown) Methodist Church Sunday School, 1924–70
- Ballakilpheric Methodist Sunday School, 1921–90
- Ballaugh Methodist Sunday School, 1972–85
- Barregarrow Chapel Sunday School, 1878–1921
- Bride Methodist Sunday School, 1969–98
- Castletown Wesleyan Sunday School, 1886–90
- Crosby Methodist Chapel Sunday School, 1976–83
- Douglas (Thomas Street) Wesleyan Sunday School, 1855–69
- Douglas (Wellington Street) Primitive Methodist Sunday School, 1871–3, 1875–8
- Hillberry Methodist Sunday School, 1899–1900
- Kerrowmoar Primitive Methodist Sunday School, 1910–43
- Peel Wesleyan Sunday School (boys), 1849–1961
- Rosemount Methodist Church Sunday School, 1898–1910

An attendance register for a girls' Methodist Sunday school class taught by Miss A.M. Joughin in an unidentified Ramsey chapel in 1903 is held as MS 11422.

See also:
✿ Periodicals

SHIPPING COMPANY RECORDS

The records of the IOMSPCo (the world's oldest shipping line still in existence) are held on behalf of the company by MNH. The bulk of the collection consists of Way Books for the company's vessels. These are effectively the ships' logs and record the journeys made by the vessels. The detail within these books is variable. A sad irony of history is that the most interesting periods of the company's past, for example, the Dunkirk evacuation, are amongst the most sparsely recorded. Those books covering the ships involved in Operation Dynamo are simply endorsed 'Admiralty Charter' with no further details recorded on those pages.

The Merchant Marine identity card of John William Hawkins, of the Howe, Port St Mary, from January 1919. Hawkins worked for the IOMSPCo for many years between the wars. (Courtesy of Southampton Arts and Heritage Service)

Other records include plans and layouts of the company's ships, though apparently not those that were lost to enemy action in the two world wars. These plans were apparently destroyed as no longer relevant. Extensive records of the company's shareholders exist within the collection and these cover the period roughly 1889 to 1919. There are also probate registers for deceased shareholders. The value of these records to Manx family historians may be somewhat limited however as an initial survey of the

C.R. 10.   No. of Identity Certificate 30.7.1.34

M.N.S. Region N.Western Regional No.9

Surname Hawkins

Christian Name John William

Rating A.B. R.N.R. No.

No. and Grade of B/T Certificate

Date and Place of Birth 8.9.87. Port St Mary I.O. Man

Nationality British Father British

Height 5' 10" Colour Hair Black Eyes Grey

Tattoo Marks

Dis. A No. 348025 N.H. Insurance No.

Name and Address of Next of Kin Elenor E. Hawkins Howe Port St Mary Isle of Man

(32281) Wt. 20167—23. 100m. 8/18. Av. P. (503).

shareholders suggests that the vast majority (though not all) of the shareholders were not local and came from all parts of Britain. There are no personnel records within the company files. The only information on individual crew members likely to be found in these records comes from the minutes of the Board of Directors, which record the appointments of senior officers such as captains and commodores.

MNH holds some records from other companies, for example, the Castletown Steam Navigation Company Register of Shareholders is at F73. Another local line is the Ramsey Steamship Company, the company that still operates the 'Ben' line cargo vessels in the coastal trade, and which has operated from Ramsey for over ninety years. Its ships are engaged mainly in carrying bulk cargoes in the Irish Sea and near-Continent trade, and range from 750 to 1500 tonnes cargo capacity. In addition, the company also provides ships' agency and stevedoring services at all Isle of Man ports, for every class of vessel including cruise liners. It also has a marine-engineering department able to undertake engine overhauls, steel fabrication, welding work and emergency repairs. Amongst its archives are the service records of the company's personnel (MS 10952). These records however are still covered by the Data Protection Act, and only those records relating to personnel who can be proved to be deceased will be produced.

The other important shipping company associated with the Isle of Man is the Karran Fleet, a family owned company which operated from Castletown between 1860 and 1913. The company began operation with one vessel, the *Enigma*, which the founder of the company John Karran purchased at auction after she was seized for non payment of debts. Vessels belonging to the company, *Lady Elizabeth*, *Manx King* and others, traded all over the globe, captained by Karran's sons. They frequently took their families on long voyages with them and Tessa Kinvig, daughter of Captain George, was born aboard the *Manx King* when passing through the dangerous waters off Cape Horn. Her reminiscences of life at sea, entitled *The Children of the Manx King* (MS 10884/2), and those of her brother T.W. Karran, published in 1944 as *A Tale of the Seas* (B158/2), can both be consulted in the MNH Reading Room. She recalled, 'Few children could have had a happier or more thrilling life'. The hulk of the *Lady Elizabeth* still rests outside Port Stanley in the Falkland Islands, where she was wrecked on her last voyage. No logs or personnel records for the company are known to survive, however other publications have covered the story of this famous company. Billy Stowell's *Latitude 54* (2010) contains extensive information on the ships of the fleet.

Information on ordinary seamen can also be found up to 1913 in the crew lists

The Mercantile Marine War Medal, awarded to merchant sailors who served in a war zone between 1914 and 1918.

(2007-0006/1)

discussed elsewhere in this book. Beyond these records, those seeking information on a forebear who served with the IOMSPCo in particular, either in peacetime or wartime will need to consult centrally held records. The records of merchant sailors engaged between 1918 and 1941 are held by Southampton City Archives, in the Central Index Register of Merchant Seamen. This is a collection of over a million and a quarter Merchant Navy service record cards. It has details of men and women serving on board British-registered ships between the end of the First World War and the beginning of the Second World War.

The Register gives the name, date and place of birth of a seafarer. It records their rating, discharge number and details of any certificates they hold (for example, master or mates certificates). Sometimes the Register has a physical description of the mariner, even down to details of their tattoos. One part of the Register, which covers 1918 to 1921, includes a passport-style photograph of the seafarer. The Central Index Register has details of a mariner's dates of engagement or discharge on board particular vessels.

As well as British seafarers, the Register also has service details of foreign merchant

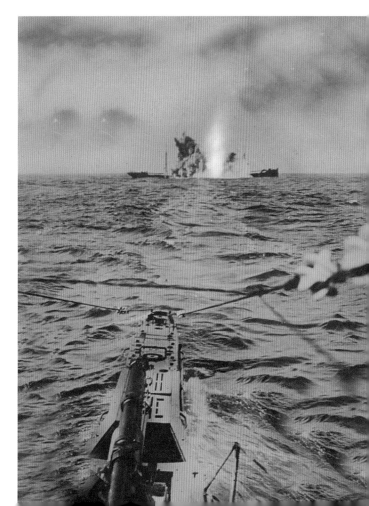

U-boats took a devastating toll on British merchant shipping in the First World War. Manx merchant sailors were often on the front line of this conflict. (Courtesy of the University of Leeds)

seamen serving on board British-registered ships. All sections of a ship's crew are included – deck crew, engine crew and victualling crew. Most of the Register includes both men and women. Unfortunately, the part of the Register that has photographs (called CR10 cards) does not usually include women. The Register can be consulted in the Reading Room of Southampton Archives. If you are unable to travel in person to search the Register, Southampton Archives offer a research service; there is a fee for this. To request a search write to:

Southampton Archives
Civic Centre
Southampton
SO14 7LY

Telephone: 02380 832251
Email: city.archives@southampton.gov.uk

TNA also holds copies of this material on microfilm under reference BT 350. Photocopies of the documentation, including the index cards (most of which carry a photograph of the individual concerned), may be obtained from this source at TNA but it is important to be aware that if you are particularly interested in the photograph, the quality of a copy from the microfilm will not be as good as a scan from the original card held at Southampton.

Merchant seaman's records created prior to 1918 were destroyed in the 1960s. However, records of campaign medals awarded to merchant seamen during the First World War still survive.

Awards of the British War Medal, Victory Medal and 1914–15 Star to men of the Mercantile Marine Reserve, of which many Manx sailors were members, and to officers and men of the Royal Naval Reserve are available on microfilm at TNA and are in ADM 171. Records of the Mercantile Marine War Medal, awarded to those with sea service of not less than six months between 4 August 1914 and 11 November 1918, and who served at sea on at least one voyage through a danger zone, are also available on microfiche in BT 351. All recipients of the Mercantile Marine War Medal were automatically entitled to the British War Medal; details are also in BT 351.

Many Merchant Navy officers and men received naval gallantry awards during the First World War. Records of these can be found in the series Admiralty and Secretariat Cases (ADM 116, code 85). Lists and indexes to these records are in Admiralty and Secretariat: Indexes and Compilations Series III (ADM 12). Further material may be found in ADM 137. Rolls of Honour for 1914–18 covering the personnel of the Merchant Marine fleet are in BT 339. For the period 1921–41 the Register of Seamen survives, again held by TNA. The register consists of two large card indexes (BT 348 and BT 349) which are available on microfilm. They give place and date of birth, ships served on and, sometimes, next of kin.

In 1941, when the next register was being prepared, cards were extracted from BT 348 and BT 349 for seamen who intended to serve during the Second World War. These extracted cards can be found in series BT 364 and BT 372. BT 395, the claims made by merchant sailors for Second World War campaign medals, are searchable online through TNA's DocumentsOnline website at: www.nationalarchives.gov.uk/ documentsonline. A fee is payable to view scans of the actual records, but it is possible to collect useful information just by using the search facility. Simply inputting the name 'Cregeen', for example, brings up five 'hits' and each are shown with full name and date of birth. Often this is all the information that a family history researcher will require.

At some time in the past, a partial attempt was made to bring BT 348, BT 349 and BT 350 together, resulting in a further class of records known as BT 364. Cards are organised in Discharge 'A' number sequence. If you know a ship on which a seaman sailed, and can find the agreement and crew list, this may provide you with the Discharge 'A' number. For the period 1941 to 1972 a fifth Register of Seamen was compiled, comprising seamen's pouches and docket books. The docket books (BT 382) contain place and date of birth, discharge book (Discharge 'A') number, rank or rating (with certificate numbers for officers), other qualifications, a list of ships with date and place of engagement, F or H (for Foreign or Home trade voyage), date and place of discharge and character.

Supplementary documents were placed in the seamen's pouches (BT 372), some of which may include details dating back to 1913. These documents are searchable by surname using TNA online catalogue.

For details of merchant sailors after 1973 it is necessary to contact:

Registry of Shipping and Seamen
MCA Cardiff
Anchor Court
Ocean Way
Cardiff
CF24 5JW

Telephone: 02920 448800
Email: rss@mcga.gov.uk

The Registry of Shipping and Seamen also holds details of the Second World War medal entitlements of merchant sailors, covered by BT 395 above.

The MNH Library and Archive Service holds a number of interviews with Manx merchant sailors collected as part of the Cruel Sea project. The Cruel Sea was a major reminiscence programme, recording the memories and experiences of Liverpool's Second World War Merchant Navy veterans. It was organised by the Culture Company in partnership with the Everyman & Playhouse, Age Concern and Age Exchange. Over a period of three months in 2005, reminiscence artists conducted interviews with surviving veterans about their experiences in arctic convoys and in the Battle of the Atlantic.

Lastly, though they were not employees of any shipping company, lighthouse keepers have for nearly 200 years been vital to the safe navigation of the coasts around the Isle of Man. Most of the lighthouses on the main Island and also on the Calf of Man are now automated, but for many years they were operated as well as manned by the Northern Lighthouses Board. Personnel records for keepers of Manx lighthouses are held by the National Archives for Scotland, with copies of earlier records held by:

Museum of Scottish Lighthouses
Kinnaird Head
Fraserburgh
AB43 9DU

Telephone: 01346 511022

Later records for still-living keepers are closed in accordance with data-protection legislation.

See also:
✿ Crew Lists

SHIPPING RECORDS

Some of the earliest records relating to Manx shipping are held by MNH under MS 06847, and these are extracts from Admiralty records of Manx vessels requesting protection in the years prior to 1793. From a similar era are extracts from the Port of Liverpool muster rolls of 1774 to 1809, covering vessels with a Manx connection, either from a Manx port or with a Manx captain. Some of these vessels were engaged in the slave trade, in which the Port of Liverpool and numbers of Manx captains, such as John Tobin and Hugh Crowe, were involved. These documents are held by MNH as MS 10199. Other extracts from the Liverpool records are held as MS 09005 (a list of Manx-built vessels registered at Liverpool Customs House in the nineteenth century) and MS 09981 (similar information relating to steamers). A return of vessels arriving at Douglas, Ramsey, Castletown and Peel between the years 1846 and 1854 is held at MS 00144.

A register of Manx ships, showing the master and owner, and covering the dates 1863 to 1913 is held under MS 08131. However, the most significant collection of shipping records held by MNH are under MS 10046 and these cover the 1820s to the 1930s. The records are organised by home port of the vessel, and those for Castletown actually go up to 1971. These ledgers contain information about where a

The fishing vessel CT 51 in Castletown harbour. Records in MNH archives show her to be the *Isabella Dodd*, whose master was Thomas Cringle. (Pc6854)

vessel was built, what her means of propulsion was (for later entries), what type of work she was engaged in, the eventual fate of the vessel and what her port registration code was, together with information about who owned the vessel and who the master was. There is no information recorded about crew members. Vessels were added to the register chronologically so a certain amount of searching is required to find a record. There also appear to be gaps in the sequences at various points.

The records cover vessels over a certain size. Although a large percentage of the vessels registered are fishing boats, such as the iconic Manx Nobbies and Nickies which made up the greater part of the fishing fleet in the nineteenth century, all Manx-registered craft should be recorded, so, for example, in 1842 we find a record for the paddle steamer *King Orry*. The registered owners are shown as the IOMSPCo, and the vessel is recorded as finally broken up at Glasgow.

More recent records of Manx-registered vessels are held by the Isle of Man Government at:

Isle of Man Ship Registry
St George's Court
Upper Church Street
Douglas
Isle of Man
British Isles
IM1 1EX

Telephone: 1624 688500
Website: www.gov.im/ded/shipregistry/

Details of shipping movements were frequently reported in the Manx newspapers, and a search of the digital copies held in the iMuseum will often yield results. The *Ramsey Courier*, for example, carried a column for many years entitled 'Nautical Briefs', reporting on shipping movements in and out of the port, cargoes carried and suchlike. The *Manks Advertiser* in the early nineteenth century often carried advertisements for vessels and craft offered for sale, as well as a regular column entitled 'Shipping Intelligence', again reporting upon arrivals in port and giving details of ship's name, owner and cargo.

See also:
❁ Shipping Company Records
❁ Customs Records

The arrival of Lieutenant Governor Francis Pigott Stainsby Conant aboard SS *King Orry I*, in 1860. *Mona's Queen I* lies alongside. (2005-0270)

SPORTING HISTORY

Sport has always played an important part in the life of the Isle of Man. Whether researching the career of a sporting ancestor or the history of a local football team, there is a rich variety of records upon which to draw. Few people now fully appreciate the range of sporting activities that have taken place on the Isle of Man in the past. In the early twentieth century, horse racing was popular with a course at Belle Vue. Either side of the Second World War the Gaiety Theatre was a popular venue for boxing, whilst the Villa Marina staged wrestling bouts. Many of the Island's football teams have a long and proud history, whilst cycling has been strong throughout the twentieth century and remains so. MNH holds an impressive collection of literature relating to the Island's football teams. This includes the 1911 *Isle of Man Times Football Annual*, copies of the Isle of Man *Examiner Football Annual* from the interwar years, through to a run of the Rushen United programme *The Spaniard*. Football results are also covered by the *Green Final* newspaper. Although the run of this newspaper is incomplete, those copies up to 1960 that are held have been digitised and are available through the iMuseum. Coverage is as follows:

- *Green Final*, 1924–6
- *Green Final*, 1935–6
- *Green Final*, 1937–40
- *Green Final*, 1947–53
- *Green Final*, 1953–8
- *Green Final*, 1959–60.

Athletics are also well covered. The MNH Library holds the minute books of the Northern Athletics Club, archives relating to Boundary Harriers (later Manx Harriers), many programmes for athletics meetings and much material relating to the Parish Walk. Amongst the printed material are booklets such as 'Island on the Run', giving the history of the first twenty-five years of the Manx Athletics Club. Typical amongst the unpublished literature is material relating to the 1970 Manx Mountain Marathon on 28 March that year, including an article from *Climber & Rambler* May 1970, an entry form, route description, route map, a list of entrants, a report from 1971 and an article from an athletics magazine. Similar material exists for this event for the following three years.

There is much material on the Isle of Man's participation in the Commonwealth Games and Island Games, including for the former many team handbooks that list members of the team and their respective disciplines. Some editions of the handbook, for example, that for the 1990 Auckland Games, also include a brief biography of each competitor.

Information can be found concerning horse racing on the Isle of Man, both at Derbyhaven and at Strang. Bowling is well covered, including programmes and fixture lists deposited by the Isle of Man Crown Green Bowling Association. D. MacFarlane's *Crown Green Bowling on the Island from 1892 to 2000* (2007) offers a comprehensive history of this sport in the twentieth century.

The photographic archives (in particular the Manx Press Pictures series and collections from the Department of Tourism) cover athletics and cycling events.

See also:
- Newspapers
- Tourist Trophy and Manx Grand Prix Races

TITHE RECORDS

Tithes (derived from the biblical concept of 'tenths') were originally rents payable to the Established Church, which were collected in the form of portions of crops or harvests. For generations tithes were hated by the agricultural population, and were thought of as hypocritical and unfair. Even Methodists and other Nonconformists were obliged to contribute in this way to the upkeep of the Established Church. At various times there have been protests against tithes, one of the earliest recorded incidents being in 1643 when a farmer was thrown into Castle Rushen gaol for refusing to pay. The worst discontent flared up in 1825 when the Church attempted to impose tithes on the potato crop, the staple diet of the Manx rural poor. It had been a bad harvest that year and the attempt by the Church to seize the provisions needed for the coming winter led to an angry mob armed with pitchforks gathering at Bishopscourt. Bishop Murray was forced to flee to the safety of Douglas and the attempt was abandoned. However, two of the ringleaders of the disturbance, John Kermode and William Hudgeon, were arrested and sentenced to transportation for life to Australia. A small number of early Tithe Books have survived for individual parishes and years, but these are sufficient to illustrate the nature of the records:

- 1776 – Patrick
- 1783 – Braddan and Onchan
- 1816 – Braddan.

In 1841 the Tithe Commutation Act was passed by Tynwald. It was an Act following the precedent of similar legislation in Britain in the 1830s, which allowed the Church to receive a cash sum, instead of the payment in kind which had been the case up to that point. In order to enable this, plans of lands and dwellings were drawn up by agents, in order to assess their value. For the Isle of Man these plans are now lodged at the General Registry. Accompanying the plans were Tithe Composition Books, listing the names of landowners, details of their properties and the tenants who farmed them. The original books are held by the IOMPRO, but copies are held in the MNH Reading Room. Collection of tithes continued in the Isle of Man until they were abolished for good in 1951. Even into the 1930s, if tithes were not paid it was not unknown for police and bailiffs to arrive to seize cattle or other goods.

MNH has extensive holdings in this area as part of the Diocesan Records. Tithe records are held with other material under MS 09309. Broadly speaking, the

See also:
✿ Land and
    Property
    Records

records fall into two groups: Composition Books, covering the years 1839 through to 1945, and cash books which appear to run up to about 1950. The Composition Books show the amount levied on each piece of land, the land owner, the occupier, a description of the land or premises, the acreage and the money value of the tithes payable on this. They also include the name of the person who paid the money and the value of the crops.

The cash books are arranged by parish and take the form of a day book recording monies received each day and from whom. There is also extensive correspondence within this archive, together with plans and other miscellaneous documents. On the whole, the potential usefulness of these records to the family historian is somewhat limited, as much of the information that they contain is paralleled by records of land holdings. However, the value may instead be considered as descriptive, giving as they do information on the relative prices of crops year on year, for example, or for their content concerning the nature of the land or property in question. Thus they offer considerable scope to those interested in agricultural or local history, or the history of a particular farm or estate.

Isle of Man Newspapers farming correspondent Harvey Briggs has worked on the land all of his life, and has written of his own personal experience of tithes:

[In the twentieth century] opposition to paying tithes continued but without the violence of the 1600s or 1800s. It was compulsory for every farm and tithe agents travelled the Island setting up collecting centres in every town and parish amounting to 17 in all, the same number as the total of parishes. Often the local railway station was used although Douglas and Onchan had their own tithe offices. Failure to pay between January 20 and February 20 could lead to produce or animals being seized by the police and I remember one farm in Onchan parish being treated in this way. The rodeo with the coroner's men and police attempting to round up cattle which I watched from a distance was a spectacle I will never forget. The farmer, as to be expected, gave no help! Under Tynwald legislation there was a clause which enabled the owner of the farm to redeem the tithe with one bulk payment and in 1945 our new landlord did so on the 100 acres of Ballakilmartin. One payment of £199 by him relieved the farm of tithe for all time. This appeared a generous gesture on his part but made little difference to us really because he added the interest on the capital sum he had expended to our annual rent. When tithes were finally abolished in 1951 he forgot to remove the extra from our rent, in effect he collected the tithe for himself until we bought the farm in 1964. [Isle of Man Examiner, 4 February 2008]

TOURIST TROPHY AND MANX GRAND PRIX RACES

The Isle of Man's association with motorcycle racing is a unique aspect of its heritage. Because of the distinct political system on the Isle of Man it was possible in 1904 to obtain an order from Tynwald to close roads for motor car racing. In 1907 the first motorcycle Tourist Trophy (TT) was held. In 1911 the Isle of Man's Mountain Circuit was used for the first time – the oldest motorcycle racing circuit in the world which is still in use. In the 1930s the races were the most prestigious events of their kind in the world, whilst in the 1950s and 60s the Island hosted the British rounds of the world championship series. Over the one-hundred and more years that the races have been run, many thousands of competitors have taken part in the event. A few of them, like Mike Hailwood, have become household names but the vast majority will simply have made up the field. In addition to the TT races at the beginning of summer, in August the Isle of Man stages the Manx Grand Prix (MGP) races. These races were originally conceived as amateur versions of the TT races, and have always provided a stepping stone towards riding in the June races. They none the less have a huge following in their own right and attract many thousands of visitors interested in classic machinery. Although the events are male dominated, several women have made a name for themselves in racing. Beryl Swain became the first female solo competitor in 1962, when she raced in the 50cc TT. In 2009 Carolynn Sells became the

The start of the 1960 Lightweight TT race.

Percy Evans, winner of the 1911 Junior TT, with the magnificent Mercury Trophy. (Pg6756)

first woman to win a race on the Mountain Circuit when she took victory in the Ultra Lightweight Manx Grand Prix.

The best source of information about the races is the programmes, an almost complete run of which are held by MNH. Additional information may be found in the stewards' reports, race guides and in the mass of other published material that has been produced in connection with the event, from the Salon cartoons of racing personalities which appeared in the 1930s and 40s, to the modern glossy magazines such as *Island Racer*.

In the 1920s it was a requirement that motorcycles that had been brought to the Isle of Man for racing had to have a temporary Isle of Man registration number for the two-week period in which they were on the Island. In reality this was a way for the Manx Government to raise much-needed revenue as there was a small fee required to do this, but the registrations are recorded in the registers together with the name of the entrant, the owner of the motorcycle and other details. These records are held as part of MS 09765.

MNH maintains a TT database as part of its website (www.gov.im/mnh/collections/tt/welcome.xml). This allows users to search by year, race, rider name, manufacturer or a combination of these. The database allows researchers very quickly to build up a picture of a rider's TT career from his first race to his last, with finishing positions shown and also race times and speeds.

Many historians on the trail of a racing ancestor are keen to find a photograph of him taken whilst competing. MNH holds the Manx Press Pictures series, which cover the 1950s through to the mid-1970s. Probably the most comprehensive archive however is the Keig Collection which covers TT riders from approximately the 1920s through to 1960s. A four-volume index of the collection has been published, making searching for a rider fairly straightforward. If you are still unable to find a photograph, it is worth contacting Fottofinders Bikesport Archives (www.fottofinders.co.uk), the collections of which cover the TT, MGP, Southern 100 and other events from 1907 to the present day.

Inevitably, with a sport of this nature there have been fatalities over the years. Sometimes families are interested in finding out more about an ancestor who died whilst competing in the racing, and several publications have appeared in recent years reflecting upon the courage of the young men (and women) who compete in this most thrilling of sports. *Isle of Man Tourist Trophy Circuit Memorials Revealed* by Paul Copparelli and Peter Mylchreest (2009) examines the many small shrines that have appeared along the circuit to riders from around the world who have raced on the Isle of Man, not all of them fatalities, whilst several websites carry a full list of those who have lost their lives.

Some marvellous personal memoirs are available for those keen to know more about what it feels like actually to compete in this most exhilarating of sporting events. Two of the best were co-written by British motorcycle racing's greatest star Mike Hailwood, with Ted Macaulay – *Hailwood* (1969) and *Mike the Bike – Again* (1980). The latter chronicles Hailwood's remarkable return to the TT in 1978 after an eleven-year absence, and his farewell TT in 1979. Although the TT races have a strong international flavour, with riders from America, Australia and New Zealand regularly competing, the Isle of Man has produced numbers of riders who have been able to hold their own at the top level. The first Manxman to win a TT race was Tom Sheard in 1922. Sheard's life has been admirably documented by his granddaughter Ruth Sheard in *The Modest Manxman* (2006). It contains the memorable quote that during the 1922 Junior TT, '*The mist was so thick on the mountain that even as a local man I had difficulty in finding my way.*' The most successful sidecar racer in the history of the event is Manxman Dave Molyneux, who also builds his own race-winning outfits. Molyneux has also penned his memoirs with Matthew Richardson, published as *The Racer's Edge* (2011), in which he describes the highs and lows of TT racing.

Finally, newspapers and periodicals provide an excellent source of information and commentary about the races, riders and results. TT and MGP editions of *Motor Cycle*, *Motor Cycling* and *Motor Cycle News* are all held by the MNH Library. Manx newspapers also give excellent coverage of the races and results. Those up to 1960 are searchable through the iMuseum. In addition, Collections Online at the iMuseum features biographies of notable TT riders.

See also:
❂ Newspapers
❂ Sporting History

> **Dave Molyneux in *The Racer's Edge* has written of his feelings following his first TT win:**
> *We got to the Park Ferme [after the race] well happy at the thought we'd finished second, and then somebody, I think it was Geoff Cannell the roaming commentator, came and said, "Something's wrong here, Dave has won it, he ain't second." There was a lot of confusion, but then it was announced over the tannoy that we'd actually won the race on corrected time, because there had been this cock up on the start line. So it was official that we'd actually won the race! It was a rollercoaster of emotions for me. Deep down I was a little disappointed in the fact that the bike had not gone as well as it had done in practice, and with such a small margin of losing out, I thought, you know if it had been right we could have walked that race, but then at the same time I figured, 'What the hell, we're second, it's my first podium position ever, so that'll do for today. We'll have better luck next time . . .'. And the next thing I know, I've won it! Luckily this was all sorted out in the Park Ferme, before we went up onto the rostrum, so we went up there as winners! We got the champagne, and the winners' laurels on our first time up there. But my memories of that first win are hazy really. It's something I remember very little of. People might find that a little bit strange I suppose, and also the fact that when I look back on it, I think it was quite hard to enjoy that moment.*

VEHICLE REGISTRATION AND DRIVING LICENCE RECORDS

Vehicle registration and licensing of drivers were introduced by an Act of Tynwald into the Isle of Man. Under the Highways Act Amendment Act, 1905 every motor car had to be registered with the Highway Board and a separate number given to each vehicle. The registers start in January 1906 and the system continues to this day at the Vehicle Licensing Section of Treasury, Government Offices, Bucks Road, Douglas. The MNH Heritage Library and Archive Service holds the registers from 1906–65 at accession reference number MS 09765. The deposit includes the earliest register for driving licence holders (1906–21).

As a brief guide to the numbering system, the following index mark sequences for vehicles were used for the years 1906–65:

- MN 1–MN 9999, 1906–35
- MAN 1–MAN 999, 1935
- BMN 1–YMN 999, 1936–59
- 1 MN–9999 MN, 1959–64
- 1 MAN–999 MAN, 1964
- 1 BMN–999 CMN, 1964–5.

The number plate from the Riley motorcar owned by Janet Gibb, of the Grove, Ramsey. Records in MNH archives show that she relinquished the vehicle (and the number) in 1940, probably due to wartime petrol restrictions. (2008-0325)

However, since numbers were reused frequently after cancellation of a vehicle registration, tracing a vehicle can be complicated, and the covering dates are for the first use of each number. The dates of re-registration may be many years after the original allocation of the number. For a more in-depth account of the numbering sequences see Appendix 1 in the *Fleet History of Isle of Man Department of Tourism and Leisure and its Predecessors* (Library reference: B192/2/53).

The registers typically consist of motor cars to the front with heavy motor vehicle entries recorded at the rear using the same number sequence. Information is usually arranged by plate number, name and address of owner, vehicle description, weight, wheel diameter and width and material of tyres.

Heavy agricultural and road-making machinery such as traction engines and steam rollers had initially been exempt from registration, but a change in the law required these vehicles to be registered from 1933. Thus the register for that year contains a swathe of such machinery, and provides an interesting snapshot of both the number and types of machinery in use on the Island.

WAR MEMORIALS

In 2008 the Isle of Man Government's Council of Ministers established a Committee for the Preservation of War Memorials. This was in response to growing public concern over the condition of many of these monuments. Most of these, in common with their counterparts in Britain, had been erected after the First World War but had not been endowed with funding to maintain them, nor in many cases was there any clear cut responsibility for maintaining them. Other people were acutely aware that as churches had closed or buildings had changed their usage, local memorials that formed part of the Isle of Man's collective memory were in danger of being lost.

The Douglas war memorial is unveiled in 1921. (Pg6239/15)

The Committee employed no paid staff, but received assistance from Mr Roger Christian and Mr Hector Duff, who had already begun to record and photograph the Island's body of war memorials as part of the Imperial War Museum's survey of extant memorials. Their tireless efforts both to document the information stored on the memorials, as well as their locations and any other details that they could uncover about who had paid for them, designed them or unveiled them, amounted to a substantial body of work. The Committee was keen both to assist in the preservation of this information and also to make it publicly available in some way.

Accordingly, they approached MNH. The information gathered is now being collated, and it is envisaged ultimately that a database system will hold the information recorded on the memorial, the location of the memorial in terms of geographical coordinates, together with additional data about its history and information regarding its condition. Information recorded on the memorials, in particular the names of individuals, is available to the public through the iMuseum.

The genealogical and historical information contained on these memorials is quite significant. Numbers of church memorials in particular list the name of every member of the congregation who was serving, not just those who fell. This can provide invaluable information. Although some 6 million men and women served overseas in the First World War, approximately a further million, although in uniform, may not have served overseas and thus may not appear in official records, such as the Medal Index Cards (see **Military and Naval Records** above). Sometimes additional details are noted on memorial panels such as 'wounded' or 'prisoner of war' and this again may not be recorded elsewhere. The repetition of surnames on memorials highlights the enormous contribution – and sacrifice – made by numerous families and communities. Many a school child has been introduced to this era of history – and its impact – by a project to research the names on a local war memorial and the iMuseum offers the potential to discover these names and also to link them to photographs and to other records such as census returns. These monuments also provide a unique snapshot of the involvement of a community in the conflicts of the twentieth century. Those from churches that have closed or been demolished, for example, Bucks Road Methodist church, often reflect once vibrant communities that have dispersed. Their architectural and artistic significance should also not be overlooked. A number of war memorials on the Isle of Man were designed by Archibald Knox, and represent a significant portion of his body of work.

See also:
✿ Military
  and Naval
  Records
✿ Newspapers

WEB RESOURCES

The greatest revolution in family and local history research in the past twenty years has undoubtedly been the growth and development of the World Wide Web, and the resources that it can offer to researchers and historians. It is no exaggeration to say that the amount of historical material that is on the web is expanding on a monthly if not weekly basis. Many of the larger repositories such as TNA have discovered that by digitising discrete collections and releasing these via the Internet on a pay-per-view basis they can generate considerable additional income. This in itself is fuelling the drive to release more material. That from TNA is available via the DocumentsOnline web page at: www.nationalarchives.gov.uk/documentsonline. This material should be used in conjunction with the main TNA website, which contains the main TNA catalogue

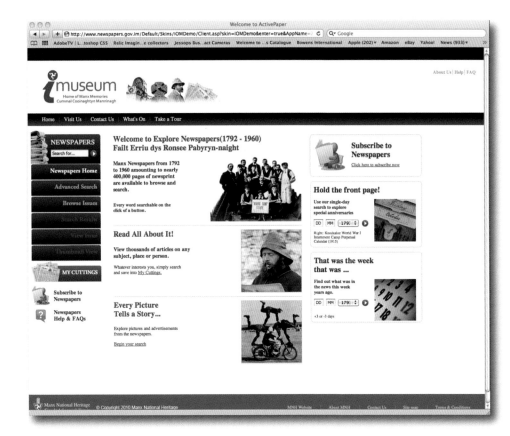

The home page for searching Manx newspapers online, via the iMuseum.

and also a series of user guides which give the researcher a fuller picture of what is available off line by visiting TNA. In addition to their own digitisation programme, TNA have worked in partnership with the largest of the genealogy websites, www.ancestry.co.uk, to make further quantities of material available to the user at home, either on a pay-per-view or subscription basis. Not far behind Ancestry is www.findmypast.co.uk. Although there is some overlap between the two sites, on the whole the two complement each other.

Aside from purely commercial websites such as those described above, an enormous amount of material has been made available by dedicated individuals, working often alone to transcribe material from paper records and making it available electronically. Some invaluable historical resources have been rescued from obscurity in this way and brought to the attention of a wider audience. From the perspective of Manx historical research, one website stands head and shoulders above others and that is Frances Coakley's Manx Note Book at: www.isle-of-man.com/manxnotebook. This website contains a wealth of material including obscure nineteenth-century publications and otherwise hard to access sources. The real beauty of the site of course is that everything is searchable almost instantly, meaning that references and facts are readily at the fingertips. The contents page lists bibliography, cartobibliography, family history, monographs and biographies amongst its contents.

Other useful sites for the Manx researcher are www.manxbmd.co.uk, a site giving access to Manx civil registration records. Most of these records will not be available on the main genealogical websites, because Manx records form a separate series from their British counterparts. Those researching births, marriages and deaths will find www.freebmd.org.uk a useful site. The information has been uploaded entirely by volunteers and for some areas the coverage is not complete. The IOMFHS website at: www.iomfhs.im contains useful resources, as does that of the Manx Heritage Foundation at: www.manxheritage.org. In the future, one of the greatest resources available to the Manx historian will undoubtedly be the iMuseum website at: www.imuseum.im, providing as it will unrivalled access to newspapers, census returns, photographs, deeds and other material. Access to much of the material by online users will be on a subscription basis. The site will also allow users to order high-quality photographic prints, as well as view historic objects from the collections of MNH, view film footage and listen to audio files.

WILLS AND PROBATE

Wills figure much more prominently in Manx family history research than in that from other parts of Britain. This is because, unlike many other parts of the British Isles, in times gone by most people in the Isle of Man made a will, regardless of their station in life. Wills invariably provide information on family relationships, and of course an inventory of a person's possessions. Indeed, it is no exaggeration to say that from 1780 onward wills are crucial to the study of Manx genealogy.

The MNH Library holds original wills from around 1600 to 1910, and microfilm copies up to 1916. The IOMFHS has compiled an index to the microfilms which makes searching them considerably easier. This paper record is available in the MNH Reading Room. The majority of the wills have been indexed, but not comprehensively so, and thus if it is strongly suspected that a person made a will but it is not listed, it is still worth searching the microfilm for the relevant year. These wills have also been digitised for MNH by the Genealogical Society of Utah, and will be made available through the iMuseum. Wills made after 1916 can be consulted at the Deeds and Probate Registry, but may need to be ordered in advance.

As late as the nineteenth century, many Manx people, especially those living in the countryside away from the main towns, spoke little or no English. It would not therefore be unusual for a clerk to have to translate into English a person's will that had been dictated to him in Manx. The will however would always be written in English. Wills on the Isle of Man can take a number of different forms, the main ones being:

- Those made in the normal way and undisputed in the courts

- Those which have been contested, such as wills challenged in court by those excluded from them who might be considered heirs. These are often of greater value as they may mention relatives other than those named by the deceased

- Petitions to the court made by the relatives of persons who died intestate, for example, without having left a valid will

- Nuncupative wills. These are wills that have no signature and were in fact drawn up after the death of the testator (person who has left goods or property after their death). In these cases a number of witnesses were

An inventory of the possessions of John Clarke, a private in the Royal Manx Fencibles who died in 1795, from the Episcopal Wills series, held by Manx National Heritage.

required to swear to the fact they had heard the deceased, at any time prior to death, make a statement regarding the distribution of his assets subsequently. This system was open to abuse and corruption and after an attempt to impose stricter controls upon their usage in 1777, in 1869 they were abolished altogether.

Wills from the earliest times to 1847 were 'proven' either in the Archidiaconal Court or the Episcopal Court (in effect they were read aloud and deemed by the court to be valid). There is in reality very little difference between the two procedures. It was essentially the same church court, presided over for part of the year by the Vicar General (Episcopal Court) and for the rest of the year by the Archdeacon. The two series were indexed separately. Archidiaconal wills are sub-numbered, whereas Episcopal Wills are not, but a running order to the microfilm copies has been prepared, which greatly assists finding an Episcopal will. The IOMFHS website also contains the will index prepared by the late Brian Lawson. Searching microfilms can be a time-consuming process, but following digitisation it will soon be possible to search all wills together, a much quicker procedure. From 1847 to 1874 wills were still proven in one or other of the two courts, but were subject to a different index. Again, digitisation will render this distinction largely irrelevant. Between 1875 and 1883 the Episcopal Court dealt with all wills, until finally in 1884 all wills were proven in the Civil Court. Records of wills (and Grants of Administration for those who died intestate) from 1900 onwards are held by the General Registry.

In addition to the wills held by MNH, the IOMPRO holds the Deemsters' Testamentary Minutes. The Deemster himself recorded in a form of a diary the minutes of the Probate Court proceedings from 1884 onwards. Where wills were proved in the High Court 'in solemn form', for example, by a Court hearing, the evidence as to who was the next of kin would generally be given verbally of which these minutes (and secondary sources such as the newspapers, if it was reported) will be the only evidence. Access to these records is not available under the Public Records Act because they are regarded as the property of the Deemster. However, this is not a final position and requests for access should be directed to IOMPRO. Each case will be judged on its merits.

CASE STUDIES

The Miner's Story

James A. Clague's story begins with a set of stereoscopic photographs, showing underground scenes in a mine, donated by a family to the Manx Museum in the 1980s. They came with two pieces of information. The first was that the photographs were taken at Langlaagt Deep Gold Mine in South Africa. The second was the name of the original owner, James A. Clague. This of course is a classic Manx surname.

The inference from this was that here was a Manx miner, who like so many of his contemporaries had emigrated to South Africa to work in the expanding South African goldfields. In 2004 when the Great Laxey Wheel celebrated its 150th anniversary, a special temporary exhibition was held at the Manx Museum in Douglas. It was felt that an important part of the exhibition should be the story of a typical miner, so the quest began to find out more about James A. Clague.

The first step was to check the indexes for the late nineteenth-century census returns to try to find a match, using the index held in the MNH Reading Room or online in the iMuseum. The first match was in the 1881 census, where a James A. Clague was found. He was aged 8 (and therefore born c. 1873) and living at 7 Beach Road, Laxey, the son of Henry Clague, a 34-year-old lead miner and his wife Jane, who was two years older than him.

James A. Clague as seen in one of the stereoscopic photographs from Langlaagt Deep Gold Mine. (Pg7808)

The Clagues had six children, their oldest son William E., then James, a daughter Catherine, another son George U., a daughter Louisa Jane and a third son Thomas Charles. Jumping forward ten years to 1891, three J.A. Clagues are found in the index. One is a Joseph Clague, born in Ramsey, who is discounted at once. The second James A. Clague was born in Lezayre and was aged 12, so he also failed to match up with the known facts. This left James A. Clague, aged 19, whose age correlates to that of James in the previous census. Further investigation of the actual census entry on microfiche in the Reading Room revealed this James to be a lead miner by occupation, and he was the son of Henry Clague, living at 44 Old Laxey. James now had four brothers, George A. Clague, Thomas C., John H. and Robert.

At the same time a search was made of memorial inscriptions in the three churchyards in Lonan parish. The index, again in the Reading Room, revealed a tombstone inscribed:

In affectionate remembrance of William Henry eldest son of Henry John
and Jane Clague of Laxey Beach who died 5 Feb 1890 aged 19 years and 10 months
Also in loving memory of George Albert third son of the above who was found drowned in the outer basin Capetown South Africa Oct 23rd 1899 aged 25 years also the above Henry John (beloved husband of Jane) who died June 24th 1917 aged 67 years also Jane beloved wife of the above died February 13th 1936 aged 92 years

Searching for background information in the Manx Museum's Folklife Survey brought forth a remarkable piece of information in the recollections of David Borland, a former miner:

Men of my generation, when they came to 18 or 20 years of age, could find very little to do here, unless they became miners. That was why so many of them went away. £1 a week was the highest wage they could hope for here and the £4 or £5 a week that they heard reports of in the South African mines seemed wonderful to them. It was the El Dorado of those days. The passage to Cape Town didn't cost much – a man could go for £9 or £10. They used to go out in batches of ten or a dozen . . . with their mining experience the men from Laxey could always get a job out there . . . I can recall whole families of men going out. The Lawsons Robert John, Teddy and Willie, five Kewley brothers, who all died out there of Miner's Phthisis. James, George, Tommy Charles and Franklyn Clague. The first two died also.

A search through the index of memorial inscriptions in Lonan revealed there were about five J. Clagues, but only one with initials J.A. The reference quickly revealed an epitaph for James A. Clague in Lonan 1871 churchyard, showing that he died in 1911. The full inscription reads:

In loving memory of James Alexander Clague of King Orry, Laxey, who died Dec 12th 1911 aged 39 years. In the midst of life we are in death. Also James Henry, son of the above who died April 22nd 1948 aged 47 years also Annie wife of J.A. Clague who died October 28th 1970 aged 97 years.

Next port of call was the index of wills in the MNH Reading Room or online at the iMuseum. This revealed that James Alexander Clague's will was proved in the year 1912 and was number 41 of that year. The index indicated that James' will would be found on microfilm reel no. JG 47. After the customary legal

The Clague family home, 'Sea Level' at Laxey Beach. (Pg5111/10)

preamble came the interesting part in which James lists his possessions and what he would like to happen to them: 'I direct my wife as such executrix to sell and dispose of the house I have lately built at Kensington, Johannesburg, South Africa for the best price obtainable.' He then directs her to sell his shares in various South African gold mines and to sell a plot of land belonging to him at South Cape, Laxey. Finally he adds, 'I direct that my gold watch and chain be preserved and given to my oldest son when he attains twenty one years.'

But James' story does not end there. A search through the MNH photograph collection turned up a remarkable photograph of the Clague family home, Sea Level Cottage on Laxey Beach, with the family standing outside. Furthermore, as research progressed independently on another object in the museum collections, a black dress belonging to a miner's widow, it transpired that this had in fact belonged to a Mrs Jane Clague. Further investigation showed that she was the widow of Henry John Clague of Sea Level, The Beach, Laxey and was actually James A. Clague's mother, the dress having arrived in the museum collections via another branch of the family. The death certificate of Henry John Clague was obtained from the General Registry. This showed that he was a miner and, typically, that he had died of phthisis (a disease of the lungs commonly caused by working in dusty conditions). Moreover, it revealed that the death had been registered by the deceased man's son, T.C. Clague, further confirming the family connection.

When members of the Clague family visited the exhibition and learned of the museum's interest in James A. Clague, his daughter donated further items which helped to fill in some of the gaps in Clague's story. One of these was a spoon inscribed 'Lead, S.D.'. Research on the Internet revealed that Lead (pronounced 'Leed'), in the Black Hills of South Dakota was a gold-mining town, and the family believed that James and his brother had travelled to the United States in search of work. The genealogy website Findmypast contains passenger list information and a search of this database for 'James Clague' shows a James A. Clague born in 1872 travelling to New York from Liverpool aboard SS *Majestic* in June 1893. He is listed as single and his occupation as miner. In fact, the original passenger manifest shows that he was travelling with a William Henry Quayle, approximately the same age and also a miner.

This information was cross referenced with the Ellis Island immigration records where the *Majestic* is documented as arriving in New York in July 1893. James Clague and William Quayle, for reasons best known to themselves, gave their occupations to the Ellis Island authorities as 'none' and stated that their destination was Philadelphia. The Find My Past search revealed another passage for a James A. Clague born in the same year, this time from Liverpool to Cape

Town, South Africa in November 1901, aboard the SS *Runic*. This journey tied in with another object that the family brought into the museum.

This other item was a military medal, the Queen's South Africa, dating from the Boer War (1899–1902). This like most British medals is impressed with the recipient's details around the edge. In this case the wording reads 'Pte J.A. Clague Rand Rifles'. Other items related to the Transvaal Manx Association. Further research revealed that the Rand Rifles were a kind of Home Guard, raised in South Africa during the Boer War to protect the gold mines. James Clague had in fact risen to the position of Mine Captain at Langlaagt Deep, and was a prominent figure in the Transvaal Manx Association. Clague's daughter also revealed that James had returned from South Africa with enough money to buy a plot of land and build a house, a fact confirmed by his will, though the illness he contracted in the mines meant that he would not live to enjoy the new life that he had worked so hard to secure, as was the case for many of his mining contemporaries.

Finally, a search of the Manx newspapers for 1911 (either in the MNH Reading Room or online at the iMuseum) produced a lengthy obituary for James A. Clague in the *Isle of Man Examiner* of 16 December 1911, which fleshes out the story of much of his life. Under 'Death of Well Known Manx South African' it reads in part:

Of generous disposition, and taking an active part in the Transvaal Manx Association, he was ever ready to extend a helping hand to his less fortunate fellow-countrymen, and if possible find them employment. On the expiry of his term of office of president of the association, he was presented by the members with a beautifully illuminated testimonial. For seven or eight years he was employed on the Langlaagte Deep Mine, during the last three years of which he was mine captain, and upon leaving there some three years ago, he was presented with a suitably inscribed gold watch and chain and a silver tea and coffee service by the employees.

The Soldier's Story

Robert Oates' story begins with a photograph, a typical studio portrait of the Edwardian era (sometimes called a cabinet card), showing a soldier with a military moustache. He was wearing a smart uniform, with collar badges showing an acorn. The only information initially known about Robert Oates was that he came from Douglas, and that he had served with the Cheshire Regiment (which was confirmed by identification of the collar badges). The first port of call when tracing a soldier of the First World War era is usually the Medal Index Card. A card exists for every soldier who served overseas in the First World War, and who earned campaign medals. A set is held by TNA and copies can be purchased online from the DocumentsOnline website. Alternatively, a set is held by www.ancestry.co.uk and copies can again be downloaded. The Index Card holds vital information such as the soldier's service number. This number is often crucial in tracing other military documents, and the Index Card must always be the starting point for research as it also (usually) confirms the soldier's Christian name. In this case, the Index cards show that only one Robert Oates served with the Cheshire Regiment, that his number was 6797 and that he was entitled to the 1914 Star (and in fact served overseas from 12 September 1914). From the date one can deduce that he served with the 1st Battalion, as no other battalion of the Cheshires was in France at this early point in the war. Other crucial pieces of information are the letters 'SWB' (standing for Silver War Badge). This badge was issued to honourably discharged soldiers. Also, the date of discharge is given as 8 March 1915. Such an early date, together with the badge, usually indicate that the soldier sustained serious wounds.

The next step is to try to locate Robert's service record. The so-called 'burnt' series

A sepia-toned portrait of Robert Oates in military uniform. The collar badges are those of the Cheshire Regiment. (Pg7516)

Cheshire 4 / 48 / 8th

Army Form E. 504.

MILITIA ATTESTATION OF

No. 8243 Name. R J Oates Corps. 3rd R L R

Questions to be put to the Recruit before Enlistment.

1. What is your Name? .... 1. Robert James Oates
2. In what Parish, and in or near what Town, and in what County were you born? .... 2. In the Parish of St. Matthews in or near the Town of Douglas in the County of Isle of Man.
3. Are you a British Subject? .... 3. yes
4. Where do you now reside? Lodgings 30, Third Avenue Rd. 4. In the Parish of Bolton in or near the Town of Manchester in the County of Lancs.
5. Where have you resided for the last twelvemonth? 7. Drury Lane Lodgings 5. In the Parish of St. Matthews in or near the Town of Douglas in the County of Isle of Man
6. What is the Name and Residence of your present (or former) Master? Joiner & Builder 6. Mr. Tyson in or near the Town of Bolton in the County of Lancs.
7. What is your age? .... 7. 19 Years 4 Months
8. What is your Trade or Calling? .... 8. Joiner

(You are warned that you are liable to heavy Punishment if you make a false answer to any of the following nine questions.)

9. Are you an Apprentice? .... 9. No
10. Are you Single, Married, or a Widower? .... 10. Single
11. If Married, or a Widower, how many Children have you under 14 years of age? .... 11. None
12. Have you ever been sentenced to imprisonment by the Civil Power? .... 12. No
13. Do you now belong to Her Majesty's Army, the Marines, the Militia, the Militia Reserve, the Royal Navy, the Volunteers, the Yeomanry, the Army Reserve, or the Naval Reserve Force? If so, to what Corps? .... 13. Yes 7th V.B. Liverpool Regt.
14.* Have you ever served in Her Majesty's Army, the Marines, the Militia, the Militia Reserve, or the Royal Navy? If so, state which, and cause of discharge? .... 14. No except as above.
15. Have you truly stated the whole, if any, of your previous Service? .... 15. yes
16. Are you in receipt of a pension for any such Service? .... 16. No
17. Have you ever been rejected as unfit for Her Majesty's Service? If so, on what grounds? .... 17. No
18. Are you willing to be vaccinated or re-vaccinated? .... 18. yes
19. Did you receive a Notice and do you understand its meaning, and who gave it to you? .... 19. yes Name Sgt. Harvey Corps R.L.O.
20. Are you willing to be attested for the term of † six years (provided Her Majesty should so long require your services), as a Militiaman for the County of ‡ Lancashire to serve in the § R. Lancaster Regt. .... 20. yes

I, Robert James Oates do solemnly declare that the above answers made by me to the above questions are true and that I am willing to fulfil the engagement made.

Robert James Oates Signature of Recruit.

Signature of Witness.

OATH TO BE TAKEN BY MILITIA RECRUIT ON ATTESTATION.

I, Robert James Oates do solemnly promise and swear that I will be faithful to Her Majesty Queen Victoria, her heirs and successors, and that I will faithfully serve in the Militia, until I shall be discharged.

CERTIFICATE OF MAGISTRATE OR OF A COMMISSIONED OFFICER.

The Recruit above-named was cautioned by me that if he made any false answer to any of the foregoing questions he would be liable to be punished.

The foregoing questions were then read to the Recruit in my presence.

I have taken care that he understands each question, and that his answer to each question has been duly entered as replied to, and the said Recruit has made and signed the declaration and taken the oath before me at MANCHESTER on this 28 day of May 1900

Lt. Col. R. S. Signature of Magistrate or Commiss. Officer of Regular Army or Militia.

* If so, the Recruit is to be asked the particulars of his former service, and to produce (if possible) his Parchment Certificate of Discharge, and Certificate of Character, which will be returned to him conspicuously endorsed in red ink, as follows, viz.:—(Name) enlisted as Militiaman for the County of on the
† Here insert 6 years, except in the case of a re-enlisted man, as defined by the Militia Regulations, who will be attested for 4 years.
‡ Here insert a "County," as defined in Sections 48 to 53 of the Militia Act (1882). § Here insert the "Corps" as defined by Royal Warrant.

If any alteration is required on this page of the Attestation, the Officer who attested the Recruit, or a Justice of the Peace, should be requested to make it and initial the alteration under Section 30 (6), Army Act.

The Recruit should, if he require it, receive a copy of the Declaration on Army Form E. 507.

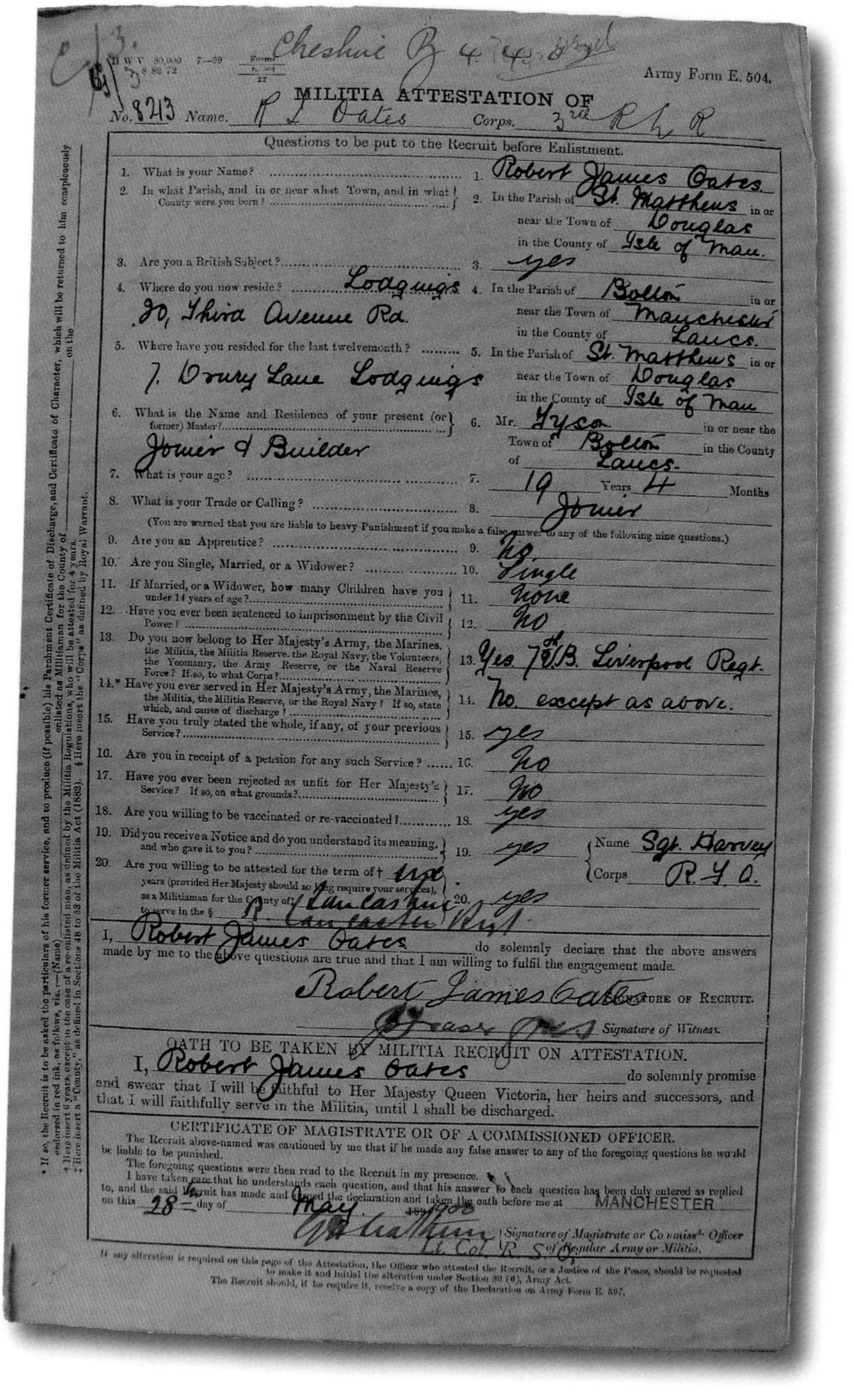

The attestation of Robert Oates for the Royal Lancaster Militia, in May 1900. (Courtesy of The National Archives)

for discharges between 1913 and 1920 is held on microfilm at Kew, or online at: www.ancestry.co.uk. Even though this series is not complete, a search for Robert Oates of the Cheshire Regiment immediately brings up a hit, showing a Robert Oates with the right service number born in St Matthew's, Douglas in 1881. Bordering the harbour, St Matthew's was the poorest parish in Douglas and contained some of its worst slums. The link on the website takes one to the scanned copies of his papers, and it is worth pointing out here that as with many other entries on the Ancestry index, the link takes the researcher to the middle of the papers. Having found the correct soldier it is necessary to page backwards as well as forwards to ensure nothing has been missed. Robert's attestation form shows him enlisting on 4 April 1902. It is always worth noting any previous service shown, and Robert stated here that he had formerly served with the 3rd Battalion Royal Lancaster Regiment (Royal Lancaster Militia). This detail might easily have been missed, but it explains why he is absent from the both the 1901 British census and 1901 Isle of Man census. This battalion, along with other Militia battalions, served on garrison duty in South Africa during the Boer War. Robert would have qualified for a medal for this service, and it is worth checking the rolls for nineteenth-century campaign medals also available via www.ancestry.co.uk. This confirms that 8213 Private R. Oates, 3rd Battalion Royal Lancaster Regiment received the Queen's South Africa Medal with clasps Cape Colony and Orange Free State. As he was not a Regular soldier at this point, this service though in a war zone was not pensionable, and therefore was not recorded in full later on in his service papers. In the late nineteenth century prior to the welfare state the Militia acted as a safety net for the urban poor. It was possible to enlist for short periods of time, recruits received a retainer and there was no compulsion to serve overseas. Many Militia soldiers subsequently transferred to the Regular Army if they found Army life to their taste. Militia attestations are held separately at TNA under WO 96, and these records will also be available online at: www.findmypast.co.uk from late 2011. Oates' Militia attestation reveals that his middle name was James, when he enlisted in May 1900 he was living in lodgings at 20 Third Avenue, Bolton and was employed by a Mr Tyson, a joiner and builder. His previous residence is shown as lodgings at 7 Drury Lane, Douglas and his previous service is recorded as being with the 7th Volunteer Battalion King's Liverpool Regiment (Isle of Man Volunteers). Armed with this information it is also possible to find Oates on the roll of the Isle of Man Volunteers held by MNH (MS 00789c). This records that he joined the volunteers on 27 March 1899, his home address was Drury Lane, his occupation was shown as 'joiner' and his reason for quitting the corps was given as 'enlisted in Lanc Regt'.

Returning to the service papers, other pages tell the researcher much about

Robert's temperament. On one page his character is described as 'exemplary' and some of the papers concern his enrolment into the Section D Army reserve at the end of his normal period of service. Only those soldiers with a clean conduct sheet could apply to join the Section D reserve, for which a retainer was paid. Other clues come from what is not stated. In spite of the fact that he has served in India, there is no mention anywhere of venereal disease, which was common amongst British Regular soldiers at this time and which is frequently mentioned in service papers, so Robert was clearly a man of temperate habits.

Scroll forward a couple of pages and there is family history treasure. The section relating to his next of kin shows his mother with her address, and also his wife with her address. Further down are details of his marriage at St George's church, Douglas on 23 January 1911. Further down still are details of the children born up to that time. His mother is shown as Elizabeth Oates of 12 Wesley Terrace, later 33 Nelson Street. Robert's wife's address is shown as 47 Athol Street, Douglas. In addition to details of his physical appearance (including a

The countryside around La Bassee in 1914 was dotted with ruined factories such as this, the Sucrerie at La Houssoie, which the Germans turned into strongholds.

description of his tattoos), there is also information about his pension entitlement and the reason he was claiming one: a bullet wound to the left leg involving amputation at the knee. As the records show that Robert served in France from 12 September to 29 October 1914 we can assume that it was on or just prior to this latter date that he was wounded.

Turning to local records it is now possible to fill in some more detail about Robert Oates and his background. The information contained in the Army service record is confirmed and enhanced by a search of the St George's marriage register held by MNH (MS 10309), in which Robert is shown as living at that time at Hills Cottage, Circular Road, Douglas, whilst his bride Emily May Cunningham is shown as living at that time at 31 Athol Street, Douglas. Robert's father was by this time deceased. The 1911 census, which was conducted shortly after Robert was married, shows the two living at Emily's address, 31 Athol Street. Whilst he is a joiner, Emily is described as caretaker of offices. The Electoral Roll for the 1914 House of Keys election (south Douglas roll) shows Robert now living at 47 Athol Street.

A check of the manuscript books held by MNH, at MS 10003, which list Douglas soldiers during the early part of the war, immediately turns up a hit. Robert Oates of 47 Athol Street is shown as a private of the 3rd Battalion Cheshire Regiment (this discrepancy is not unusual, the 3rd Battalion was used as a holding battalion for reservists and convalescents). The entry reads: 'Reservist. Married 3 children. Wounded early in war, in Nov. No 5 Military Ward R.Infirmary Manchester. Parcel sent. Letter received. Reported Dec 7. Leg amputated Jan. Home Feb 27. Seen often. Difficulty about paperwork. Discharged. Worked at Knockaloe but had to give it up. Has pension of about 32/- per week Sept.'

The *Isle of Man Examiner Yearbook* for 1916 contains a brief report about Oates and states that he was wounded at La Bassée. However, a search of the Manx newspapers themselves is also usually productive, especially for the early part of the First World War. The pages are literally filled with soldiers' letters and accounts of what Manx soldiers had been doing at the front. Censorship it seems had not yet been thought of! Scrolling through the microfilm copy of the *Isle of Man Weekly Times* of 7 November 1914 we find a remarkable letter from Oates himself, written to his brother in Douglas from hospital, which reads:

Just a few lines to let you know how I am getting on. Well I have had an awful time of it. I have been up at Lille and La Bassee . . . well I have had my share of fighting for a bit. We have been taking position after position, just a little at a time and it has been awful, I can tell you . . . Well, we were at some village near Lille, and we had fought our way right up, bit by bit, gaining ground, then entrenching ourselves at night, so as to hold what we had gained against an attack in the morning. One afternoon, about five o clock we got an order to advance. We had to take a factory in the village, which the Germans had occupied, and had a Maxim gun there, which was doing a lot of damage. We were told to take it at all costs. I was in the first company to advance, and we got about 150 yards off them, and then it was like hell – bullets flying all over us, so we had to take cover, and the Germans had men on the tops of houses and in trees, sniping at us. They had the range of all places of cover. I got hit when taking cover. I had to run across an open space, and while crossing this space one of the German snipers got me in the leg and smashed two bones. I think it was a dum-dum bullet; it made such a terrible hole when it came out. I have a compound fracture of the leg between the knee and ankle, and it will be some time before it is alright. It was awful lying there wounded, with shells flying all around. The agony was terrible. The stretcher bearers could not get near me, the fire was too heavy.

This letter is superb, but not wholly unexpected given the level of media interest in Manx soldiers at the time. A further nugget comes to light however from the *Isle of Man Weekly Times* of 29 June 1940. Under the heading 'A Forgotten Hero Joins up for His Third War' we find a photograph of Oates and a report that states that he is a widower with four children, he is living in Pulrose (which explains why he does not appear on the 1927 Douglas Electoral Roll), that he had been present at the coronation of King Edward VII and that he has just volunteered for the Local Defence Volunteers (Home Guard). It adds:

He was discharged from the army with a disability pension of 24s per week for the loss of a leg . . . He is a joiner by trade, but now earns a somewhat precarious livelihood by being engaged sometimes as a night watchman, and at the moment is working two days a week in the river near Union Mills.

Looking into his background, in the 1891 census there is confirmation of the middle name, for Robert is here shown as Robert James Oates, the son of Frederick and Elizabeth E. Oates. He has an older brother and sister, and the family are living in three rooms at 3 Gelling's Court, in the parish of St Matthew's, Douglas, a building they apparently share with three other families. Frederick is shown as a joiner. A search of *Brown's Directory* of 1894 (which is organised on a street by street basis) shows only two families living at Gelling's court, neither of which are Oates. The 1894 directory is useful as it lists members of the working classes as well as professional people, and is good for tracing people between the census returns. Clearly, the family were itinerant and moved from rented accommodation to rented accommodation in this period. By 1901, Elizabeth Oates is shown as a widow, living at 11 Hill Street, Douglas, as a boarding house keeper. Her husband, Frederick Oates (Robert Oates' father), died in 1899.

In the 1881 census, Robert appears as a 2-month-old baby. His parents and older siblings were at this stage living at 6 Drury Lane, St Matthew's, again a shared building. The 1882 *Brown's Directory* lists Frederick Oates as a joiner, still living at 6 Drury Lane, Douglas. Ten years further back in 1871, and Frederick Oates, is shown living with his father James Oates, a market gardener, and his wife Maria Oates at 14 New Bond Street, Douglas. Both Frederick and his brother Robert are shown as joiners, so the family had been able to afford to apprentice two of their sons to tradesmen. In the 1882 directory, James is shown as a greengrocer at 14 New Bond Street, so it would appear that he is both growing and selling his own vegetables. In 1861, James Oates and his wife are living at 6 Alms Lane, this time he is shown as a gardener. In 1851, they are living on Drury Lane in Douglas, with James Oates shown as a Common Porter. The 1847 Electoral Roll shows James Oates living at 12 New Bond Street. In over sixty years, the family had lived in the same approximately 1 square mile of Douglas, though by the First World War they had moved to the slightly better area of Athol Street. Gelling's Court faced onto the old Douglas marketplace opposite Old St Matthew's Church. This area was demolished in the first phase of the Douglas slum clearances, in the 1890s.

Next a search through the death indexes shows how easy it can be to turn down a blind alley with family history, as it shows a Robert Oates who died in 1942. The index for Braddan new burial ground (one likely to be in use for Douglas residents at this time) shows this Robert Oates buried in grave 3470, and a search through the volume of memorial inscriptions records Robert Oates buried with his wife Elizabeth May Oates who died after him. However, we know that our Robert Oates was a widower, and his wife was in fact Emily May Oates. The correct Robert Oates is buried in Douglas Borough Cemetery. His age, 67, at the time of his death on 29 March 1948 tallies with his known age from other records. The grave has no headstone. A final piece of information comes once again from the newspapers – Robert Oates' obituary which states that his death occurred: 'On March 29th at 97 Heather Crescent, Pulrose, Robert James, beloved husband of the late May Oates, in his 67th year, after a long illness. Interred at the borough cemetery.' Finally, Robert's death certificate obtained from the General Registry confirms the known details of age, occupation and place of death.

The Broadcaster's Story

Mark Kermode has made his name as a journalist and film critic, broadcasting on BBC Radio One and latterly on BBC television on the *Culture Show*. A graduate of Manchester University where he obtained a PhD in film studies, he was born in London and educated at the respected Haberdashers' Aske's Boys' School. Born Mark Fairey, he later adopted his maternal grandfather's surname of Kermode.

Mark Kermode, film critic and broadcaster, has appeared on television as well as BBC Radio One (photo by Rex Features).

The first thing to note when researching Kermode's family tree is that whilst his birth can be readily identified using online sources, there being only one Mark Fairey born in the 1960s whose mother's maiden name was Kermode, his parent's marriage cannot be found by searching British marriage registers. This is because they married in the Isle of Man, and a search of Manx marriage registers shows Michael John Fairey marrying Audrey Edwina Kermode at Rosemount Methodist church in Douglas in 1958.

Searching through Manx birth indexes approximately twenty years previously reveals Audrey Edwina Kermode born in Douglas in 1933. As she was later married at Rosemount church it is worthwhile checking baptisms there as well as this may have been the family church, and indeed Audrey Edwina was baptised on 24 December 1933. Her father is shown as James Stanley Kermode and the family lived at Wyndholme, Bray Hill, Douglas.

It is reasonably safe to assume that James was born in the early 1900s, and the next stop is the 1911 census. There is only one James Stanley Kermode listed, and he is shown aged 9 living with his parents James Quayle Kermode and Eleanor Jane Kermode. His father James is recorded as a House Carpenter.

Searching twentieth-century Manx newspapers immediately brings up two hits for a J. Stanley Kermode, one a report of his retirement published in the *Isle of Man Examiner* of 27 October 1960, and another being his obituary from the

Caption: The
Snaefell Mine,
where Thomas
Kermode may have
worked. (Pg4419/6)

Weekly Times of 28 January 1975. The latter records that Mr Kermode was aged 73, so this tallies with the known age from the census. It further records that: 'Mr Kermode, a former partner in the accountancy firm of Shannon, Kneale & Co [was] chairman of several leading companies.' The report in the *Weekly Times* states that Mr J. Stanley Kermode was Chairman of the directors of the Sefton Hotel Ltd and the Hotel Metropole Ltd. It also records that he was a commissioned officer in the 1st Manx Battalion Home Guard during the Second World War, and that he began his business career as an accountant in 1917. It also confirms that his daughter married in 1958, and adds that she had graduated from Cambridge University and was a doctor living in London. MNH holds some records relating to the Manx Home Guard, MS 11320 containing a partial roll of the 1st Manx Battalion. Corporal J.S. Kermode is listed under Lieutenant H.S. Cain's Number 5 section in December 1940, his address at that time shown again as Wyndholme, Bray Hill, Douglas. Later on in this document Kermode is shown as holding the rank of sergeant. Turning to Bertram Sergeaunt's *A Military History of the Isle of Man*, J.S. Kermode is again listed under 1st Manx Battalion and recorded as commissioned Second Lieutenant 10 March 1943, promoted Lieutenant 10 September 1944.

Returning to the 1911 census entry, this reveals that James Stanley Kermode's

Caption: The Snaefell Mine, where Thomas Kermode may have worked. (Pg4419/6)

parents had been married for seventeen years at the time the census was taken, and this gives a date for their marriage as 1894. Searching marriage indexes for this year reveals that a Kermode married a Kermode, for this was also Eleanor's maiden name.

A copy of their marriage certificate, available from the General Registry, shows that James senior's father was Thomas Kermode, a miner. James senior was at the time of his marriage living at 8 Hill Street. His bride Eleanor meanwhile is shown as the daughter of Ceasar (*sic*) Kermode, a shoemaker. On the 1891 census her father Ceasar is shown as a Shoemaker and Postman, living with his wife and another daughter Emily, who is also a witness on her sister's marriage certificate. It is often worth scrutinising the names of witnesses, as they frequently turn out to be a brother or married sister. Ceasar appears to have inherited his father William's shoemaking business, which in 1861 was located on Chester Street in Douglas. By 1871 he was at 45 North Quay, Douglas. At the time of her marriage Eleanor was living at 10 Kingswood Grove, where she was a housekeeper. A search of the 1894 *Brown's Directory* reveals a

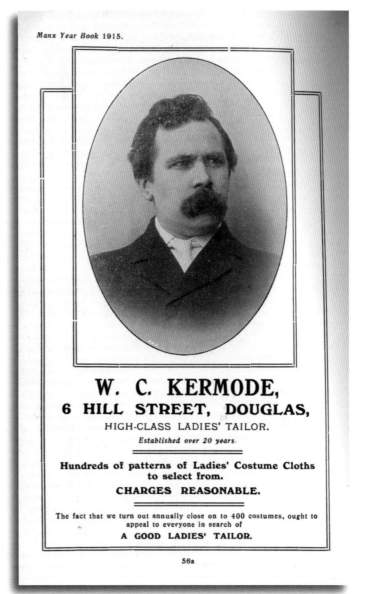

Manx Year Book 1915.

W. C. KERMODE,
6 HILL STREET, DOUGLAS,
HIGH-CLASS LADIES' TAILOR.
Established over 20 years.

Hundreds of patterns of Ladies' Costume Cloths to select from.

CHARGES REASONABLE.

The fact that we turn out annually close on to 400 costumes, ought to appeal to everyone in search of

A GOOD LADIES' TAILOR.

56a

number of interesting facts. First, 10 Kingswood Grove is shown as the business address of Kermode Brothers, Painters. Secondly, the rateable value section of the directory shows the proprietor of this property to be Evan Kermode. Evan Kermode also appears on the 1891 census at 10 Kingswood Grove as a 48-year-old widower, by trade a painter and decorator, born at Malew. If we go back as

William Kermode's full-page advertisement in the 1915 *Norris Modern Press Yearbook*.

far as the 1851 census, we find that Evan and Ceasar Kermode are in fact brothers, and are the sons of William Kermode the shoemaker, who at that time was living on Castletown Road, Ballasalla. So Eleanor Kermode was the housekeeper for her widowed uncle.

The marriage certificate gives an approximate date of birth for James Kermode senior as 1869, and shows his father Thomas Kermode as a miner. Turning to the 1871 census, we find James Q. Kermode aged 2 years and living with his father Thomas, again recorded as a miner, and his mother Elizabeth. He has an older brother John Thomas Kermode, who also appears as a witness on the marriage certificate, so this further confirms we are dealing with the right family. These Kermodes are living at Ballachosney in the parish of Lonan. Their near neighbours were also Kermodes, and may also have been related. By the 1891 census, Thomas Kermode is living in a three-roomed cottage on Glen Roy Road, Agneash, so he may well have been working at the nearby Snaefell Mine. What is more interesting however is that another son, William C. Kermode, is still living at home, but is shown as a tailor by trade. By 1901, William had moved to Douglas and had his own tailoring business at 8 Hill Street in the town. It is at this address that James Q. Kermode was living at the time of his marriage, so he had clearly followed his brother to Douglas. So successful did William's business become that by 1915 he was able to afford a full-page advertisement in the *Norris Modern Press Yearbook*.

What emerges most clearly from this case study is evidence, from both sides of the family, of the move of a significant portion of the population from rural areas into Douglas, as the town gained in popularity as a holiday resort. Both James Kermode as a joiner and Evan Kermode as a house painter would have been involved in the massive expansion of the town in the last two decades of the nineteenth century, as it grew to meet the unprecedented demand of the Victorian holiday visitors. The degree of social mobility within Manx society at this time is also evident. Prosperity that the trade brought with it undoubtedly enabled both sides of the family to move from being poor rural labourers through to middle-class tradesmen and members of the commercial classes, and finally to the professional classes, within about three generations.

The Housekeeper's Story

Samplers are unusual in terms of objects that are passed down through families because they are rarely anonymous, and often provide a wealth of information for the family historian or genealogist.

So what exactly is a sampler? In its simplest form, a sampler is a piece of fabric with an alphabet sewn onto it in cross-stitch, often with the date and the maker's name sewn underneath. In its more extravagant form, a sampler can include several decorative alphabets and motifs together with a morally uplifting verse. Sampler

The sampler made by Julia Ann Skelly in 1883, held in the collections of Manx National Heritage. (2007-0037)

making was an important part of a young girl's education and they could be made both at home and at a variety of institutions such as charity, board and private schools. The production of a sampler could be used to teach practical (needlework) and academic (reading) skills and was also seen as part of moral and religious education.

Whether one is researching a treasured family heirloom or an 'anonymous' sampler picked up at a local auction or charity shop, the research paths are the same – one begins with the name on the sampler. In this particular case the inscription on the sampler reads 'Kirk German Parochial School. St John's. Isle of Man. Julia Ann Skelly. Age 12 years. May 1883' with a Three Legs of Man and a small flower design.

The sampler maker, Julia Ann Skelly, appears to have been born around 1870–2, depending on whether she was only just 12 years old or almost 13 in May 1883. A review of the Manx baptismal records shows a Julia Ann Skelly was baptised on the 14 August 1870 at Patrick parish church. The combination of two Christian names, a relatively uncommon surname and a baptism record in Patrick means that one can be confident that they are one and the same person. The baptism record also provides details of Julia Skelly's parents who are listed as John and Catharine Skelly. If, though, there had been several potential candidates listed in the baptismal records, a second route would have been through the 1881 census or the 1882 *Brown's Directory* entries for the St John's area. In this case, these two sources provide both supplementary and additional information by providing details of her home address, her father's occupation, her parents' ages and place of birth together with details of her siblings. In this particular instance, the 1882 trade-directory entry is also helpful in providing the spelling for the family smallholding, as handwritten place names in census entries can be relatively difficult to decipher. It records: 'Skelly, John, Miner, Ballahigg (Patrick)'.

The 1881 census for the parish of Patrick, Enumeration District 5 (covering Ballahigg near Slieu Whallian) shows John Skelly as head of household. He is married, aged 49 and his occupation given as Lead Miner and Farmer. He was born in Patrick, Isle of Man. His wife is Catherine Skelly, aged 46, also born in Patrick, Isle of Man. Their children are shown as Rebecca, unmarried aged 21, formerly a servant, Richard, unmarried aged 20, like his father a lead miner, George, unmarried aged 17, a lead miner, Evan unmarried aged 14 and a Scholar, and Julia who is unmarried aged 10. She is also a Scholar. All the children were born in Patrick, Isle of Man. Also shown on the census is John Kinnish, a boarder aged 4 and a Scholar born in Malew, Isle of Man.

From this well-documented point, it should now be possible to trace Julia Skelly's life story and family history both forward and backward in time. The 1871 census provides further information about the Skelly family and confirms that Julia Skelly was born July–early August 1870. It also highlights the need to look at several census entries, to discover the full story about a family. Whilst the eldest daughter, Rebecca, is listed in the 1881 census as having been born in Patrick, both the 1861 and 1871 censuses show that she was born in England. This indicates that the Skellys lived for a short period in Lancashire before moving back to live in Patrick, a fact that would have been lost if only the 1881 census had been studied.

By searching for the record of their marriage, one can discover that John Skelly and Catherine Moore were married on 13 May 1858 in Kirk German and appear to have moved to England shortly afterwards. A search of the FreeBMD website for England and Wales lists a Rebecca Jane Skelley (*sic*) born in the Apr–May–Jun quarter in 1859 in the Ulverston district, in the county of Lancashire. It might therefore be speculated that John Skelly, with his new wife, had moved to the Ulverston area so that he could find work in one of the iron-ore mines. However, the fact that subsequent children were born on the Isle of Man, and that they are listed in the 1861 census on the Isle of Man, shows that they returned to the Island within two years.

Evidence that spellings of surnames have not always been consistent can be discovered if Julia Skelly's father, John, is traced further back to the 1851 and 1841 censuses, where the family name was spelt as Scelly (1851) and Skeally (1841). This may be a possible indication of its pronunciation in the earlier part of the nineteenth century, before the introduction of consistent and standardised spellings for various Manx surnames. The variations in the spellings of 'Skelly' are further highlighted when the baptism records for John Skelly and his siblings are traced, indicating how vicars in different parishes thought the surname was (or should be) spelt:

John Skelly, son of Henry Skelly and Jane Kelly, baptised 26 June 1831, German

Robt (Robert) Skeally, son of Henry Skeally and Jane Kelly, baptised 31 March 1833, Malew

Catharine Skeally, daughter of Henry Skeally and Jane Kelly, baptised 23 August 1835, Malew

Thomas Skeaylley, son of Henry Skeaylley and Jane Kelly, baptised 6 July 1841, St Marks

Edwin Skeaylley, son of Henry Skeaylley and Jane Kelly, baptised 28 April 1844, St Marks

It can be seen that the surname is spelt as Skelly in the parishes of Patrick and German but is spelt as Skeally or Skeaylley in Malew, in both the parish register and the census. In a period of limited literacy and transition from a Manx Gaelic to an English-speaking community, it is not wholly unexpected that Manx surnames will have a variety of spellings or that there may be some local variation to these names.

Returning to the sampler, it is fortunate that this gives us the additional information that Julia Skelly in 1883 was a 12-year-old pupil at the German Parochial School. Compulsory education had been introduced on the Isle of Man in 1872 and the existing Church-funded parochial schools were replaced (if only in name) by state-funded Board Schools. So it is interesting to see that Julia still refers to her school by its original name, which may have been common practice regardless of an earlier change in legal and funding status. *Brown's Directory* (1882) provides the more accurate title for the school by listing Thomas Caine as the master of the Board School in St John's. We are fortunate in that the Kirk German Parochial School is one of the few on the Isle of Man for which detailed records and admission registers survive. The records of this school are held in the MNH archive under MS 09604. It is described as having 3 rooms, 1 of which is an infants' room, and there is accommodation in the school for a total of 217 pupils. Amongst the registers we find Julia Skelly recorded as pupil number 477. The register states that she was born on 26 July 1870. Her residence was Foxdale. She was admitted to the school in 1878, but the register records that she left on 25 June 1880. The stated reason is 'bad attendance' which rather implies that she was expelled. However, a note next to this states, 'readmitted July 1880'. It is likely that Julia Skelly would have left school for good at around 12 or 13 years of age and her main options on leaving school would have been to help her mother at home, enter domestic service at a neighbouring farm or possibly train for a trade such as dressmaker.

A search of the 1891 census finds Julia Skelly employed as a general servant (domestic) in Douglas working for the Cubbon family, at 7 Circular Road. The head of the household, Thomas Cubbon, is listed as a car proprietor, whilst his wife, Margaret Cubbon, is listed as a boarding house keeper. Entries in the 1894 *Brown's Directory* show Thomas Cubbon as one of several car proprietors and livery stables operating in Douglas, although Mrs Cubbon is not listed as operating a boarding house. These occupations, car proprietor and boarding house keeper, show the importance of and growing reliance of the Manx economy upon the tourist industry.

In Patrick by the time of the 1891 census, all of Julia's siblings have left home and her father, John Skelly, had died, leaving her mother 'living on own means' with a 7-year-old nephew and two children who were boarding with her. It may be that Catherine Skelly, prior to the introduction of National Insurance legislation and increased welfare provision, may have derived her income by payment for the boarding or 'fostering' of children, although her source of income may be from a variety of sources including her adult children and/or her late husband's membership of a friendly society such as the Oddfellows.

The burial records and monumental inscriptions for St Paul's Church, Foxdale provide further details about the death of John Skelly, together with additional family history information, such as his eldest daughter's married name:

*In affectionate remembrance of John Skelly of Foxdale who departed this life November 2nd 1882 aged 52 years/ tis hard to part with those we love but parting days must come but let us hope to meet again for this is not our home/ also Evan Thomas Faragher second son of Robert and Rebecca Faragher and grandson of the above who died Feb 28th 1887 aged 1 year and 8 months safe in the arms of Jesus/ also Catherine beloved wife of the above who died February 27th 1917 aged ** years life's work well done life's race well run now rest.*

By the time of the 1901 census, Julia Ann Skelly was married to Thomas Christian, a Grocer employing others, and living at 5 Queen's Terrace, Douglas, with her husband and young son but also her widowed mother and older brother Evan. The 1901 census provides additional information (and less obvious family history) by showing that whilst Julia, her husband and brother are all English speakers, her 66-year-old mother, Catherine Skelly, can speak both English and Manx Gaelic – important evidence of the changing linguistic landscape of the Island by the early twentieth century.

The family do not appear on the 1911 census for the Isle of Man or Britain. There are two possible reasons for this: death or emigration. It seems unlikely that an entire family would have died, and a search of online passenger lists available through the Ellis Island website reveals a Thomas Christian travelling from Liverpool to New York aboard the Cunard liner SS *Carmania* on 24 April 1906. SS *Carmania* carried many immigrant families to start new lives in the United States around this time. The passenger lists show that Thomas Christian was married, he could read and write, his place of origin was Douglas and his occupation is given as Grocer. He was heading for Colorado, where he had a friend by the name of Frank Kelly, living at 743 North Walnut Street, Colorado Springs. The same sources show that his wife and two children followed him in October 1906 and their entry in the Ellis Island immigration records is even more detailed, including height, hair, complexion and eye colour. Curiously, Julia Christian is here shown as 'Jessie', but all other details match with known facts, and this appears to have been the name by which she was known for the rest of her life. She is described as a 'housekeeper' 5ft 6in tall, with brown hair, grey eyes and fair skin. She was travelling to meet her husband in Colorado, but a search of US Federal Census records via www.ancestry.co.uk reveals that in 1910 the family had settled in King County, Washington State. The actual census entry, available from Washington State Archives website, reveals that the family were living at Summit Avenue North, in the city of Seattle. Thomas Christian, unsurprisingly, is shown as a clerk in a grocery store but was working for himself. The family seem to have settled permanently in the United States, and according to US Federal death records, Julia (or Jessie) Christian, the maker of a sampler so many years earlier in the Isle of Man, died in Seattle on 13 July 1920. Information from the Washington State Archives death records confirms that her husband was Thomas, and her father was John Shelly (Skelly).

The Cunard liner *Carmania*, which carried many immigrant families across the Atlantic to America.

The Blacksmith's Story

This case study begins with an American lady who was keen to discover more about her Manx ancestry and who, it transpired, was related to one of the best known blacksmiths on the Isle of Man. It also demonstrates the way by which land transfers and other records can be used to build a pedigree. The story begins in the later part of the twentieth century with the lady's last known family in the Isle of Man, who lived in a cottage named Killey's Croft, West Nappin in Jurby in the north of the Island. The property was owned by Mr and Mrs J.R. Gill.

The Jurby sales index held by the Registry of Deeds shows that the Gills purchased Killey's Croft from Mrs Gill's brother Humphrey Joughin (pronounced 'Jockin') for £1,000 on 12 September 1954. Humphrey Joughin (a blacksmith) was acting as trustee for his father Andrew Joughin, who died on 9 January 1952. Andrew Joughin's will shows that Humphrey was appointed a trustee of his estate until the death of his mother Margaret in June 1954, when he was to dispose of the assets. Andrew Joughin (or Andy, as he was known) was also a well-regarded blacksmith, and by chance an informant of the Manx Museum's Folk Life Survey. He was interviewed in December 1948, when he was aged 75, and recounted that:

My father and his father before him were smiths. I don't suppose any smith in the Island made more ploughs than my uncle Humphrey Joughin – he lived in St Jude's all his days . . . My father was one of the best scholars in the Island and was a great copper-plate writer. My father was a Greek scholar and . . . knew Latin too. My grandfather was a schoolmaster for 40 years in Jurby West – his name was Andrew Joughin and he came from Andreas, the home of the Joughins . . . My father was a great man with ould Tom

Andy Joughin, the Jurby blacksmith. He was an informant of the Manx Museum's Folk Life Survey. (Pg12858)

Brown [T.E. Brown the Manx national poet]. He used to say to my father, 'Ould Johnnie boy, give us a tale'.

He goes on to describe many of the working practices of the rural blacksmith at this time, the equipment that he made, and also the superstitions associated with the craft, for example, washing a weak baby in the water in which hot iron had been cooled, in the belief that it would make them strong.

Using the *Liber Vastarum* from the Manorial Rolls one finds that Andy Joughin had acquired the property in 1902 upon the death of his father, John Thomas Joughin. In the directories of the last decades of the nineteenth century John T. Joughin is shown both as a smith and postmaster, living at the Nappin, Jurby. On the 1901 census, John T. Joughin is shown as Sub Post Master, living at the

The Old Post Office at Jurby, home of the Joughin family, seen in the 1980s. (Courtesy of Nigel Crowe)

same address. A widower, he lived with his son (the blacksmith) and daughter-in-law. He in turn had acquired half the property in the will of his father, Andrew Joughin, which was probated in 1867. The other half had been left to his widow but she later passed this to her son. In 1896 J.T. Joughin also purchased another parcel of land near the family home, this was behind the existing cottages on the north-east of the crossroads.

Andrew Joughin was according to the 1861 census a farmer of 30 acres, living at West Nappin, employing seven men and by trade a master blacksmith. In 1847 he purchased a plot of land lying north-west of Jurby West crossroads from William Killey and his wife Elizabeth. Here he built a house, now known as the Old Post Office, which became the family home. Two-and-a-half years later he purchased the remainder of Killey's croft for a further £198, including the Killey cottage. The cottage appears on the 1847 tithe plan, and it was from William Killey that the property acquired its name. It is possible that William Killey was Andrew Joughin's cousin, as the latter's maternal grandparents were named Killey.

Andrew Joughin's father was a schoolmaster, also called Andrew Joughin. This neatly illustrates the care that must be taken with oral testimony, for Andy Joughin had stated that his grandfather was the schoolmaster, whereas it would appear that it was in fact his great-grandfather. Andrew Joughin the schoolmaster died in 1839, and we know from his will that he was at this time living with his son and his son's wife. He had by this time sold his own property, which sales documents show was Croit Paddy also in Jurby. A deed dated 18 January 1793 and recorded in the North Side Sales shows that Andrew paid £100 to William Kneale for 'the croft or parcel of land called . . . Crott Paddy'. Later he added to this holding, by purchasing for £6 a small piece of land from his neighbour. This is recorded in a deed dated 30 December 1799 when John Callister sold 'a certain parcel of land known as cooil ne ping' which joined the Joughin's land on the west and north-west, and was bounded by the highway on the south-east. *Liber Vastarum*, the Manorial Rolls, record this latter transaction in the October 1798 Court, but strangely there is no mention of the former.

Prior to this, the family had lived in the parish of Andreas. In 1755 Andrew's father Charles Joughin made a purchase from an Arthur Lace, a piece of land known as the New Flat (in Manx 'Ffai Noa') which indicated it was a fertile piece of land close to a farmyard, where dung from animal sheds was spread. The same week, Andrew made a purchase from the same vendor. The Manorial Roll records: 'The said Chas Joughen is entered for the said iiis id by virtue of a bill of sale from the said Arthur Lace dated 10th March 1755 . . . Andrew Joughen for the said viiid by virtue of another bill of sayle dated 23rd May 1755 . . .'.

Amongst the deeds once held by the Rolls Office and now part of the archives of MNH are what might be considered early prenuptial agreements. These are marriage contracts, and are organised by parish and then by surname. Their purpose was to safeguard land interests when two families intermarried, and they shed valuable light on family relationships. The marriage contract of Charles Joughen and Mary Cleater dated 10 November 1722 reads as follows:

Articles of marriage concluded and agreed upon by and betwixt Bahey Joughen als Lace in behalf of hir son Charles Joughen on the one part and Jo Cleater and his wife Jony in behalf of their daughter Mary Cleater [on] the other partie [all of the parish of Kirk Andreas] as follows

First it is agreed upon that the said Charles Joughen and Mary Cleater shall enter into the holy estate of matrimony within a month next ensuing the date hereof if God and Church permit thereof

Secondly it is agreed upon and the said Bahy Joughin doth hereby settle and estate upon her said son all her lands whatsoever and its aparrtinances after her decease and during her natural life she and her said son are to enjoy all the lands and houses of Balladaugherdy belonging to them now and that shal become due to them after her father in law Charles Joughen Senior his decease equally between them half and half as above said also all incumbrances and immediately after marriage he is to enjoy half the crop of corn and half of the husbandry gears in consideration whereof the said Charles Joughen doth bind himself to pay the children what his said mother owes them for what she has formerly received of their deceased father's goods due to them being three pounds two shillings and four pence after the expiration of three years next ensuing the date hereof

This tells us a number of things. First, Charles Joughen's own father appears to have died before his son's marriage in 1722. Secondly, his mother's father-in-law (his paternal grandfather) is referred to by name, as Charles Joughin senior. Charles Joughin senior and his wife Ann had made a settlement of their lands on their son John, on the occasion of his marriage to Bahee Lace of Ballaseyr. The couple were to live at Ballaseyr during the lifetime of Bahee's parents. The marriage contract of John Joughin and Bahee Lace, dated 12 December 1698, reads:

Att the matrimonial contract of John Joughin son of Charles Joughin and Bahee Lace daughter of John Lace of Balnasear all the said parties being of the parish of Kirk Andreas as is concluded and agreed upon as follows

1 That the said John and Bahee shall proceed into the Holy Eastate of Matrimony at or before the first of January next God permitting

2 That Charles Joughin and his wife doth promise and covenant to give unto their said son and daughter in law half of all their land of what nature soever with half the crop of corn and husbandry gears as soon as their occasion requires and the other half of the premises (save the crop of corn) after the death of the longer liver of the said Charles or his wife the said John paying the sum of one pound and ten shillings to the assigns of the said Charles Joughin and his wife, with the proviso that if there is no issue begotten betwixt the said John and Bahee to enjoy the said lands then the same is (after the death of the said John and Bahee) to return to the next of kindred from when it came

Charles Joughin is mentioned in the will of his mother dated 1669, found in the Andreas Archidiaconal wills:

This is affirmed to be the last will and testament of Katherin Joughin als Christian who comited her soule to god and her body to Christian buryall: Item she bequesthed to her daughter Margt Joaghin a blanket legacie. Item she bequesthed to her son Joh: 4 pottles of corne. Item she bequeathed to her husband her part of the cow and a petticoat. Item she constituted ordained her son Charles Joughin sole executor of all the rest of her goods moveable and unmoveable whatsoever.

Her husband is mentioned by name further on in the will as Christopher Joughin. No will seems to exist for Christopher but he appears to have died before the Manorial Composition Book of *c.* 1704 was compiled. Charles is shown as the holder of land known from other surviving records to have been purchased by his father. Christopher is a comparatively unusual name for this period and this makes him relatively easy to track using other documents.

A deed dated 5 April 1652 conveys a piece of land purchased by him on the outskirts of the present-day village of Andreas. Here he is recorded as Christopher Joughen 'of the parish of Kirk Bride'. His name was shortly afterwards entered in the manorial records, in accordance with the provisions of the deed. His name appears in *Liber Assedationes* in 1671 as 'Xpher Joughin'. By 1675 this had been rendered as 'Christo Joughin'. In 1676 the name is rendered as 'Christian Joughin', an apparent slip as in this era Christian was a female name. By 1686 the name had been contracted to 'Xtin'. The Manorial Composition Books shed further light on the Joughins. That for Kirk Bride in 1657 states: 'William Joughin houlds certain intacks in K Bride and certain intacks in Kk Christ for the lives of the said Will and of Donald and Xopher his bretheren'. That for Kirk Bride in 1691 records 'Christo Joughen' as being aged 69 years. His unusual name also allows us to identify his parents, as he is mentioned in two other wills held in the Episcopal registry. From 1643 the will of Christian Cowle:

In dei nomine Amen the last will and testament off Christian Cowle. First she committed her soule to god and her bodie to the earth Item her son Wm Joughen 6d to her daughter Bessie 6d to Tho: Crinelts children I Ianbe [sic] betwixt them if there bee any Item constituted her sons Christopher & Do: Joughen executors off all the rest off here goods movable and unmoveable.

Also the will of Donald Joughen, from 1647:

In dei nomine Amen The last will and testament of Donald Joughen First he committed his soule to god and his bodie to the earth Item for his son Donald four yards of raw cloath and a chist Item to his son Wm Joughen and to his grandchild Bahie Costen four yards of raw cloath Item to his son Christopher one hogg Item hee constituted his said son Christopher and his daughter Bessie executors off all the rest of his goods moveable and unmoveable.

This may be as far as it is possible to go (and to prove) using written sources. Although Andy Joughin stated in the Folk Life Survey that it was family tradition that the Joughins were of Norse descent, and came to the Isle of Man with King Orry, this must perhaps remain in the realms of speculation! However, A.W. Moore records the earliest use of the surname in 1422 in the form of Mac Joychene, whilst Leslie Quilliam in *Surnames of the Manks* identifies its origin as being derived from MacJaghan, meaning 'son of the Deacon'. He also identifies the strongest concentrations of the surname as occurring in Bride and Maughold, confirming that it is traditionally a 'northside' name.

CONCLUSION

For those researching in the field of family history, or for those interested in the grass roots history of a locality or district, these are exciting times. Never before has there been such a level of interest in the subject, with several primetime television programmes such as *Who Do You Think You Are?* reflecting the current public passion for genealogy. Fuelling this interest – or perhaps to some degree resulting from it – is a previously unprecedented degree of access to the records from which such histories are fashioned. In the past forty years we in the British Isles have moved from a situation in which authorities only reluctantly conceded that 'history from below' was a valid subject for study, and that some records might be of value to 'ordinary' people and so grudgingly preserved them, to that today in which the incredible power of computers, scanners and databases are being actively harnessed to make the searching, analysing and studying of these records by ordinary people easier and more rewarding than ever before.

In the Isle of Man, the sterling work of the Isle of Man Family History Society over the past thirty years, in parallel with the efforts of the Genealogical Society of Utah, has produced indices to census records, burial registers, monumental inscriptions and a host of other invaluable sources. It has recently been joined by Manx National Heritage, which, through Tynwald support and the financial backing of its Trustees, has embarked upon an ambitious programme of digitising and indexing the many and varied records which it holds. The presentation of these newly accessible collections in the purpose-built iMuseum, a part of the Manx Museum complex in Douglas, is one of the most exciting developments in Manx local and family history in the early twenty first century.

As the iMuseum continues to develop, new material will be added on a regular basis, so it is important to check back often to see what is new and whether it can help you in your research. Updates on iMuseum content can be found on the website www.imuseum.im. Manx National Heritage staff are also keen to receive suggestions for new bodies of material suitable for digitisation, and information about new sources of information about Manx history (perhaps held in other institutions). Above all, the iMuseum encourages users to share their own knowledge and information, perhaps by leaving feedback or by using the 'Add Your Story' feature which accompanies the digital records.

As a valediction to this book, there can be no more appropriate sentiment than that of Nigel Crowe in encouraging those engaged in research to make a permanent written record of their findings, in order to enrich the resources upon which future generations may draw.

FURTHER READING

Anon, *Fleet History of Isle of Man Department of Tourism and Leisure and its Predecessors,* s.l.: PSV Circle (1991)

Anon, *The Isle of Man Charities*, Liverpool: D. Marples (1830)

Anon, *Maps of the Isle of Man 1280–1760*, Douglas: Shearwater Press (1975)

Barry, Ivy, *Something Different*, Onchan: Streetscene Publications (1993)

Bird, Hinton, *The Island that led – The History of Manx Education,* 2 volumes, Port St Mary: Hinton Bird (1991, 1995)

Blundell, William, *History of the Isle of Man*, Volume I Manx Society, Volume XXV, Edinburgh: Manx Society (1876); Volume II Manx Society, Volume XXVII, Edinburgh: Manx Society (1877)

Broderick, G., *Placenames of the Isle of Man*, 7 volumes, Tubingen: Max Niemeyer Verlag (1994–2005)

Cashen, William, *Manx Folk-Lore*, Douglas: G. & L. Johnson (1912)

Chappell, Connery, *Island Lifeline*, Prescot: T. Stephenson & Sons (1980)

Chappell, Connery, *Island of Barbed Wire*, London: Robert Hale (2005)

Clague, Curwen, *Ack Ack*, Douglas: Old Comrades Association, 15th (IOM) LAA Regt RA (1981)

Cohen-Portheim, Paul, *Time Stood Still*, London: Duckworth (1932)

Copparelli, Paul and Mylchreest, Peter, *Isle of Man Tourist Trophy Circuit Memorials Revealed*, Douglas: Copparelli and Mylchreest (2009)

Cottle, Val, *Gold Dust and Calm*, Douglas: MHF (2007)

Creer, Hampton*, Never To Return,* Douglas: MHF (2000)

Cresswell, Yvonne, *Living With The Wire*, rev. edn, Douglas: MNH (2010)

Crow, Hugh, *Memoirs of the late Captain Hugh Crow of Liverpool*, Oxford: Bodleian Library (2007)

Crowe, Nigel G., *The Survey of Douglas: Quarterland and Cottage Rents of Douglas c1705*, Douglas: N.G. Crowe (2001)

Cubbon, A.M., *Early Maps of the Isle of Man*, Douglas: MNH (1994)

Dickinson, J.R., *The Lordship of Man under the Stanleys*, Douglas: Centre for Manx Studies (1997)

Everingham, F.R., *The Isle of Man and Child Emigration*, Ontario: Fred Everingham (1994)

Feltham, John and Wright, Edward, *Memorials of God's Acre being Monumental Inscriptions in the Isle of Man*, Douglas: Manx Society, Volume XIV (1868)

Francis, Paul, Isle of Man *20th Century Military Archaeology*, Douglas: Manx Heritage Foundation (2006)

Gill, W.W., *A Manx Scrapbook*, London: Arrowsmith (1929)

Hicks Beach, Susan, *The Yesterdays Behind The Door*, Liverpool: Liverpool University Press (1956)

Hoy, Michael, *A Blessing to this Island, The Story of King William's College and The Buchan School*, London: James & James (2006)

Karran, T.W., *A Tale of the Seas*, s.l. (1944)

Kelly, Dollin (ed.), *New Manx Worthies*, Douglas: MHF (2006)

Kermode, D.G., *Offshore Island Politics*, Liverpool: LUP (2001)

Kermode, P.M.C., *Manx Crosses*, repr. with introduction by D.M. Wilson, Balgavies: Pinkfoot Press (1907)

Killip, Margaret, *The Folklore of the Isle of Man*, London: Batsford (1986)

Kneen, J.J., *Personal Names of the Isle of Man*, Oxford: OUP (1937)

Lamplugh, G.W., *The Geology of the Isle of Man (Memoirs of the Geological Survey)*, London: HMSO (1903)

Macaulay, Ted, *Hailwood*, London: Cassell & Co. (1969)

Macaulay, Ted, *Mike the Bike Again*, London: Cassell & Co. (1980)

MacFarlane, D., *Crown Green Bowling on the Island from 1892 to 2000*, Port St Mary: D. MacFarlane (2007)

Molyneux, Dave and Richardson, Matthew, *The Racer's Edge*, Barnsley: Wharncliffe Books (2011)

Moore, A.W., *The Manx Note Book*, Douglas: G.H. Johnson (1885–7)

Moore, A.W., *History of the Isle of Man*, London: T. Fisher Unwin (1900)

Moore, A.W., *Manx Worthies*, Douglas: S.K. Broadbent & Co. Ltd (1901)

Moore, A.W., *Manx Names*, London: Elliott Stock (1906)

Moore, R.B., 'The History of Education in the Isle of Man', in *The Handbook of Education Week*, Douglas: S.K. Broadbent & Co. (1926)

Morrison, Sophia, *Manx Fairytales*, London: David Nutt (1911)

Narasimham, Janet, *The Manx Family Tree*, s.l.: IOMFHS (1986, 3rd edn 2000)

Norris, Samuel, *Manx Memories and Movements*, Douglas: Norris Modern Press (1938)

Owen, E.C., *A Hundred Years of Education*, Douglas: Brown & Sons (1930)

Poole, Steve, *Rough Landing or Fatal Flight: a History of Aircraft Accidents On, Over and Around the Isle of Man*, Laxey: Amulree Publications (1999)

Quayle, George E., *Legends of a Lifetime,* sl George Quayle (2nd edn 1979)

Quilliam, Leslie, *Surnames of the Manks: a review*, Peel: Cashtal Books (1989)

Quilliam, N.D., *Keys and Cuffs,* s.l.: N.D. Quilliam (2009)

Quirk, John, *The Manx Connection*, Onchan: Manx Experience (2007)

Radcliffe, Constance, *Ramsey 1600 to 1800*, Ramsey: C. Radcliffe (1986)

Radcliffe, Constance, *Shining by the Sea Ramsey 1800 to 1914*, Douglas: Nelson Press (1989)

Rawcliffe, Roger, *No Man is an Island*, Douglas: MHF (2009)

Scarffe, Andrew, *The Great Laxey Mine*, Douglas: MHF (2004)

Sergeaunt, Bertram, *The Isle of Man and the Great War*, Douglas: Brown & Sons Ltd (1920)

Sergeaunt, Bertram, *The Manx Fencibles*, Aldershot: Gale & Polden (1947)

Sergeaunt, Bertram, *A Military History of the Isle of Man*, Arbroath: T. Buncle & Co. Ltd (1949)

Sheard, Ruth, *The Modest Manxman*, sl: R. Sheard (2006)

Skillicorn, Pat, *Wave to Your Daddy*, Onchan: Manx Experience (2006)

Slack, Stuart, *Streets of Douglas – Old and New*, Douglas: Manx Experience (1996)

Stoffa, Paul, *Round the World to Freedom*, London: Bodley Head (1933)

Stowell, Brian and O'Breaslain, Diarmuid. *A Short History of the Manx Language*, Beal Feirste: An Clochan (1996)

Stowell, Billy, *Latitude 54*, sl: B. Stowell (2010)

Teare, Alfred, *Reminiscences of the Manx Labour Party*, Douglas: Island Development Co. Ltd (1962)

Train, Joseph, *Historical and Statistical Account of the Isle of Man*, Douglas: M.A. Quiggin (1845)

Turnbull, G., *History of the Isle of Man Constabulary*, s.l.: Kathleen Turnbull (1984)

Underhill, Arthur C., *A Policeman's Lot*, Douglas: Manx Experience (1993)

various authors, *Skeealyn Vannin – Stories of Mann*, Douglas: MNH (2003)

West, Margery, *Island at War*, Laxey: Western Books (1986)

Wilkins, Frances, *The Isle of Man in Smuggling History*, Kidderminster: Wyre Forest Press (1992)

Wilkins, Frances, *Manx Slave Traders*, Kidderminster: Wyre Forest Press (1999)

Wilkins, Frances, *2000 Manx Mariners, an Eighteenth Century Survey*, Kidderminster: Wyre Forest Press (2000)

W. C. KERMODE,
6 HILL STREET, DOUGLAS,